The Irish Revolution, 1916–1923

This Seminar Studies volume is a concise study of the Irish revolution of 1916 to 1923, during which Ireland changed from a unified island that was an integral part of the United Kingdom to an island divided into an effectively independent 26-county Free State and a devolved government in Northern Ireland which remained within the UK.

Marie Coleman covers the key events from the Easter Rising to the Irish Civil War and incorporates the most recent historiography on the subject. The book treats key themes such as labour, gender, sectarianism, the nature of revolutionary violence and the social background and motivation of revolutionaries.

Irish Revolution includes a document section that will introduce students to the principal primary sources relating to the events and themes covered in the text and further reading sections, all of which makes this the ideal introduction to the subject.

Marie Coleman is a Lecturer in the School of History and Anthropology at the Queen's University of Belfast. She teaches on aspects of Irish history and the Irish revolution at second- and third-year undergraduate level, and is the author of two books, *The Irish Sweep: A History of the Irish Hospitals Sweepstake, 1930–1987* (2009) and *County Longford and the Irish Revolution, 1910–1923* (2003).

Introduction to the series

History is narrative constructed by historians from traces left by the past. Historical enquiry is often driven by contemporary issues and, in consequence, historical narratives are constantly reconsidered, reconstructed and reshaped. The fact that different historians have different perspectives on issues means that there is also often controversy and no universally agreed version of past events. Seminar Studies was designed to bridge the gap between current research and debate, and the broad, popular general surveys that often date rapidly.

The volumes in the series are written by historians who are not only familiar with the latest research and current debates concerning their topic, but who have themselves contributed to our understanding of the subject. The books are intended to provide the reader with a clear introduction to a major topic in history. They provide both a narrative of events and a critical analysis of contemporary interpretations. They include the kinds of tools generally omitted from specialist monographs: a chronology of events, a glossary of terms and brief biographies of 'who's who'. They also include bibliographical essays in order to guide students to the literature on various aspects of the subject. Students and teachers alike will find that the selection of documents will stimulate discussion and offer insight into the raw materials used by historians in their attempt to understand the past.

Clive Emsley and Gordon Martel
Series Editors

The Irish Revolution, 1916–1923

Marie Coleman

Routledge
Taylor & Francis Group

LONDON AND NEW YORK

For Aoife and Niamh Martin

First published 2014
by Routledge
2 Park Square, Milton Park, Abingdon, Oxon OX14 4RN

and by Routledge
711 Third Avenue, New York, NY 10017

Routledge is an imprint of the Taylor & Francis Group, an informa business

© 2014 Marie Coleman

British Library Cataloguing-in-Publication Data
A catalogue record for this book is available from the British Library

Library of Congress Cataloging in Publication Data
A catalog record for this book has been requested

ISBN: 978-0-415-73687-9 (hbk)
ISBN: 978-1-408-27910-6 (pbk)
ISBN: 978-1-315-81341-7 (ebk)

Typeset in 10/13.5pt ITC Berkeley
by Graphicraft Limited, Hong Kong

Printed and bound by CPI Group (UK) Ltd, Croydon, CR0 4YY

Contents

Abbreviations		*viii*
Chronology		*ix*
Who's who		*xiii*
Glossary		*xvii*
List of plates		*xxi*
General reading		*xxii*
Maps		*xxiii*

PART ONE	BACKGROUND	1
1	THE IRISH QUESTION, 1870–1916	3
	Home Rule, 1870–1912	3
	The Ulster Crisis, 1912–14	7
	Ireland and the First World War	9
	Guide to further reading	11

PART TWO	ANALYSIS	13
2	THE EASTER RISING, 1916	15
	England's difficulty and Ireland's opportunity	15
	Easter Week	19
	The Proclamation	24
	Reactions	26
	Guide to further reading	29
3	THE REPUBLICAN RESURGENCE, 1917–19	31
	The 1917 and 1918 by-elections	31
	The post-Rising Volunteers	34

The Irish Convention   36
The conscription crisis   37
The 1918 general election   40
Guide to further reading   44

4   THE POLITICAL CAMPAIGN FOR INDEPENDENCE, 1919–21   45
The first Dáil Éireann   45
Foreign policy   48
Domestic policy   55
Social conflict in revolutionary Ireland   63
Guide to further reading   65

5   THE MILITARY CAMPAIGN FOR INDEPENDENCE, 1919–21   67
The Irish War of Independence   67
The social composition and motivation of the IRA   74
The geography of war   78
Guerrilla warfare and violence   81
Intelligence   88
Gender in the Irish revolution   90
Sectarianism   93
Guide to further reading   94

6   PEACE AND CIVIL WAR, 1921–3   96
British policy in Ireland, 1919–21   96
The partition of Ireland, 1920–1   97
The truce and the treaty   100
The treaty split   104
The Irish Civil War, 1922–3   112
Epilogue: The consolidation of the two Irelands, 1923–5   116
Guide to further reading   119

PART THREE   DOCUMENTS   121

1   The third home rule bill   122
2   The Ulster Solemn League and Covenant and the
    women's Declaration   123
3   John Redmond's Woodenbridge speech   123
4   Fianna Éireann and the Rising   124
5   The 1916 Proclamation   125
6   The Democratic Programme   126
7   John Dillon criticises the British response to the Rising   128

8	The extension of conscription to Ireland	129
9	Irish Roman Catholic bishops oppose conscription	130
10	Extracts from Sinn Féin's manifesto for the 1918 general election	131
11	The constitution of Dáil Éireann	131
12	The Declaration of Independence	133
13	The Message to the Free Nations of the World	134
14	Excerpts from the *Irish Bulletin*	135
15	Arthur Griffith on national courts of law	136
16	Extracts from Kevin O'Shiel's memoir of the Dáil land courts	137
17	The munitions strike, 1920	138
18	The Restoration of Order in Ireland Act	139
19	Extracts from the diaries of Mark Sturgis	139
20	Extracts from *An tÓglach* on guerrilla warfare	140
21	Violence against women during the War of Independence	143
22	Unionist acceptance of the Government of Ireland Act	144
23	The Government of Ireland Act (1920)	145
24	The Anglo-Irish Treaty	147
25	Extracts from the Dáil Treaty debate	150
26	Document No. 2	152
27	The Army Emergency Powers Resolution	153
	REFERENCES	155
	INDEX	163

Abbreviations

AARIR	American Association for the Recognition of the Irish Republic
BMH	Bureau of Military History
CBS	Christian Brothers school
CID	Criminal Investigation Department
DMP	Dublin Metropolitan Police
FOIF	Friends of Irish Freedom
GHQ	General Headquarters
GPO	General Post Office
ICA	Irish Citizen Army
IPP	Irish Parliamentary Party
IRA	Irish Republican Army
IRB	Irish Republican Brotherhood
ITGWU	Irish Transport and General Workers Union
IVF	Irish Volunteer Force
LGB	Local Government Board
MP	Member of Parliament
PRSTV	Proportional representation (by single transferable vote)
RIC	Royal Irish Constabulary
RUC	Royal Ulster Constabulary
ROIA	Restoration of Order in Ireland Act
SF	Sinn Féin
TD	*Teachta Dála*
USC	Ulster Special Constabulary
UVF	Ulster Volunteer Force

Chronology

1912

11 April   The third home rule bill is introduced in the House of Commons.

28 September   Over 200,000 unionists sign the Ulster Solemn League and Covenant in opposition to home rule and over 200,000 women sign a similar declaration.

1913

31 January   The Ulster Volunteer Force (UVF) is established to resist home rule.

26 August   Dublin tram drivers go on strike in support of trade union recognition sparking a lock-out of 20,000 industrial workers that lasted until early 1914.

25 November   The Irish Volunteer Force is founded in Dublin.

1914

5 April   Cumann na mBan, the women's auxiliary of the Irish Volunteers, holds its inaugural meeting.

24–5 April   The UVF lands over 35,000 rifles and five million rounds of ammunition in the Larne gun-running.

25 July   The Irish Volunteers land guns at Howth and three Volunteer supporters are shot dead by British soldiers at Bachelor's Walk in Dublin.

18 September   The third home rule bill becomes law but is suspended for the duration of the war. Provision will be made for the exclusion of part of Ulster.

20 September   John Redmond makes a speech at Woodenbridge, County Wicklow, encouraging Irish Volunteers to enlist in the army.

1916

21 April   Roger Casement is arrested at Banna strand on Good Friday.

23 April   Eoin MacNeill's countermanding order is published in the *Sunday Independent* on Easter Sunday.

24 April	The Easter Rising starts when the GPO is occupied and the Irish Republic declared.
29 April	Patrick Pearse surrenders, signalling the end of the Easter Rising.
3–12 May	Fourteen rebels are executed in Dublin and Thomas Kent is executed in Cork.
23 June	A majority of the Irish Party's supporters accept the offer of home rule for 26 counties.
20 July	The home rule negotiations collapse.
3 August	Roger Casement is hanged in Pentonville Prison.

1917

3 February	Count Plunkett (SF) wins the Roscommon North by-election.
9 May	Joseph McGuinness (SF) wins the Longford South by-election.
10 July	Eamon de Valera (SF) wins the Clare East by-election.
10 August	W. T. Cosgrave (SF) wins the Kilkenny City by-election.
25 September	Thomas Ashe dies from the effects of force-feeding.
25 October	The Sinn Féin *ard fheis* takes place in Dublin.
27 October	The national convention of the Irish Volunteers is held in Dublin.

1918

2 February	The IPP wins the Armagh South by-election.
6 March	John Redmond dies.
22 March	William Archer Redmond (IPP) wins the Waterford City by-election.
16 April	The Military Service Act passes and the IPP withdraws from Westminster.
21 April	Protests against conscription are held at Catholic churches.
23 April	A general strike against conscription is observed widely outside Ulster.
17–18 May	Seventy-three leading Sinn Féin members are arrested as part of an alleged German plot.
20 June	Arthur Griffith (SF) wins the Cavan East by-election.
14 December	The general election is held in which Sinn Féin wins 73 seats, Unionists 26 and the IPP 6.

1919

21 January	Dáil Éireann sits at the Mansion House in Dublin. Two RIC constables are shot dead by the IRA at Soloheadbeg, County Tipperary.
10 April	Dáil Éireann decrees a peaceful boycott of the RIC.
13 May	Two RIC officers are shot dead by the IRA during the rescue of Seán Hogan at Knocklong railway station, County Limerick.

11 June	Eamon de Valera arrives in America, where he remains until December 1920.
7 September	One soldier is killed and four injured in an attack by the IRA at Fermoy, County Cork, resulting in a reprisal attack on business premises in the town.
12 September	Dáil Éireann is proclaimed an illegal assembly.
19 December	The IRA fails in an attempt to assassinate the Lord Lieutenant, Lord French.

1920

2 January	Black and Tan recruits join the RIC.
15 January	Elections for urban local authorities take place.
20 March	The Sinn Féin Lord Mayor of Cork, Tomás MacCurtain, is shot dead by policemen in disguise.
3–4 April	The IRA destroys 350 government buildings, including police stations and taxation offices.
20 May	The munitions strike by dock and rail workers begins.
2–3 June	Elections for county councils and rural district councils take place.
21 July	Catholic workers are expelled from Belfast shipyards by loyalist co-workers.
23 July	Recruitment of the Auxiliary Division of the RIC begins.
9 August	The Restoration of Order in Ireland Act is passed at Westminster.
20 September	Balbriggan, County Dublin, is attacked and property destroyed by Black and Tans and Auxiliaries as a reprisal for the death of an RIC head constable.
25 October	The Sinn Féin Lord Mayor of Cork, Terence MacSwiney, dies in Brixton prison on the 75th day of a hunger strike.
1 November	Kevin Barry is hanged in Mountjoy Prison.
21 November	Bloody Sunday. A total of 41 people are killed, 36 of them in Dublin, including a number of intelligence officers shot dead by the Squad, civilians killed in police reprisal at Croke Park and leading IRA figures, Dick McKee and Peadar Clancy, while in custody in Dublin Castle.
28 November	Seventeen Auxiliaries are killed in an IRA ambush at Kilmichael, County Cork.
11–12 December	Widespread damage is done to Cork City and a number of prominent civic buildings are burned in a reprisal carried out by Auxiliaries.

1921

2 February	Four Auxiliaries are killed in an IRA ambush at Clonfin, County Longford.
3 February	Eleven RIC officers and Black and Tans are killed in an IRA ambush at Dromkeen, County Limerick.
20 February	Twelve members of the IRA's east Cork flying column are killed and eight are arrested at the Battle of Clonmult.

19 March	Nine soldiers and one Auxiliary are killed by Tom Barry's west Cork flying column at Crossbarry.
25 May	The Custom House in Dublin is attacked and burned by the IRA resulting in the arrest of nearly 100 members of the Dublin Brigade.
22 June	The Northern Ireland Parliament is opened by King George V in Belfast.
30 June	Richard and Abraham Pearson are shot dead by the IRA in Coolacrease, County Offaly.
11 July	A truce is agreed ending the War of Independence.
6 December	The Anglo-Irish Treaty is signed in 10 Downing Street.

1922

7 January	The Dáil accepts the Anglo-Irish Treaty by 64 votes to 57.
16 January	Dublin Castle is handed over to the Provisional Government.
24 March	The MacMahons are murdered in Belfast by members of the RIC and B Specials.
26 March	The army convention takes place, effectively splitting the IRA.
13 April	An anti-treaty IRA unit led by Rory O'Connor occupies the Four Courts.
27–9 April	Eighteen Protestants are killed in the Bandon area of west Cork.
16 June	The southern Irish general election is held.
17 June	Six Protestants are killed by the IRA in Altnaveigh and Lisdrumliska, County Armagh.
22 June	Sir Henry Wilson is assassinated in London by two IRA members.
28 June	The shelling of the Four Courts marks the start of the Civil War.
12 August	Arthur Griffith dies of a brain haemorrhage.
22 August	Michael Collins is shot dead in an IRA ambush in Beal na Blá, County Cork.
28 September	Dáil Éireann passes the Army Emergency Powers resolution establishing military courts that have the right to impose the death penalty.
6 December	The Irish Free State comes into existence one year after the signing of the treaty.
8 December	Rory O'Connor, Liam Mellows, Dick Barrett and Joe McKelvey are executed.

1923

7 March	Eight IRA men are killed by a Free State mine in Ballyseedy, County Kerry.
10 April	Liam Lynch is shot dead by the Free State army.
24 May	Frank Aiken orders an IRA ceasefire.

Who's who

Anderson, Sir John (1882–1958): Joint Under Secretary at Dublin Castle May 1920–January 1922.

Asquith, H. H. (1852–1928): British Prime Minister 1908–16.

Barry, Kevin (1902–20): Medical student and IRA volunteer hanged in Mountjoy Prison in November 1920.

Barry, Tom (1897–1980): Leader of the IRA's west Cork flying column in the War of Independence.

Birrell, Augustine (1850–1933): Irish Chief Secretary 1907–16.

Breen, Dan (1894–1969): Tipperary IRA leader during the War of Independence and author of a memoir of the revolution.

Broy, Ned (1887–1972): Detective in G Division of the Dublin Metropolitan Police who was one of Michael Collins's most important spies.

Brugha, Cathal (1874–1922): Minister for Defence in the First Dáil and an opponent of the treaty who was killed in the Civil War.

Carson, Sir Edward (1854–1935): Leader of the Ulster Unionist Party, 1910–21.

Casement, Roger (1864–1916): Former British diplomat who acquired guns in Germany for the Easter Rising, after which he was executed.

Ceannt, Eamon (1881–1916): Leader of the Easter Rising.

Childers, (Robert) Erskine (1870–1922): Sinn Féin propagandist, secretary to the Irish treaty delegation and subsequent opponent of the treaty who was executed in November 1922.

Clarke, Thomas (1858–1916): Senior IRB figure and leader of the Easter Rising.

Collins, Michael (1890–1922): Minister for Finance in the First Dáil; IRA Director of Organisation and Intelligence; signatory of the Anglo-Irish Treaty; chairman of the Provisional Government of the Irish Free State and Commander-in-Chief of its army.

Connolly, James (1868–1916): Socialist, trade unionist and leader of the Easter Rising.

Cope, Alfred W. 'Andy' (1877–1954): Joint Assistant Under Secretary at Dublin Castle 1920–2 and go-between for Lloyd George with Sinn Féin.

Cosgrave, William Thomas (W. T.) (1880–1965): Minister for Local Government in the First Dáil and chairman of the Provisional Government of the Irish Free State.

Craig, Sir James (1871–1940): Leader of the Ulster Unionist Party and first Prime Minister of Northern Ireland.

de Valera, Eamon (1882–1975): Leader of the Easter Rising and president of Sinn Féin and Dáil Éireann. An opponent of the treaty and later Taoiseach and President of Ireland.

Devlin, Joseph (1871–1934): IPP MP for Belfast Falls.

Dillon, John (1851–1927): IPP MP; succeeded John Redmond as leader in 1918.

French, Field Marshal Lord (1852–1925): Lord Lieutenant May 1918–April 1921.

Greenwood, Sir Hamar (1870–1948): Irish Chief Secretary April 1920–October 1922.

Griffith, Arthur (1871–1922): Journalist and founder of Sinn Féin; acting president (1919–20) and president (1922) of Dáil Éireann; signatory of the treaty.

Johnson, Thomas (1872–1963): Trade unionist and leader of the Irish Labour Party.

Lloyd George, David (1863–1945): British Prime Minister 1916–22.

Lynch, Liam (1893–1923): IRA leader in Cork during the War of Independence and Chief-of-Staff of the anti-treaty IRA 1922–3.

MacCurtain, Tomás (1884–1920): Sinn Féin Lord Mayor of Cork shot dead by police in March 1920.

MacDermott (MacDiarmada), Seán (1883–1916): IRB organizer and leader of the Easter Rising.

MacDonagh, Thomas (1878–1916): Poet, academic and leader of the Easter Rising.

MacNeill, Eoin (John) (1867–1945): Founder of the Irish Volunteers, Sinn Féin TD and Irish representative on the Boundary Commission.

MacPherson, Ian (1880–1937): Irish Chief Secretary January 1919–April 1920.

Macready, General Sir Nevil (1862–1946): Commander of the British Army in Ireland 1920–2.

MacSwiney, Mary (1872–1942): Sinn Féin TD and sister of Terence MacSwiney, who was a vociferous opponent of the treaty.

MacSwiney, Terence (1879–1920): Sinn Féin Lord Mayor of Cork who died on hunger strike in October 1920.

Markievicz, Countess Constance (1868–1927): ICA commander during the Easter Rising, Sinn Féin TD and Minister for Labour in the First Dáil and an opponent of the treaty.

Mulcahy, Richard (1886–1971): Sinn Féin TD, IRA Chief-of-Staff during the War of Independence, Commander-in-Chief of the Free State Army.

O'Connor, Rory (1883–1922): Anti-treaty IRA leader who occupied the Four Courts in April 1922 and was executed on 8 December 1922.

O'Flanagan, Fr Michael (1876–1942): Catholic priest from County Roscommon who was active in organising Sinn Féin after the Easter Rising.

Pearse, Patrick (1879–1916): Educationalist and leader of the Easter Rising.

Plunkett, George Noble, Count (1851–1948): Father of Joseph Mary Plunkett and Sinn Féin TD.

Plunkett, Joseph Mary (1887–1916): Planner and leader of the Easter Rising.

Redmond, John (1856–1918): Leader of the Irish Parliamentary Party 1900–18.

Sheehy-Skeffington, Francis (1878–1916): Pacifist, journalist and suffragist controversially shot dead during Easter Rising.

Sheehy-Skeffington, Hanna (1877–1946): Wife of Francis Sheehy-Skeffington and Sinn Féin activist.

Sturgis, Mark (1884–1949): Diarist and joint Assistant Under Secretary at Dublin Castle, May 1920–2.

Treacy, Seán (1895–1920): Tipperary IRA leader during the War of Independence.

Tudor, Hugh (1871–1965): Police adviser 1920–2, who recruited the Black and Tans and Auxiliaries.

Wilson, Field Marshal Sir Henry (1864–1922): Irish-born former Chief of the Imperial General Staff of the British Army and security adviser to the Northern Ireland Government assassinated by the IRA in June 1922.

Glossary

Act of Union: Political, economic and religious union of Ireland with Great Britain from 1801 until 1921.

Anglo-Irish Treaty: Treaty signed in December 1921 between Britain and Southern Ireland that created the Irish Free State as a dominion of the Commonwealth.

An tÓglach: Journal of the Irish Volunteers/IRA, edited by Piaras Béaslaí.

Ard fheis: Annual national convention of Sinn Féin.

Auxiliaries (Auxiliary Division of the RIC): Paramilitary police force recruited largely from ex-soldiers brought to Ireland in August 1920 to bolster the RIC.

Belfast boycott: Boycott of Ulster businesses introduced by Dáil Éireann in protest at partition and sectarian attacks on Catholics in Ulster.

Black and Tans: Paramilitary police force recruited largely from ex-soldiers and introduced to Ireland in January 1920.

Bloody Sunday: 21 November 1920. Forty-one people were killed including British Intelligence agents, civilians attending a football match at Croke Park and senior IRA prisoners in Dublin Castle. Not to be confused with Bloody Sunday in Derry in January 1972.

Boundary commission: Commission established under the Anglo-Irish Treaty to delineate the border between Northern Ireland and the Irish Free State. Its 1925 report was suppressed and the border left unchanged.

B Specials: see *Ulster Special Constabulary*.

Ceann Comhairle: Chairman or speaker of Dáil Éireann.

Christian Brothers: An Irish Catholic teaching order founded in the nineteenth century.

Criminal Investigation Department (CID): Free State intelligence unit that operated during the Civil War and earned a reputation for ill-treatment and controversial killings of republicans.

Cumann na mBan: The women's auxiliary of the Irish Volunteers/IRA, formed in 1914.

Cumann na nGaedheal: Political party formed in 1922 from pro-treaty Sinn Féin.

Curragh Mutiny: Threat by Irish officers in the British Army stationed at the Curragh in County Kildare to resign their commissions rather that use force against Ulster during the home rule crisis in March 1914.

Dáil Éireann: Irish Parliament, established by Sinn Féin in January 1919.

Document No. 2: De Valera's alternative to the treaty that envisaged an external association relationship between the Free State and Britain, under which the King would not be recognised as Irish head of state.

Dominion status: The sovereignty granted to the Irish Free State under the Anglo-Irish Treaty, under which the King remained as head of state, similarly to Australia, New Zealand, Canada and South Africa.

Dublin Castle: The administrative centre of British government in Ireland.

Dublin Metropolitan Police (DMP): Police force for Dublin until 1925.

Fenians: see *Irish Republican Brotherhood*.

Fianna Éireann: Republican boy scouts and youth wing of the Irish Volunteers, many of whose members took part in the Easter Rising.

Fianna Fáil: Political party formed by Eamon de Valera in 1926 following a split in Sinn Féin.

Flying column: Mobile active service unit formed by the IRA during the War of Independence to wage guerrilla warfare.

Friends of Irish Freedom (FOIF): Irish-American organisation led by John Devoy and Daniel Cohalan that supported Irish independence and split with de Valera's American Association for the Recognition of the Irish Republic (AARIR) in October 1920.

Frongoch: Prison camp in north Wales where many of the 1916 prisoners were interned.

Gaelic Athletic Association: Association formed in 1884 to codify and regulate Gaelic sports. It was infiltrated by the Irish Republican Brotherhood (IRB) and many prominent revolutionaries were members.

Gaelic League: Organisation formed in 1893 by Eoin MacNeill and Douglas Hyde to revive the Irish language. Became increasingly politicised and included many revolutionaries including Patrick Pearse.

Government of Ireland Act (1920): Legislation partitioning Ireland into the six counties of Northern Ireland and the 26 counties of Southern Ireland that later became the Irish Free State.

Home rule: Devolved government for Ireland within the United Kingdom. Existed in Northern Ireland 1921–72.

Irish Bulletin: Propaganda newspaper of Dáil Éireann.

Irish Citizen Army (ICA): Militia formed by James Connolly to protect striking workers in Dublin city during the 1913 lock-out which played a key role in the Easter Rising.

Irish Parliamentary Party (Irish Party/IPP): The Irish home rule party.

Irish Republican Army (IRA): see *Irish Volunteers*.

Irish Republican Brotherhood (IRB): Secret oath-bound society formed in 1858 to achieve an Irish republic by revolutionary means. Responsible for planning the Easter Rising.

Irish Transport and General Workers Union (ITGWU): Trade union founded by Jim Larkin in 1908.

Irish Volunteers (Irish Volunteer Force): Paramilitary body formed on 25 November 1913 in response to the formation of the Ulster Volunteers. It split in September 1914 into Redmond's National Volunteers and MacNeill's Irish Volunteers, which carried out the Easter Rising. It was rejuvenated in 1917 and 1918 and fought the guerrilla campaign in the War of Independence (1919–21), by which time it was more commonly known as the Irish Republican Army (IRA).

Lord Lieutenant: The King's representative in Ireland under the Act of Union.

Northern Ireland: Six-county home rule entity created by the Government of Ireland Act (1920) comprising Counties Antrim, Armagh, Derry, Down, Fermanagh and Tyrone.

Proportional representation by single transferable vote (PRSTV): An electoral system based on multiple-seat constituencies, in which voters vote numerically in order of preference (1, 2, 3 . . .), and votes are allocated accordingly until all seats are filled. Favours smaller parties.

Representation of the People Act (1918): Legislation extending the vote to women over 30 and widening the franchise generally.

Revisionism: A term used to describe a critical re-evaluation of history that emerged in Ireland from the 1930s. In the context of the Irish revolution it is often a pejorative term applied to historians seen as critical of the traditional nationalist interpretation of the period.

Royal Irish Constabulary (RIC): The police force for Ireland outside of Dublin, which was disbanded in 1922.

Sinn Féin: Political party formed by Arthur Griffith in 1905, adopted a republican constitution in 1917 and split in January 1922 into pro-treaty (later Cumann na nGaedheal) and anti-treaty factions and again in 1926 with the formation of Fianna Fáil.

Solemn League and Covenant: Commitment to resist home rule signed by over 200,000 men in Ulster in September 1912. A corresponding declaration was signed by over 200,000 women.

Squad: A death squad controlled by Michael Collins that targeted British Intelligence agents and was responsible for high-profile killings such as Bloody Sunday.

Teachta Dála (TD): Member of Dáil Éireann.

Third home rule bill: Irish home rule bill introduced in April 1912 and passed in September 1914 but suspended for the duration of the war and subsequently abandoned and replaced by the Government of Ireland Act in 1920.

Ulster Provisional Government: Plans for a breakaway government drawn up by the Ulster Unionists in the event of home rule being imposed against their will in 1914.

Ulster Special Constabulary (USC): Special constabulary formed to deal with violence in Ulster in 1920 that contained a large number of Ulster Volunteer Force (UVF) members and was associated with high-profile sectarian attacks and killings of Catholics.

Ulster Unionist Party: The political party representing unionists in Ulster.

Ulster Volunteer Force (UVF): A paramilitary force formed in Ulster in January 1913 to resist home rule by force, many of whose members were killed in the First World War.

Plates

The following plates appear between pages 95 and 96.

1   John Redmond delivering a speech on the third home rule bill, April 1912

2   The destruction of the GPO after the Easter Rising, 1916

3   The Irish Citizen Army outside Liberty Hall

4   Arthur Griffith (1871–1922)

5   Eamon de Valera (1882–1975)

6   Constance Markievicz (1868–1927)

7   Anti-conscription pledge poster

8   Auxiliary recruits

9   The Irish Army taking over Portobello Barracks, Dublin, in 1922

10   Sir James Craig, first prime minister of Northern Ireland at the opening of the Northern Ireland Parliament in City Hall, Belfast, June 1922

General reading

Bartlett, T. (2010) *Ireland: A History*. Cambridge: Cambridge University Press.

Boyce, D. G. (1992) *Ireland 1828–1923: From Ascendancy to Democracy*. Oxford: Blackwell.

Boyce, D. G. (1995) *Nationalism in Ireland*, 3rd edition. London: Routledge.

Boyce, D. G. (1996) *The Irish Question and British Politics, 1868–1996*. Basingstoke: Palgrave.

Boyce, D. George (ed.) (1988) *The Revolution in Ireland, 1879–1923*. Dublin: Gill and Macmillan.

English, R. (2003) *Armed Struggle: A History of the IRA*. London: Macmillan.

English, R. (2007) *Irish Freedom: A History of Nationalism in Ireland*. London: Macmillan.

Fitzpatrick, D. (1998) *The Two Irelands, 1912–1939*. Oxford: Oxford University Press.

Jackson, A. (1999) *Ireland, 1798–1998*. Oxford: Blackwell.

Lyons, F. S. L. (1971) *Ireland Since the Famine*. London: Weidenfeld & Nicolson.

Smith, J. (1999) *Britain and Ireland: From Home Rule to Independence*. Harlow: Longman.

Townshend, C. (2013) *The Republic: The Fight for Irish Independence, 1918–1923*. London: Allen Lane.

Vaughan, W. E. (ed.) (1996) *A New History of Ireland, Vol. VI: Ireland Under the Union II, 1870–1921*. Oxford: Oxford University Press.

Walsh, O. (2002) *Ireland's Independence, 1880–1923*. London: Routledge.

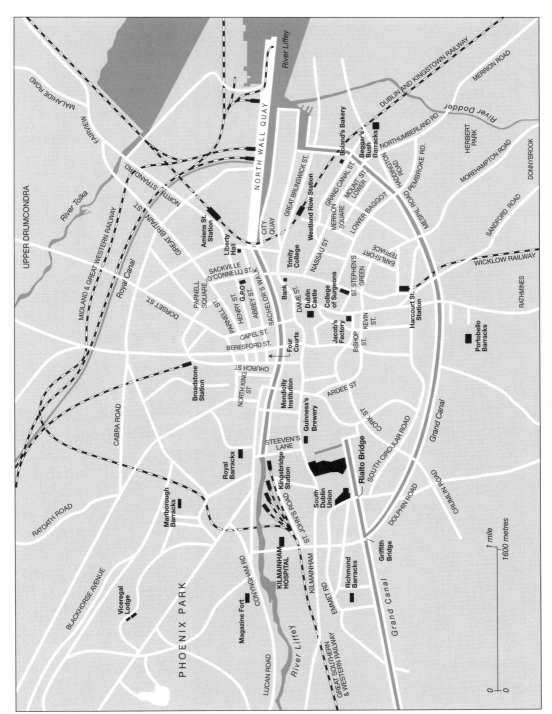

1 Map of central Dublin showing the principal locations of action during the Easter Rising.

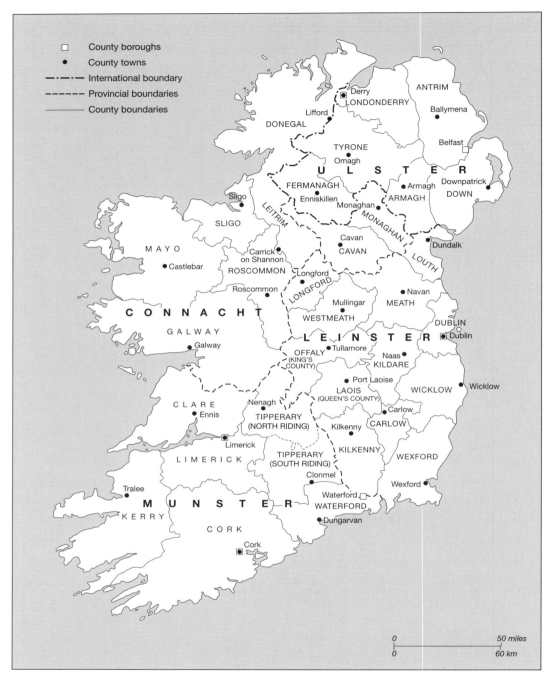

2 Map of Ireland showing county boundaries and the border between Northern Ireland and the Irish Free State.

Part 1

BACKGROUND

1

The Irish Question, 1870–1916

HOME RULE, 1870–1912

In the last quarter of the nineteenth century a vigorous political movement emerged in Ireland seeking home rule, a form of devolved government that would give Ireland control of its own affairs while remaining within the imperial framework. Ireland would remain part of the United Kingdom with Great Britain that was formed in 1801 but the Westminster Parliament would not have sole legislative jurisdiction for Ireland. **Home rule** was the latest manifestation of a nineteenth-century tradition of using constitutional means to achieve some modification of the **Act of Union** and was preceded by O'Connell's emancipation and repeal movements in the 1820s and 1840s, and the Independent Irish Party in the 1850s.

A second impetus for the emergence of the home rule movement was the campaign for an amnesty for Fenian prisoners. The **Irish Republican Brotherhood (IRB)**, popularly known as the Fenians, was a secret revolutionary organisation. Following an abortive uprising in 1867 many of its members were imprisoned and an Amnesty Association was formed, comprising Fenian sympathisers and constitutional nationalist politicians, to seek a reprieve for them. The president of the association was a Protestant lawyer from Donegal, Isaac Butt, who had defended Fenian prisoners. Initially a Tory who opposed repeal of the union, the experience of the famine in the 1840s and of defending nationalists gradually brought him around to supporting a measure of Irish self-government.

In 1870 Butt formed the Home Government Association, which was essentially a Dublin-based pressure group, initially composed mostly of Protestants. It had a very limited appeal and did not enjoy much success (O'Day, 1998: 29). A broader-based Home Rule League was formed in 1874, enjoying immediate success with the return of 59 home rule candidates in that year's general election. The parliamentary strength of the league was somewhat illusory as many of those elected were former Liberals who had

Home rule: Devolved government for Ireland within the United Kingdom. Existed in Northern Ireland 1921–72.

Act of Union: Political, economic and religious union of Ireland with Great Britain from 1801 until 1921.

Irish Republican Brotherhood (IRB): Secret oath-bound society formed in 1858 to achieve an Irish republic by revolutionary means. Responsible for planning the Easter Rising.

simply switched over to the increasingly popular new political movement. In reality, only about one-third of those elected in 1874 were committed home rulers, and many abandoned their short-lived dalliance with home rule as soon as election had been secured (Thornley, 1964: 195–6).

The Fenian uprising also had a significant impact on British politics. The Liberal Party leader, William Gladstone, who became Prime Minister in 1868, saw the rebellion as an indication that reform was badly needed in Ireland to assuage the discontent that had precipitated it. For the next 25 years Ireland became a 'preoccupation' for Gladstone. The policy he adopted towards Ireland was aimed at drawing a line 'between the **Fenians** and the people of Ireland and to make the people of Ireland indisposed to cross it'. In pursuit of this policy he sought to introduce a level of reform that would detract support from revolutionary nationalism while preserving Ireland's place within the union. His first government sought 'justice for Ireland' through disestablishment of the Church of Ireland, land reform and solving the issue of university education for Catholics, but was still a long way from supporting home rule (Matthew, 1986: 192–6).

The first Irish Home Rule Party made very little impression at Westminster between 1874 and 1877. The first home rule resolution introduced by Butt in July 1874 was defeated soundly by 458 votes to 61 and his land reform bill met a similar fate in 1876. In 1877 a group of Irish Members of Parliament (MPs), including Joseph Biggar and Charles Stewart Parnell, resorted to the tactic of obstruction, essentially filibustering and delaying the workings of Parliament with long speeches and frequently tabling amendments to legislation. The stratagem which was opposed by Butt divided the party and by the time of his death in May 1879 it had little to show for five years in parliament (Thornley, 1964: 233, 274, 335).

Butt's failure was partly due to his own personality, which was unsuited to political life, and his precarious personal finances, which required him to spend much of his time on the legal circuit in Ireland to the neglect of his leadership of the parliamentary party. The perceived Protestant dominance of the early home rule movement made essential allies such as the Roman Catholic clergy, tenant farmers and the remnants of the Fenians suspicious of it. Even if Butt had garnered greater support in Ireland and been a more effective party leader, it would have been to little avail as there was no significant support in Britain for Irish home rule, which was an essential prerequisite for its success. Nevertheless, Butt bequeathed an important legacy to his successors; a distinct **Irish Parliamentary Party (IPP)** existed at Westminster and home rule had been established as the minimum demand of Irish nationalists (Thornley, 1964: 380–7).

By the late 1870s home rule had also been over-shadowed by the emergence of the Land War. An economic depression in the late 1870s,

Fenians: See *Irish Republican Brotherhood.*

Irish Parliamentary Party (Irish Party/IPP): The Irish home rule party.

caused by unusually bad weather and a succession of bad harvests, resulted in a decline in both crop and livestock production. An influx of cheap grain from the USA, the curtailment of credit and the refusal of landlords to lower rents resulted in an increase in evictions and a generally precarious situation for Irish tenant farmers. In 1879 the Land League was formed in County Mayo, initially to protect tenants during the immediate crisis, but with the long-term aim of replacing landlords. As the rising star of Irish nationalist politics, Parnell accepted the presidency of the League and much of the period from 1879 to 1882 was taken up with the land issue.

Gladstone introduced a Land Act in 1881 that granted the basic demands of tenants, known as the three 'f's – fair rent, free sale and fixity of tenure. Parnell's response to it was ambiguous and when he attacked it at public meetings in Ireland he was arrested and held in Kilmainham Jail. After reaching a compromise with Gladstone in 1882, whereby the Prime Minister agreed to amend the Act to make better provision for leaseholders and tenants in arrears with rent in return for Parnell using his influence to quell agrarian agitation, Parnell was finally in a position to bring home rule back to the centre of the Irish and British political stages.

When Parnell established the Irish National League in 1882, to replace the outlawed Land League, home rule became its primary aim. He also formed a much more cohesive and disciplined parliamentary party, insisting that prior to standing in an election all candidates were required to take an oath pledging themselves to 'sit, act and vote with the Irish Parliamentary Party' and to resign their seats if found to be in breach of this promise. As a result, the 86 home rule MPs elected in the 1885 general election were loyal home rulers (O'Day, 1998: 70–80).

The overall result of the election – 335 seats for the out-going Liberal government and 249 for the Conservatives – meant that the Irish Party, whose 86 seats represented the exact difference between the two main parties, was in a position to make or break the government. The Irish Party eventually pledged its support to the Liberals early in 1886 when Gladstone announced that he had come around to supporting home rule for Ireland, a decision that appears to have stemmed from a belief that there was a strong moral argument for it as well as a feeling that such a measure of reform was needed to head-off serious social disorder in Ireland (Loughlin, 1986: 284–7).

The first home rule bill, which was introduced in parliament in April 1886, provided for a unicameral legislature with jurisdiction over domestic affairs, the Irish bureaucracy and the judiciary. There would no longer be any Irish representation in the House of Commons at Westminster, a controversial provision in light of the significant powers to govern Ireland that were retained by the imperial parliament, including trade, defence and taxation. Opposition to the measure from Liberal-Unionists within Gladstone's own

Party, who wished to protect the union and the interests of the Protestant minority in Ulster, resulted in the bill's defeat in the House of Commons by 341 votes to 311 (O'Day, 1998: 106–16).

Gladstone's second home rule bill in 1893 proceeded one step further, making it through the Commons, only to be rejected by the House of Lords, an institution whose implacable opposition would need to be overcome for Irish home rule to have a chance of success. By that time the IPP was in disarray, riven by the O'Shea divorce case that ousted Parnell as leader, and left rudderless by his death in 1891. Gladstone's government was forced out of office soon afterwards and replaced by a Conservative government and Gladstone was replaced as leader of the Liberal Party by Lord Rosebery, who did not commit the party to home rule (O'Day, 1998: 165–70).

Although the Irish Party re-emerged united in 1900, the obstacle of British opposition to home rule remained. The Conservatives tried to quell demands through a policy of constructive unionism, also known as 'killing home rule with kindness', that included new Land Purchase Acts, local government reform and renewed efforts to solve the university question. The post-Gladstone Liberals were wary of home rule for having split the party in 1886, supported constructive unionism, were alienated by elements of the Irish Party's support for the Boers during the South African Wars and did not want to be dependent on a small party as they had been after the 1885 election. Therefore, when the Liberals were returned to power with a large majority in 1906 under Henry Campbell-Bannerman, who was replaced as party leader and prime minister by Herbert Asquith in 1908, it was the first Liberal government since 1886 not to introduce an Irish home rule bill. Given the size of their majority (245 more seats than the Conservatives), the government could probably have successfully introduced a home rule bill. The House of Lords would have had difficulty opposing the will of a government with such a huge mandate, and if it had done so it would have triggered a latent confrontation with the Commons over the veto powers of the unelected peers.

This confrontation finally happened in 1909 when the Lords rejected aspects of David Lloyd George's 'people's budget' that introduced higher taxes to fund national insurance, resulting in the introduction of the Parliament Act in 1911 that severely curtailed the ability of the Lords to reject legislation indefinitely. One major obstacle to home rule, which had prevented its implementation in 1892, had now been removed. The remaining barrier of Liberal indifference had also been overcome in the meantime, as the general elections of 1910 reduced the Liberals' working majority, replicating the situation of 1886 where they required the support of the Irish Party, the *quid pro quo* for which was a third home rule bill. The introduction of the **third home rule bill** on 11 April 1912 triggered a political crisis in the United Kingdom.

Third home rule bill: Irish home rule bill introduced in April 1912 and passed in September 1914 but suspended for the duration of the war and subsequently abandoned and replaced by the Government of Ireland Act in 1920.

THE ULSTER CRISIS, 1912–14

The third home rule bill envisioned a devolved bi-cameral parliament in Ireland with limited jurisdiction that excluded land purchase, old age pensions, national insurance, policing, taxation and postal services as well as imperial concerns such as defence and foreign policy [**Doc. 1**]. Limitations were also to be imposed on the Home Rule Parliament's right to legislate over matters relating to religion and education. These clauses were inserted to assuage unionist fears, which were heightened at the time by the *Ne Temere* papal decree of 1908 requiring the children of mixed marriages to be raised as Catholics. Unionists were not convinced by such safeguards and were more fearful than ever of home rule becoming a reality as their traditional protectors in the House of Lords could no longer veto the bill indefinitely. Under the terms of the Parliament Act the Lords could reject the bill twice. If it passed the Commons a third time it would become law. Unionists, especially in the commercialised regions of the north-east and the major urban centres, were also concerned that a Home Rule Parliament, which would inevitably be dominated by the agrarian interests of the IPP, could be detrimental to their business interests. The union had already been tampered with when Gladstone disestablished the Church of Ireland in 1869 and they feared any further dilution of it would distance them further from their co-religionists in Britain, with whom they felt a closer ethnic affiliation.

The prospect of home rule by 1914 led unionists to resort to an intensive campaign of political, extra-parliamentary and military tactics to defeat it. While there was opposition within southern unionism, this was a declining force, and much of the focus of the campaign against the bill was centred on Ulster, in the process further distancing the Ulster Unionists from their southern brethren. Under its new leader, the Dublin-born lawyer, Sir Edward Carson, the Unionist Party forged a close alliance with the Conservative Party to attack the bill during its parliamentary passage. The Conservative leader, Andrew Bonar-Law, whose family had Ulster-Scots heritage, was personally opposed to home rule but also saw a good opportunity to unite his party, which was recovering from a debilitating split over free trade, around a major political issue (Smith, 2000: 5–8).

The unionists also brought their campaign to a wider public audience with a series of large demonstrations held throughout Ulster and Britain, including gatherings at Craigavon, County Down, the family seat of the influential unionist Sir James Craig, and Blenheim Palace, the ancestral home of the Churchills. The initial hope of unionists was to defeat home rule entirely. However, with its enactment a strong possibility since the removal of the Lords' veto, contingency plans were drawn up to exclude Ulster from it. In September 1913 plans were put in place for the formation of an

Ulster Provisional Government: Plans for a breakaway government drawn up by the Ulster Unionists in the event of home rule being imposed against their will in 1914.

Solemn League and Covenant: Commitment to resist home rule signed by over 200,000 men in Ulster in September 1912. A corresponding declaration was signed by over 200,000 women.

Ulster Provisional Government that would breakaway from the Irish Home Rule Parliament.

The most telling demonstration of Ulster's intention to resist home rule was the signing of the Ulster **Solemn League and Covenant** in September 1912. Drawing its inspiration from the covenant signed by the opponents of Charles I in 1643, more than 200,000 men signed the Ulster Covenant and reaffirmed their loyalty to the king, promised to defend their rights as citizens of the United Kingdom and declared their intention to 'defeat the present conspiracy to set up a Home Rule Parliament in Ireland' and refuse to recognise it should it be established. Over 200,000 women signed a declaration expressing similar sentiments [**Doc. 2**]. The covenant was signed throughout Ulster on 28 September 1912, which was declared as Ulster Day (Buckland, 1973: 45–67).

The unionist strategy was successful in highlighting the cause of Ulster and eventually ensuring that home rule would need to be modified to accommodate unionist opposition. The first suggestion of making some form of separate provision for Ulster arose in June 1912 when a Liberal backbencher, T. G. Agar-Robartes, proposed an amendment that would have excluded the four counties with Protestant majorities – Antrim, Armagh, Derry and Down. While unionists opposed the idea of partition initially, they were prepared to use the threat of it as a tactic to destroy home rule, in the belief that the IPP would accept nothing less than home rule for all of Ireland. However, by 1914, the home rule bill was entering the final stages of its passage having survived two defeats in the Lords, and both unionists and the government came to realise that the only solution to the Ulster crisis was excluding a part of Ulster from home rule.

In March 1914 Asquith announced that those Ulster counties which chose to do so could remain outside the workings of home rule, a solution which satisfied neither side in Ireland, with Edward Carson describing it as a death sentence with a six-year stay of execution. There was an unsuccessful attempt to negotiate the area of Ulster that would be excluded at the Buckingham Palace Conference in June 1914. The counties of Fermanagh and Tyrone, which had Catholic majorities, proved to be insurmountable obstacles. The government's ability to impose any solution without a compromise was made increasingly difficult when sections of the British Army based at the Curragh in County Kildare indicated that they would not be prepared to quell any uprising in Ulster against the imposition of home rule. Although often referred to as the **Curragh Mutiny**, no direct orders were disobeyed, but the incident was a further boost to unionist resistance and made a compromise on Ulster more likely (Laffan, 1983: 19–48).

Curragh Mutiny: Threat by Irish officers in the British Army stationed at the Curragh in County Kildare to resign their commissions rather that use force against Ulster during the home rule crisis in March 1914.

Should parliamentary and propagandist tactics fail to defeat home rule, unionists were prepared to resort to violence to protect their interests, as evidenced by the formation of the paramilitary group, the **Ulster Volunteer Force (UVF)**, in January 1913. This force, which had an estimated membership of 110,000 by mid-1914, enjoyed the support of unionist political leaders, as well as prominent business magnates and senior British Army officers. The seriousness of its intentions was made clear in April 1914 when a large consignment of arms and ammunition was imported into Larne, Bangor and Donaghadee in the Larne gun-running (Bowman, 2007: 1, 142).

The formation and arming of the Ulster unionists served as an example to nationalists in the south, who formed their own Irish Volunteer Force in November 1913. Recruitment was slow initially with an estimated 10,000 enlisting in the final two months of 1913. This figure progressed steadily throughout the first half of 1914, inspired by the Larne gun-running and Asquith's vacillation on the inclusion of Ulster in home rule. However, it was not until the summer of that year, when John Redmond succeeded in taking control of the organisation to ensure it did not derail the implementation of home rule, that the **Irish Volunteers** mushroomed to 150,000 members. The Irish Volunteers armed themselves in a similar way to the UVF with the importation of arms through Howth in County Dublin in July 1914 (Townshend, 2005: 44; Fitzpatrick, 1996: 386).

By the summer of 1914, with home rule set to become law by September, Ireland was on the brink of civil war, with two armed militias ready to use violence to fight for and against home rule and the government unsure of the loyalty of the army in Ireland to deal effectively with any such event. However, a conflict was avoided and the Irish political crisis that had consumed British politics for two years was swept aside almost overnight with the outbreak of the First World War in August 1914. On 18 September 1914, 40 years of campaigning by Irish nationalists finally resulted in Irish home rule becoming law. However, it was accompanied by two provisos – it would be suspended for the duration of the war and part of Ulster would be excluded in some form.

Ulster Volunteer Force (UVF): A paramilitary force formed in Ulster in January 1913 to resist home rule by force, many of whose members were killed in the First World War.

Irish Volunteers (Irish Volunteer Force): Paramilitary body formed on 25 November 1913 in response to the formation of the Ulster Volunteers. It split in September 1914 into Redmond's National Volunteers and MacNeill's Irish Volunteers, which carried out the Easter Rising. It was rejuvenated in 1917 and 1918 and fought the guerrilla campaign in the War of Independence (1919–21), by which time it was more commonly known as the Irish Republican Army (IRA).

IRELAND AND THE FIRST WORLD WAR

Six weeks after the start of the war, on 20 September 1914, John Redmond delivered a speech to a gathering of Irish Volunteers at Woodenbridge, County Wicklow, urging them to enlist in the army [**Doc. 3**]. Redmond had succeeded in gaining control of the Volunteer movement earlier in June 1914 to ensure it did not fall too strongly under the influence of radical nationalists and derail the chances of achieving home rule. The support of constitutional nationalism swelled the ranks of the Irish Volunteers, with membership estimated to be over 150,000 by August 1914 (Coleman, 2003: 33).

Redmond, who was a strong believer in Ireland playing a role in the empire, like Canada or Australia, believed that Ireland should make its contribution to the war effort, and hoped that its support would be rewarded with the implementation of home rule once the war ended. He entertained the hope that the experience of Irish nationalists and unionists fighting together for the same cause might heal the divisions of the preceding years. He was also aware that the UVF would immediately pledge its support and that nationalist Ireland could not afford to 'allow the Unionists to win all the credit for sacrifice in the British cause' (Bew, 1996: 38). His support for the war split the Volunteers, with the majority styled the National Volunteers remaining under Redmondite control and many of them (estimated at 24,000) enlisting. A rump of 10,000 Irish Volunteers, who were opposed to the British war effort, coalesced under the leadership of Eoin MacNeill (Fitzpatrick, 1996: 380).

Redmond's call to arms and the loyalty of the UVF explain why many young Irish men joined the British Army during the First World War. Enlistment rates were higher in Ulster, from where half of all Irish recruits came. Approximately 45 per cent of Irish recruits were Protestant, a disproportionately high figure given that the Protestant population of Ireland was 26 per cent (Boyce, 2002: 193). Irish recruitment was a noticeably urban phenomenon, possibly because there was greater economic need in cities, but also because farmers benefited economically from the war and did not want to lose their sons or labourers to the army.

Many joined for reasons other than the influence of John Redmond or the UVF, including the sense of adventure associated with soldiering, the militarism of Irish society at that time, peer influence, family martial traditions and the financial benefits that would accrue to dependents. Some held a genuine conviction that the war was morally justified, and there was considerable sympathy among Irish Catholics for their Belgian counterparts. The German actions in Belgium, where Catholic priests were targeted, also meant that the Irish Catholic hierarchy were influential supporters of the war effort in its early stages (Fitzpatrick, 1996: 388–90; Pašeta, 2008: 76).

It is estimated that over 200,000 Irish men fought in the British Army during the First World War. There was an initial rush to enlist, with 44,000 joining up in the first five months. The realisation that the war would be a prolonged and bloody one soon cooled such ardour and recruitment figures fell to 46,000 in 1915. By 1916, when the horrors of the war were being brought home by conflicts like the Somme, enlistment declined noticeably and progressively; from 1916 to 1918 the annual enlistment figures were 19,000, 14,000 and under 11,000 respectively (Fitzpatrick, 1996: 388).

The UVF was rewarded for its support with the formation of a distinct 36th Ulster Division that would endure considerable losses, especially at the

Somme in 1916 where it lost over 5,000 men. As a result, the war and the Somme, in particular, hold a very significant place in unionist political and cultural memory. The Irish casualties at the Somme were not exclusively from the Ulster Division; 4,300 men from the 16th Division also perished (Horne, 2008: 12). Redmond's hopes that the National Volunteers would be treated similarly to the UVF were dashed, although most southern Irishmen served in the 10th and 16th Divisions which played significant roles, and suffered considerable losses, in important engagements at Gallipoli, Guillemont and Ginchy (Dungan, 1997: 12). An estimated 27,405 Irish soldiers were killed in the war, approximately 14 per cent of those who enlisted, which is a similar proportion to overall British Army casualties (Fitzpatrick, 1996: 392).

The suspension of home rule created a very difficult position for the Irish Party. It had achieved its main aim in theory but not in practice. There was no longer a need to campaign for home rule, nor an opportunity to get on with the business of running a Home Rule Parliament in Ireland. The influence that the Irish Party enjoyed from 1910, with the Liberals dependent on its support, disappeared as the main British parties moved closer together, eventually forming a coalition government in 1915, in which prominent Ulster unionists were given posts, including Edward Carson as Attorney General. Redmond was treated badly by the government which refused to allow the National Volunteers to be used for the defence of Ireland or to form a specific division for them. His hopes that Ireland might benefit from some of the economic spoils of the war were also dashed when the War Office failed to award any significant contracts to Irish firms. The continued suspension of home rule, Redmond's political impotence and his continued support for a war that grew increasingly less popular in Ireland meant that his party was in a precarious position even before the events of Easter 1916 in Dublin.

GUIDE TO FURTHER READING

A detailed documentary history of unionism is contained in Patrick Buckland's *Irish Unionism, 1885–1923* (Her Majesty's Stationery Office, 1973). This work is complemented by *Ulster Unionism and the Origins of Northern Ireland, 1886–1922* (Gill and Macmillan, 1973) which provides a detailed account of the tactics adopted by Ulster unionists to resist the third home rule bill and their acceptance of home rule for six counties in 1920. Digitised copies of the Ulster Solemn League and Covenant are on the website of the Public Record of Northern Ireland, http://www.proni.gov.uk/index/search_the_archives/ulster_covenant.htm

The classic account of the political controversy created by the third home rule bill is A. T. Q. Stewart, *The Ulster Crisis, 1912–14* (Faber, 1967). There are two detailed and comprehensive accounts of the Irish home rule movement in Alvin Jackson's, *Home Rule: An Irish History, 1800–2000* (Weidenfeld & Nicolson, 2003) and Alan O'Day's, *Irish Home Rule, 1887–1921* (Manchester University Press, 1998).

The leading political figures of the period are examined in biographical studies including Alvin Jackson's, *Sir Edward Carson* (Dundalk, 1993), F. S. L. Lyons's, *John Dillon: A Biography* (Routledge and Kegan Paul, 1968) and Paul Bew's, *John Redmond* (Dundalgan, 1996). The Irish policy of the two principal British political parties is examined in Patricia Jalland's, *The Liberals and Ireland: The Ulster Question in British Politics to 1914* (Harvester Press, 1980) and Jeremy Smith's, *The Tories and Ireland, 1910–1914: Conservative Party Politics and the Irish Home Rule Crisis* (Irish Academic Press, 2000). The evolution of partition is chronicled by Michael Laffan in *The Partition of Ireland, 1911–1925* (Dundalgan, 1983).

Ireland's participation in the First World War is the subject of Tim Bowman's, *Irish Regiments in the Great War* (Manchester University Press, 2003), Myles Dungan's, *They Shall Not Grow Old: Irish Soldiers and the Great War* (Dublin, 1997), Keith Jeffery's, *Ireland and the Great War* (Cambridge, 2000) and two edited collections of essays – Adrian Gregory and Senia Pašeta (eds), *Ireland and the Great War: 'A War to Unite Us All?'* (Manchester University Press, 2002) and John Horne (ed.), *Our War: Ireland and the Great War* (Royal Irish Academy, 2008).

Part 2

ANALYSIS

2

The Easter Rising, 1916

ENGLAND'S DIFFICULTY AND IRELAND'S OPPORTUNITY

Following the defeat of the IRB uprising in 1867, radical nationalism which sought the complete separation of Ireland from Britain through force of arms went into decline for nearly 40 years. With many Fenian leaders imprisoned and exiled, constitutional nationalism came to prominence, striving for the twin goals of Irish home rule and land reform. Revolutionary nationalism re-emerged in the early twentieth century as a result of the Gaelic cultural revival that reinforced the sense of Ireland having a distinct identity separate from Britain, the sense that the constitutional movement had failed to deliver on home rule, the centenary commemoration in 1898 of the United Irish rebellion and the rejuvenation of the Fenian leadership (Lyons, 1968a: 42–3).

Although the Fenian movement had not been to the forefront of Irish political activity it had retained a dedicated cluster of activists, one of the most prominent of whom was Thomas Clarke, who had spent 15 years in prison in Britain for planning a bomb attack on London in the 1880s. His return to Ireland in 1907 was a significant factor in the revival of the IRB and coincided with efforts by new younger leaders to reorganise the movement and plan a new insurrection to achieve Irish freedom. In Belfast, Denis McCullough had succeeded in purging the brotherhood of its older members, including his own father who had initiated him into the movement, while in Dublin a similar process occurred in 1911 after the ousting of the city's most prominent Fenian organiser, P. T. Daly (McGee, 2005: 291, 350). Another important figure in the new revolutionary leadership was Seán MacDermott who was appointed as the IRB's national organiser in 1908.

The IRB was still a small organisation, especially in Dublin, and its regional strength varied widely; in 1911 its estimated membership was 2,000 (Kelly, 2006: 142–4; Foy and Barton, 1999: 6). It sought to extend its influence

Gaelic League: Organisation formed in 1893 by Eoin MacNeill and Douglas Hyde to revive the Irish language. Became increasingly politicised and included many revolutionaries including Patrick Pearse.

Gaelic Athletic Association: Association formed in 1884 to codify and regulate Gaelic sports. It was infiltrated by the Irish Republican Brotherhood (IRB) and many prominent revolutionaries were members.

Sinn Féin: Political party formed by Arthur Griffith in 1905, adopted a republican constitution in 1917 and split in January 1922 into pro-treaty (later Cumann na nGaedheal) and anti-treaty factions and again in 1926 with the formation of Fianna Fáil.

through infiltrating a number of cultural and political organisations that shared its nationalist ideology, including literary societies, the **Gaelic League** (founded in 1893 to promote the revival of the Irish language), the **Gaelic Athletic Association** (the governing body of Gaelic sports such as hurling and Gaelic football) and the newly formed fringe political organisation Sinn Féin (SF). **Sinn Féin** was formed in 1905 as an amalgam of a number of small advanced nationalist bodies that had emerged around the turn of the century, including: the Dungannon Clubs founded in Ulster by Denis McCullough and Bulmer Hobson, which sought an Irish republic; Cumann na nGaedheal, a front for the IRB; the Celtic Literary Society; and the National Council formed in 1903 by the Dublin journalist Arthur Griffith. Griffith 'hated British rule' but was not as ideologically committed to a republic as some of the other members of the early Sinn Féin Party, realising that Irish public opinion was not yet ready for it. He was prepared to accept a monarchist form of government for an independent Ireland and suggested a dual-monarchist relationship between Ireland and Great Britain along the lines of Austria-Hungary, as outlined in his pamphlet *The Resurrection of Hungary: A Parallel for Ireland*, published in 1904 (Laffan, 1999: 16–24).

Griffith was one of the few nationalist thinkers to envisage what an independent Ireland might look like and many of the ideas set out in *The Sinn Féin Policy* (1906) were implemented by both the First Dáil and subsequent Irish Governments after independence, including abstention from Westminster, the establishment of arbitration courts, the creation of a foreign consular service, the abolition of the poor law system and the creation of a national stock exchange (Laffan, 1999: 16–19). Griffith's Sinn Féin enjoyed a brief period of success in 1907 when the IPP MP, Charles Dolan, converted to the party, although he lost an ensuing by-election. The Party's only serious electoral success was the election of 12 councillors to Dublin Corporation, including W. T. Cosgrave and Seán T. O'Kelly (Daly, 1997: 47). Thereafter, the movement went into decline and on the eve of the Rising amounted to little more than a Dublin-based pressure group that was probably better known for the newspaper of the same name that Griffith produced.

The formation of the Irish Volunteers in November 1913 provided another organisation through which the IRB could exert its influence covertly and one, more importantly, that could be used to implement its desire of an armed uprising against British rule. When the Volunteers split in September 1914, the rump MacNeillite Volunteers allowed the IRB to reassert its influence (Foy and Barton, 1999: 14). If the Irish Volunteers provided the means through which the IRB could execute a rebellion, the outbreak of the First World War in August provided the opportunity, and the organisation was determined to have a rebellion in Ireland before the end of the war. A military council was formed to plan it, consisting of Patrick Pearse, Eamonn Ceannt and Joseph Plunkett, who were joined subsequently by Clarke, MacDermott and Thomas MacDonagh (Foy and Barton, 1999: 15–16). This clique kept its plans secret not only from the Volunteer leaders but also from many senior figures in the IRB, including the President of the Supreme Council, Denis McCullough. The unfortunate history of informers within Irish revolutionary movements was obviously part of the reason for this. However, there was also a fear that their efforts might be opposed. This was especially true of the Volunteers, where MacNeill would only commit them to armed insurrection for defensive reasons, such as attempts to suppress them or impose wartime conscription.

In January 1916 James Connolly was co-opted onto the military council. This socialist and trade union activist had been active in organising the **Irish Transport and General Workers Union (ITGWU)** in Ireland since 1910. He played a key role in the 1913 Dublin lock-out, the mass dismissal of trade union members by Dublin employers, and following the failure of that and the departure of the ITGWU leader James Larkin to the USA, he became the recognised leader of the labour movement in Ireland. During the lock-out Connolly had formed the **Irish Citizen Army (ICA)** to protect workers in Dublin. Between 1914 and 1916, as a result of the spiralling Ulster crisis, the detrimental impact of the First World War on socialism and the weakness of the trade union movement in the wake of the lock-out, Connolly turned increasingly towards separatism and the use of militant action to overthrow British rule in Ireland. Concerned that Connolly and the ICA might take precipitate action and ruin its plans, the IRB's military council decided to include him in their conspiracy (Townshend, 2005: 93–4).

The capture of prominent buildings in Dublin City was the focus of the insurrection. The plan highlighted the lack of military or logistical training or experience among the collaborators. As a result key strategic buildings, such as **Dublin Castle** and Trinity College, appear to have been omitted and the obstacle of the River Liffey in cutting off bases on the northern and southern sides of the city from each other was not given sufficient attention (Townshend, 2005: 100–1). The extent to which the organisers intended for the rebellion to spread outwards from Dublin into the provinces is disputed, although their lack of knowledge about the Volunteers in the country and the absence of sufficient weapons to arm units outside of the city, suggests that the Dublin insurrection was always their main focus (McGarry, 2010: 210–11).

The last aspect of the planning was the acquisition of arms and ammunition. For over a year before the Rising strenuous efforts were made to acquire the necessary material from Germany. In April 1915 Plunkett and Roger Casement travelled to Berlin in an effort to convince the German Government that their plans were sufficiently serious and well-advanced to be worth the

Irish Transport and General Workers Union (ITGWU): Trade union founded by Jim Larkin in 1908.

Irish Citizen Army (ICA): Militia formed by James Connolly to protect striking workers in Dublin city during the 1913 lock-out which played a key role in the Easter Rising.

Dublin Castle: The administrative centre of British government in Ireland.

German Government's while getting involved. In addition to arming the rebels, it was hoped that Germany would also send a military force to participate in the Rising, as France had done during the United Irish revolt of 1798, though hopefully with greater success. Casement was also involved in raising an Irish Brigade from Irish soldiers who had been captured by the German Army while fighting for the British Army during the First World War, a mission that met with very little success. It soon became clear that Germany had no intention of taking part in an invasion and was only prepared to provide one shipload of 'second-rate rifles' (Townshend, 2005: 104–5, 116). The inadequacy of the German support greatly increased Casement's fears for the success of the Rising, and as he returned to Ireland in April 1916 aboard a German submarine, it was with the intention of convincing the military council to call it off.

The last remaining task of the organisers was to convince Eoin MacNeill to allow the Irish Volunteers to participate in the Rising. His initial acquiescence was achieved when the contents of a document emanating from Dublin Castle were leaked at a meeting of Dublin Corporation, indicating that the authorities planned to arrest the leaders of Sinn Féin, the Gaelic League and the Volunteers and raid these organisations' headquarters and the leaders' homes. This castle document has long been considered to have been substantially forged by Plunkett in an effort to deceive MacNeill. While it was certainly doctored, it appears to have been based on genuine plans drawn up by the administration outlining precautions to be undertaken in the event of conscription being extended to Ireland (McGarry, 2010: 117; Townshend, 2005: 131–3). By Holy Thursday 1916 the Rising was set to proceed three days later on Easter Sunday, 23 April 1916, with MacNeill having agreed to the use of the Volunteers and a consignment of arms *en route* from Germany aboard the *Aud*.

The *Aud* arrived as scheduled in Tralee on Holy Thursday. Although British intelligence was aware of it, no action was taken to intercept it. To have done so, would have revealed to the Germans that the British had broken their codes. Allowing the *Aud* to land might also have resulted in the capture of a greater number of the conspirators. It has also been suggested that permitting the landing was a propaganda ploy aimed at showing up the treachery of both the Irish revolutionaries and their German collaborators, and less plausibly that elements within the British administration wanted the Rising to proceed in order to provide an excuse for repressing militant nationalism. Whatever the reason, an opportunity to halt the Rising was deliberately passed up (McGarry, 2010: 114; Townshend, 2005: 126–7; Foy and Barton, 1999: 65–7).

A planned rendezvous with the U-boat carrying Casement failed, partly because of the absence of radio communication on the *Aud* and the poor navigation of its captain, Karl Spindler. An exhausted Casement, who had spent a week cramped in the submarine, came ashore on Banna strand on Good Friday morning, where he was arrested by police who had been alerted to the presence of a suspicious figure. The following day, aware of the failure of his mission, Spindler scuttled the *Aud* and the chances of the Rising succeeding sank along with the arms intended for the Volunteers. The local Kerry Volunteers were partly to blame for the fiasco, having failed to keep watch for the *Aud* or pick up Casement (Townshend, 2005: 128–31).

On receipt of the news that Casement had been captured and the German arms sabotaged, Eoin MacNeill decided to cancel the involvement of the Volunteers in the Rising, realising there was no chance of success. He also discovered that he had been deceived about the nature of the castle document. On Easter Sunday morning a notice was published in the *Sunday Independent* newspaper announcing that orders for Volunteer mobilisation were 'hereby rescinded, and no parades, marches, or other movements of the Irish Volunteers will take place' (Townshend, 2005: 138–9). The plans of the military council were in disarray, without either the munitions or the personnel to put their insurrection into effect.

EASTER WEEK

In spite of MacNeill's action, the military council, and Clarke and Pearse in particular, felt they had gone too far with their plans to abandon them and decided merely to postpone rather than cancel the Rising. This decision was taken with the knowledge that the Rising could not succeed but would have symbolic significance. It raises the question of whether Pearse intended the Rising to be a blood sacrifice. The man most closely associated with the Rising was a relative newcomer to revolutionary life. A trained lawyer, who had dedicated much of his career until that point to education through his Irish-language school, St Enda's, Pearse was a home ruler until the early 1910s. The strength of Ulster unionist resistance to home rule, the fear of it being defeated and the opportunity offered by the First World War drove him into the IRB and the Irish Volunteers (Augusteijn, 2010: 281). Some of his writings provide evidence of his belief in the efficacy of blood-letting: 'bloodshed is a cleansing and sanctifying thing'. However, the notion that his main aim in planning the Rising was to sacrifice himself to advance the cause of Ireland ignores the in-depth planning undertaken by the military council. Pearse was serious about trying to mount a rebellion for reasons other than a mere symbolic blood sacrifice and the decision to proceed with the doomed insurrection stemmed more from the view that 'action was preferable to inaction' (McGarry, 2010: 52, 96, 101).

Mobilisation orders were dispatched to units of the Dublin Brigade of the Volunteers to assemble on Easter Monday, but the confusion between these and MacNeill's order resulted in only about 1,600 Volunteers assembling for the delayed insurrection (Augusteijn, 2010: 308). Mobilisation was slow on Monday morning. Aside from the confusion generated by MacNeill's and Pearse's contradictory orders, some Volunteers overslept, some were at the big race meeting in Fairyhouse where the Irish Grand National was being held, while others feared the consequences of taking part in a futile exercise that was doomed to fail (McGarry, 2010: 126–8; Townshend, 2005: 153–4). Nevertheless, by about noon the rebels had occupied the buildings they had targeted. The main garrison was based in the General Post Office (GPO) on Sackville (now O'Connell) Street, Dublin's main thoroughfare, and consisted of a mixture of Volunteers and ICA commanded by Pearse and Connolly.

The four Dublin City battalions of the Volunteers occupied different geographical zones of the city. Ned Daly's First Battalion was based at the Four Courts on the north-west quays and covered the surrounding areas including North King Street, Church Street and the North Dublin Union (the Richmond Hospital). Approximately 130 men of the Third Battalion under Eamon de Valera occupied Boland's Mills and also seized Westland Row railway station. A similar sized force, led by Eamonn Ceannt, took the 50-acre South Dublin Union site (now St James's Hospital) along with the Jameson Distillery in Marrowbone Lane and the surrounding streets. The last unit, Thomas MacDonagh's Second Battalion, had intended to cover the area north-east of the city around Fairview, but much of it was redeployed back to the city centre and remained in occupation of the Jacob's factory south of the river on Bishop Street. The bulk of the ICA, which was unaffected by MacNeill's countermanding order and as such mobilised to near its full strength, took up positions in St Stephen's Green, a 22-acre public park (Townshend, 2005: 165–80).

A number of factors explain the choice of these locations. With regard to the Volunteers they largely remained within their own localities. The positions were strategically located near important transport depots. The Four Courts garrison was close to Broadstone railway station, the terminus for the trains from Athlone, where the army's artillery was housed. The original location of MacDonagh's Second Battalion included Amiens Street (now Connolly) Station, the base for the Dublin–Belfast railway service, while the South Dublin Union was close to the terminus for southern trains at Kingsbridge (now Heuston) Station. Yet, the only battalion to seize a railway station was de Valera's, which occupied Westland Row. Daly's and MacDonagh's failure to take Broadstone and Amiens Street made it much easier for the army to respond quickly by bringing reinforcements from Belfast and 18-pound field guns from Athlone that were crucial to the quelling of the rebellion.

These failures were possibly due to inadequate manpower, rather than poor strategic planning. The four city locations might also have been chosen to give the Volunteers a good vantage point to cover the four main army barracks within the city limits, Richmond, Portobello, Marlborough and the Royal (Townshend, 2005: 153–83; Hayes-McCoy, 1969: 260–1).

The non-occupation of the principal railway stations was compounded by the failure to seize the telegraph office at Crown Alley, just across the river from the GPO, or the greatest propaganda prize of all, Dublin Castle. There is still much debate about whether the Volunteers ever planned to capture the castle or were deterred in the mistaken belief that it was too well defended. The ICA garrison under Seán Connolly mistakenly opted instead for the nearby City Hall, from which they were easily ejected within a day by British reinforcements and where Seán Connolly was killed by a sniper from the castle (Townshend, 2005: 162–4; McGarry, 2010: 141).

The ease with which the rebels occupied their targeted buildings illustrates the extent to which the administration, police and army were taken unawares by the rebellion. Both the commander of the army in Ireland, General Friend, and the Chief Secretary, Augustine Birrell, were in England for Easter and there were only 400 soldiers scattered across the various barracks in Dublin City. While an armed uprising was not expected, the authorities were well aware that elaborate Volunteer manoeuvres had been planned for Easter Sunday, which makes their lackadaisical attitude to security difficult to explain. In Birrell's absence, the civilian response was handled by the Under Secretary, Sir Matthew Nathan, who appears to have underestimated the rebellion and been at a loss to respond in the absence of Birrell. Arthur Hamilton Norway, the head of the Irish Post Office, spent Easter Monday morning in Dublin Castle with Nathan, whom he described as 'a man who was not cool and steady, but rather bewildered' (Jeffery, 2006a: 44). Birrell and Nathan had adopted a tolerant approach to both the Volunteers and the ICA prior to the Rising, leaving them with no choice but to resign immediately afterwards.

The army responded more quickly and effectively than the civilian administrators. On Tuesday night martial law was declared in Dublin and extended countrywide the following day. Also on Tuesday reinforcements from within the island arrived from the Curragh and Belfast along with heavy artillery from Athlone, underscoring the disastrous effect of the rebels' failure to secure the railway stations. These were strengthened by reinforcements from Britain who arrived by boat at Kingstown (Dún Laoghaire) on Wednesday. By the end of the week there were 20,000 troops in the city. On Wednesday, the armed yacht, the *Helga*, began the bombardment of the city from the River Liffey, destroying Liberty Hall (the headquarters of the ITGWU) and much of the centre of the city around the GPO. This barrage, exacerbated by a lack of adequate supplies of food and ammunition, exhaustion and the realisation that no reinforcements were coming for the rebels from either the provinces or Germany, resulted in the collapse of the short-lived Irish Republic when Pearse surrendered on Saturday, 29 April (McGarry, 2010: 167–8, 189–94, 204–6; Townshend, 2005: 186–96).

Outside Dublin the main activity took place in Cork, Wexford, Meath and Galway. There was an initially poor turn out in Cork on Easter Sunday morning, MacNeill's countermanding order not yet having arrived, suggesting that other factors, such as fear, might also explain why mobilisation was poor in general for the Rising. The demoralised Cork Volunteers demobilised and returned home 'wet, sore and sorry' on Easter Sunday night. Wexford Volunteers held the town of Enniscorthy for most of Easter week. In Galway, a small contingent led by Liam Mellows attacked **Royal Irish Constabulary (RIC)** barracks at Oranmore and Athenry. The highest casualties outside of Dublin occurred at Rath Crossroads near Ashbourne, County Meath, where the Volunteers, commanded by Thomas Ashe and Richard Mulcahy, engaged the local RIC in a five-hour gun battle that resulted in the deaths of eight policemen and two Volunteers. Very little mobilisation occurred in Ulster, where Denis McCullough tried unsuccessfully to link up with Mellows in Connaught (McGarry, 2010: 213–9; 240–3; Townshend, 2005: 218–21, 228–9).

An unusual feature of the Rising was the participation of women and children. Approximately 200 women were involved, the majority of whom were members of **Cumann na mBan**, the women's auxiliary of the Irish Volunteers. The most prominent female rebel was Constance Markievicz, who commanded the St Stephen's Green Garrison for the ICA along with Michael Mallin and appears to have shot dead at least one policeman (McGarry, 2010: 137). Cumann na mBan was not part of the initial operations on Monday morning and was only mobilised at its own insistence that evening. With the exception of Markievicz, no other woman was given a senior role and the members of Cumann na mBan were denied any combat role at all, focusing instead on the subordinate duties of providing food supplies and first aid. Those who had medical expertise, such as Brigid Lyons, a medical student in University College Galway, Elizabeth O'Farrell, who was a nurse, and Dr Kathleen Lynn, the ICA's chief medical officer, provided essential treatment for wounded rebels. Women were also used to carry dispatches and ammunition between the rebel garrisons, a dangerous undertaking during the most intense phases of the fighting (http://www.bureauofmilitaryhistory.ie/reels/bmh/BMH.WS0259.pdf#page=1).

These activities were in line with Cumann na mBan's perception of itself as an auxiliary force for the Volunteers and with its activities prior to 1916. While Eamon de Valera is often cited for not allowing women into his garrison, he was prepared to make use of them as dispatch carriers

Royal Irish Constabulary (RIC): The police force for Ireland outside of Dublin, which was disbanded in 1922.

Cumann na mBan: The women's auxiliary of the Irish Volunteers/IRA, formed in 1914.

(Matthews, 2010: 123). Thomas MacDonagh reluctantly permitted women into the Jacob's factory. In general, the ICA women enjoyed a larger measure of equality, though their experience did not differ greatly from that of Cumann na mBan. Unlike the Volunteers, which was an all-male force supported by a female cast in its own separate organisation, women were members of the ICA, in line with Connolly's thinking on gender equality. Nevertheless, Markievicz was the only member of the force to see serious military action and Connolly refused to allow his daughter Nora to become involved, sending her on a mission to Tyrone instead. Similarly, Thomas Clarke would not allow his wife, Kathleen, to join him, an understandable decision given that they had small children; he knew that the Rising would probably result in his death and she was pregnant (and was to suffer a miscarriage later in the year) (Clarke, 2008: 112, 161). Outside Dublin women took little part in the provincial fighting, apart from acting as messengers. Seventy-nine women were subsequently arrested though most were released after a short period. Markievicz was tried by court martial and initially sentenced to death along with her fellow commanders, but this was commuted 'solely and only on account of her sex'. None of the female rebels were killed, although Margaret Skinnider of the ICA was badly wounded by a sniper while attempting to set fire to a hotel (McGarry, 2010: 162, 226–8; Foy and Barton, 1999: 358).

Children participated in the Rising as members of **Fianna Éireann** and the ICA's boys' corps, including James Connolly's son Roddy, who was only 15 and acted as an *aide-de-camp* for his father and Pearse in the GPO. Fourteen-year-old John Healy of the Fianna was probably the youngest combat fatality, though not the youngest child to die as a result of the Rising. John Francis Foster was only two years old when shot in cross-fire on Church Street, one of three children killed on Easter Monday and of 30 in total who died as a result of gun-fire during Easter week (Duffy, 2013: 34–5; McGarry, 2010: 198; Matthews, 2010: 145–6). The Fianna's most notable action during the Rising was the attempted raid on the Magazine Fort at the Phoenix Park which resulted in the shooting dead of the 23-year-old son of its commander by Gary Holohan of the Fianna (McGarry, 2010: 138) [**Doc. 4**]. Some minors who fought in the Rising subsequently became prominent figures in the **Irish Republican Army (IRA)**, including Seán Lemass and Vinnie Byrne.

Approximately 450 people were killed in the Rising, more than half of whom were civilians. Slightly more than 100 soldiers and policemen were killed, while the rebels incurred the fewest fatalities, losing approximately 60. Between 2,000 and 3,000 people – including civilians and combatants – were injured. The rebel strategy of occupying buildings in the middle of the city, and the intense street fighting that ensued, helps to account for

Fianna Éireann: Republican boy scouts and youth wing of the Irish Volunteers, many of whose members took part in the Easter Rising.

Irish Republican Army (IRA): see *Irish Volunteers.*

the high level of civilian casualties, the majority of which have been attri-
buted to the crown forces. The potential impact on civilians appears to
have been overlooked by the planners (McGarry, 2012: 50–1; Townshend,
2005: 393).

The single largest loss of civilian life took place in North King Street,
where 15 civilians were killed by the military, which had previously lost
14 men in the same area in a shoot-out with the rebels (McGarry, 2010:
187–8). The most notorious killing of an innocent civilian was that of Francis
Sheehy-Skeffington, a well-known journalist, pacifist and campaigner for
female suffrage. Arrested on Easter Tuesday night while returning home
from trying to prevent looting, he was taken to Portobello Barracks in
Rathmines where he was shot by firing squad on the orders of Captain John
Bowen-Colthurst, who was subsequently court-martialled and found guilty
but insane (Townshend, 2005: 192–5).The army suffered its highest loss
of life in the rebels' most successful action when a detachment of Sherwood
Foresters, *en route* to the city from Kingstown, was ambushed at Mount
Street Bridge on Wednesday, resulting in 230 being wounded or killed
(McGarry, 2012: 45).

The actions of men like Bowen-Colthurst highlight the psychological effect
of the violence and killing on those who took part in the Rising. Few of
the rebels had any military experience and Eamon de Valera in particular
appears to have suffered from the mental strain of commanding the garrison
at Boland's Mills (Townshend, 2005: 199–201). While they were part of
an ostensibly professional army, many of the British reinforcements sent to
Dublin were in reality recent war-time recruits or conscripts, whose training
was also fairly rudimentary. The Sherwood Foresters who were ambushed
at Mount Street Bridge were 'merely boys . . . Recruits who had not been
in uniform about 6 or 8 weeks' and 'had never fired a service rifle before'
(McGarry, 2010: 173).

THE PROCLAMATION

The general philosophy of the rebels can best be deciphered by a close
reading of their manifesto, the Easter Proclamation, read aloud by Pearse
outside the GPO on Easter Monday morning to bemused passers-by [**Doc. 5**].
Influenced by famous declarations of historic revolutionary movements, including the eighteenth-century American Declaration of Independence and the
French Declaration of the Rights of Man and of the Citizen, it also drew upon
Robert Emmet's 1803 manifesto. Drafted largely by Pearse, with input from
Connolly, the final version was ratified on Easter Sunday and signed by the
seven members of the military council. Eoin MacNeill had been invited to

sign but declined. Two thousand five hundred copies were printed hastily at Liberty Hall and distributed early on Easter Monday morning by members of the ICA (de Paor, 1997: 15–18, 29–30).

In spite of Pearse's centrality to the Gaelic League and the language revival, there were only three words of Irish in the document – the heading 'Poblacht na h Éireann', necessitating the creation of a new Irish word – 'poblacht' – literally translated as 'peopledom', that has since become the recognised Irish translation of 'republic'. The announcement that a provisional government of the Irish republic had been established echoed not only Emmet, but also the Ulster Unionists, who in 1914 had elaborate plans in place to establish a provisional government in Ulster in defiance of an Irish Home Rule Parliament (de Paor, 1997: 31–8).

Much of the Proclamation was a justification for the actions of the rebels, asserting Ireland's right to freedom, eschewing foreign domination and placing this latest bid for freedom in the tradition of armed Irish uprisings dating back to 1641. The financial assistance and support of Clan na Gael in the USA ('exiled children in America') was recognised, as was the contribution, limited though it turned out to be, of the Germans ('our gallant allies in Europe').

The influence of James Connolly was noticeable in many areas. One was the unusually inclusive nature of the language, which refers throughout to Irishmen and Irishwomen. It held out the promise of equal citizenship, promising equal rights and opportunities and universal suffrage, but also highlighted the obligations of citizenship, claiming the allegiance of all Irishmen and women for the republic, a reference that was also aimed at unionists (de Paor, 1997: 42, 72). While beginning and ending with religious references, invoking the deity in support of their actions in a similar way to which the unionists had sought divine support for opposition to home rule in the covenant of 1912, the proclamation also sought to bridge the sectarian divide by promising equality of treatment for all citizens and blaming 'an alien government' for dividing the 'minority from the majority' (McGarry, 2010: 133–4). The most socialistic aspect of the proclamation was the assertion that the people of Ireland had the right 'to the ownership of Ireland'. Aspects of it, such as this claim to public ownership, were reiterated in the Democratic Programme of the First Dáil in 1919 [Doc. 6] and some of its promises were made good after independence, such as the introduction of universal suffrage under the 1922 Irish Free State Constitution.

The proclamation has always been central to commemorations of the Rising, none of which are complete without the ritual of reading it aloud. In 1966, to mark the Rising's fiftieth anniversary, a display containing the English and Irish versions, along with pictures of the seven signatories, was sent to all primary schools in the Republic of Ireland. Approximately 50 copies are extant, a rarity reflected in the record price of €360,000 paid for one at an auction in 2008. In recent years it has been adopted by defenders of Irish sovereignty in the face of the perceived surrender of political and fiscal independence to the European Union and the International Monetary Fund (Higgins, 2012: 48, 208–9). While the Easter Proclamation has always been held in high regard by the Irish public and its political leaders as the foundation stone of the independent Irish state, much of its rhetoric is antithetical to the socially conservative, theocratic and capitalist policies pursued by successive Irish governments since independence.

REACTIONS

The deaths of more than 200 civilians and the destruction to the heart of Dublin explain why the rebellion and those responsible for it were initially despised by much of the city's population. Throughout the course of Easter week, relations between those living in the vicinity of the fighting and the rebels were poor and there was widespread looting of some of the city's leading commercial premises. The rebels both despised the motives of the looters, which reflected badly on what they perceived as their more noble aims, and worried that their actions, including incendiarism, might endanger rebel-held posts. Many families in the city also had male relatives fighting with the British Army in France, and this accounts for the particular bitterness that the rebels encountered from so-called separation women (wives who received a separation allowance while their husbands were at war) (McGarry, 2010: 142–8).

The rebels also encountered significant hostility from Dublin's commercial and propertied elite, aghast at the destruction wrought by the uprising on the commercial centre of the city. Recent research has also highlighted the role of class distinctions in underlying this antipathy, as many of the rebels, especially those in the ICA, came from working-class backgrounds and the hostility of the city's employers to trade unionism, especially during the lockout, was still fresh in their minds. Religion might also have played some part in such attitudes, as the rebels were overwhelmingly Catholic, whereas a significant part of Dublin's commercial elite was Protestant and held unionist political sympathies. Class, as well as contemporary mores, partly explains the extent of the hostility displayed towards female rebels, much of which was directed at Markievicz (McGarry, 2005: 139, 160, 164–5). However, within a short space of time, Dublin's hostility, and the general lack of public support for the political aims of the rebels, was to be transformed.

Immediately after the Rising over 3,500 people were arrested, more than 1,800 of whom were interned in prisons in Britain, although 1,200 were released within a few weeks (Foy and Barton, 1999: 347). Many of these had little or no involvement in the Rising and were rounded-up because of suspected Sinn Féin sympathies. The experience turned many into ardent republicans on their return to Ireland. Inexplicable decisions, such as the arrest of 27 people in Roscommon town, which had played no role in the Rising, illustrated the mistakes made by the authorities in Ireland that helped to galvanise support for the rebels in the aftermath of the Rising (McGarry, 2010: 265).

One hundred and eighty-seven of the most senior rebels were court-martialled in secret, under the provisions of martial law imposed during the Rising, including Markievicz, the only woman tried at the highest level. Only 11 were acquitted and 88 were initially sentenced to death by firing squad, although most of these were subsequently commuted to periods of penal servitude. The 15 subsequently executed were charged with taking 'part in an armed rebellion and in the waging of war against his Majesty, the King'. With the exception of Patrick Pearse's younger brother, Willie, all the accused pleaded not guilty. The prosecution and subsequent execution of Willie Pearse, in spite of his limited role in the Rising, has been seen as a reaction to his brother's rather than his own involvement. The courts martial relied heavily on the evidence of soldiers involved in the fighting or captured by the rebels, much of which was 'entirely circumstantial, misleading and inaccurate'. Although the proclamation was not relied upon heavily during the trials, it was a significant factor in the decision of Sir John Maxwell, effectively the military governor of Ireland, to confirm the death sentences of the seven men who had signed it (Barton, 2002: 28–40).

The executions took place in Kilmainham Jail between 3 and 12 May. In addition to the seven signatories of the proclamation and Willie Pearse, the Dublin commanders executed included Michael Mallin of the ICA, and from the Volunteers Edward Daly, Michael O'Hanrahan, John MacBride, Seán Heuston and Con Colbert. One execution took place outside Dublin, that of Thomas Kent, a Cork Volunteer who was charged with the 'wilful murder' of a policeman following a stand-off with the police at the Kents' farm in Castlelyons, near Fermoy, the week after the surrender during which Kent's brother, Richard, was also killed (Townshend, 2005: 279–80).

The final death toll from judicial executions reached the iconic figure of 16, when Roger Casement was hanged for high treason in London on 3 August. Efforts to seek clemency on his behalf were damaged by a smear campaign highlighting his homosexual activities, including the alleged use of rent boys. Two high-profile commutations took place in the cases of Markievicz, because of her sex, and de Valera, possibly as a result of his American birth but also because his trial and court martial took place later than those of the other commanders and by that time public and political outrage and the ensuing political fall-out had forced their cessation; de Valera himself was adamant that the latter reason was the true explanation for his reprieve (Ferriter, 2007: 28–9).

By the time the last executions took place, the severity of the British response to the Rising was beginning to have an effect on turning public opinion towards sympathy with the rebels. In the House of Commons on 11 May John Dillon delivered a scathing attack on the British actions. Although no supporter of the rebels, he commended the actions of 'three thousand men' in facing 'twenty thousand with machine guns and artillery' and contrasting their bravery with that of the British Army at the front: 'it would be a damned good thing for you if your soldiers were able to put up as good a fight as did those men in Dublin' [Doc. 7]. Dillon realised the effect that these repressive measures would have in generating support for republicanism at the expense of constitutional nationalism.

By late May and early June it was clear that the tide of public opinion had turned in favour of the rebels. Memorabilia commemorating the executed leaders were on sale in Dublin and masses were held to pray for them (Wills, 2009: 105–8). The details of some of the executions added to the sense of martyrdom and romance surrounding the rebels, such as the badly injured James Connolly having to be propped up in a siting position to face the firing squad and the marriage of Joseph Plunkett to his fiancée, Grace Gifford, on the eve of his execution.

By early 1917 the tragedy of the Rising was becoming established in Irish literature, with the composition of W. B. Yeats's elegiac poem *Easter 1916* (not published widely until 1920). The resonant conclusion that all had 'changed, changed utterly' and a 'terrible beauty' had been born, has become an iconic statement of how Irish public opinion was transformed by the British response to the Rising. While the Rising inspired many other literary celebrations and commemorations, it has also been criticised in literature, most notably in Seán O'Casey's *The Plough and the Stars*. As a former member of the ICA, O'Casey's plays focused on how the political events of the decade impacted on the mundane lives of Dublin city's poorest class of tenement dwellers. In *The Plough and the Stars*, the juxtaposition of prostitution, poverty and drunkenness with the Rising, the illustration of its detrimental impact on local tenement dwellers and the clearly satirical commentary on the ideals of its leaders provoked nationalist fury leading to angry protests during its first run in the Abbey Theatre in 1926 (Wills, 2009: 146–51).

The British Government tried to moderate the adverse impact of its harsh repression of the Rising by introducing home rule in the summer of 1916. The task was delegated to David Lloyd George, the Minister of Munitions. John Redmond secured the agreement of the majority of his supporters to the deal, which would have excluded the six Ulster counties with the largest

Protestant populations. However, the talks failed due to Lloyd George's duplicity in giving contradictory promises to each side as to whether or not the exclusion of the Ulster counties would be permanent and because of the opposition of southern unionists (Jackson, 2003: 166–72). This episode is important for representing the point at which the Irish Party committed itself to accepting a partitionist solution and represented the last genuine chance of implementing home rule in Ireland before the aims of Irish nationalism morphed into the demand for greater sovereignty as an independent republic and the willingness to take up arms to achieve such an end.

GUIDE TO FURTHER READING

The best documentary sources for the Easter Rising are the oral history statements of participants in the Bureau of Military History (BMH), now freely available online www.bureauofmilitaryhistory.ie. Extracts from those relating to the Rising with a contextual commentary can be found in Fearghal McGarry's, *Rebels: Voices from the Easter Rising* (Penguin, 2011) and Annie Ryan's, *Witness: Inside the Easter Rising* (Liberties Press, 2005). Liam de Paor's, *On the Easter Proclamation and Other Declarations* (Four Courts Press, 1997) provides an excellent textual analysis of the most important document relating to the Rising. The British files relating to the court martials of the executed leaders were released between 1999 and 2001 and were published by Brian Barton in *From Behind a Closed Door: Secret Court Martial Records of the 1916 Easter Rising* (Blackstaff, 2002) and republished as *The Secret Court Martial Records of the 1916 Easter Rising* (History Press, 2008).

The three best narrative accounts of the Rising are Michael Foy and Brian Barton's, *The Easter Rising* (Sutton, 1999), Charles Townshend's, *Easter 1916: The Irish Rebellion* (Penguin, 2005) and Fearghal McGarry's, *The Rising. Ireland: Easter 1916* (Oxford University Press, 2010). Clair Wills's, *Dublin, 1916: The Siege of the GPO* (Profile, 2009) recreates the experience of those inside the GPO in Easter Week.

The best biographical accounts of the Rising's leaders are Ruth Dudley Edwards's, *Patrick Pearse: The Triumph of Failure* (Victor Gollancz, 1977), Joost Augusteijn's more recent, *Patrick Pearse: The Making of a Revolutionary* (Palgrave, 2010) and Donal Nevin's, *James Connolly: A Full Life* (Gill and Macmillan, 2005). Accounts of the life of Constance Markievicz can be found in Anne Marreco, *The Rebel Countess: The Life and Times of Constance Markievicz* (Weidenfeld & Nicolson, 1967), Anne Haverty, *Constance Markievicz: Irish Revolutionary* (Harper Collins, 1988) and Diana Norman, *Terrible Beauty: A Life of Constance Markievicz, 1868–1927* (Hodder and Stoughton, 1987), all of which are now quite dated.

The best accounts of women's participation in the Rising are Ruth Taillon's, *When History Was Made: The Women of 1916* (Beyond The Pale, 1996), Margaret Ward's, *Unmanageable Revolutionaries* (Pluto Press, 1995), Cal McCarthy's, *Cumann na mBan and the Irish Revolution* (Collins Press, 2007) and Ann Matthews's, *Renegades: Irish Republican Women, 1900–1922* (Mercier, 2010).

3

The Republican Resurgence, 1917–19

In the two years that followed the Rising a sea change occurred in Irish nationalist politics, with the emergence of Sinn Féin to supplant the IPP as the largest political party in the country. The demands of Irish nationalism also changed; the decisive victory for the republican Sinn Féin Party in the 1918 general election indicated that home rule within the union was no longer acceptable to an electorate which had voiced its support for an independent state governed as a republic.

THE 1917 AND 1918 BY-ELECTIONS

The harsh British response to the Rising, and the inaccurate attribution of it to Sinn Féin, catapulted that party from relative obscurity before Easter 1916 to being the organisation around which republicans coalesced from 1917 in pursuit of Irish independence. The revival of Sinn Féin became noticeable in the latter half of 1916. In addition to gaining more support as a reaction to the harsh suppression of the Rising, it attracted constitutional nationalists dissatisfied with the leadership of John Redmond. The failure to have home rule implemented after the Rising was a serious defeat for Redmond. During these negotiations he had made a significant concession on partition that alienated many Ulster nationalists, who formed the breakaway Irish Nation League, that would eventually merge with Sinn Féin. Thus, as 1917 opened, Redmond had failed in his best chance yet of achieving Irish home rule, and in the process lost an important sector of his party's supporters.

Nevertheless, the IPP remained the largest representative of nationalist Ireland. The postponement due to the war of the 1915 general election, extended the IPP's political life for three further years. Only a general election would measure the extent to which nationalist political sentiment had swung between the IPP and Sinn Féin and this was not to take place until the war was over. However, the prolongation of the 1910 Parliament also meant that some elderly members of the Irish Party, who would most likely have retired in 1915, passed away before the next election, occasioning an unusually high number of by-elections in Ireland during 1917 and 1918. These electoral contests provided the arena for the emergent Sinn Féin to challenge the hegemony of the IPP in the crucial two-and-a-half-year period between the Rising and the 1918 general election.

The first of these vacancies arose in February 1917 in the western constituency of Roscommon North following the death of the old Fenian, J. J. O'Kelly, who had been first elected to Parliament for Roscommon as a Land League candidate in 1880. George Noble, Count Plunkett, father of the executed 1916 rebel, Joseph Plunkett, was put forward to contest the by-election and he enjoyed a comfortable victory over the IPP's T. J. Devine, polling 3,022 votes to the latter's 1,708. The extent of Plunkett's victory owed much to his status as the father of an executed rebel and the particular circumstances of County Roscommon, where there had been a large number of arrests after the Rising and a strong Sinn Féin organisation had been put in place there by Father Michael O'Flanagan. By contrast, the home rule organisation was weak and riven by internal conflict; the cantankerous editor of the *Roscommon Herald* newspaper, Jasper Tully, contested the by-election as an independent nationalist but only polled 600 votes. Plunkett's winning margin was still greater than the combined nationalist and independent nationalist vote (Laffan, 1999: 77–85).

Internal divisions in the home rule movement also contributed significantly to the IPP's defeat in the next by-election, which took place three months later in May 1917 in the neighbouring constituency of Longford South, where the contest arose from the death of another elderly nationalist MP, John Phillips. John Redmond was forced to intervene and select the party's candidate after three nationalists initially contested the nomination, and many of the supporters of the two unsuccessful candidates refused to back Redmond's choice, Patrick McKenna. Buoyed by their success in Roscommon, Sinn Féin supporters approached Joseph McGuinness, who had lived in the county previously, and was at the time serving a three-year prison sentence in Lewes Prison for his involvement in the Rising. Opinion was divided among McGuinness's fellow prisoners about whether or not he should allow his name to go forward, but his candidacy proceeded eventually and he won the seat by a slim margin of 37 votes after a tense recount. The intervention of the Roman Catholic archbishop of Dublin, William Walsh, in support of him on the eve of the poll was the decisive factor in his success (Coleman, 2003: 45–67).

The death of John Redmond's brother, Willie, from wounds suffered while fighting with the army in Belgium in June 1917 soon led to another parliamentary vacancy in Clare East. The contest which took place in July was significantly different from the two previous ones because it took place after the release of the remaining 1916 prisoners in June and the most prominent of these, Eamon de Valera, won the election for Sinn Féin, gaining over 70 per cent of the votes cast. The loss of the seat, which had been held by John Redmond's brother since 1892, to the new leader of nationalist Ireland was a significant symbolic defeat for the IPP. Sinn Féin completed its successful electoral sweep in 1917 when W. T. Cosgrave won the Kilkenny City by-election in August. In line with stated Sinn Féin policy, all of the MPs elected in 1917 abstained from the Westminster Parliament (Laffan, 1999: 106–13).

By the end of 1917 it was clear that a major shift was taking place in Irish nationalist politics. The electorate was losing patience with the IPP's failure to deliver home rule. Many of the local leaders of the Irish Party had defected to Sinn Féin (Fitzpatrick, 1977: 138). Public anger at the harsh British reaction to the Rising was expressed in support for Sinn Féin's candidates in the four by-elections held that year. The shadow of 1916 hung over all of these contests; Plunkett's son had been executed, de Valera had been lucky to escape with his life and he, along with McGuinness and Cosgrave, had been imprisoned for taking part in the insurrection. The Longford contest took place at the time of the first anniversary of the executions, and during all of the campaigns recently released prisoners, including Michael Collins, and relatives of executed or imprisoned rebels, played an important role in canvassing for Sinn Féin. The significance of the by-elections in rejuvenating Sinn Féin is clear from the fact that by the end of 1917 three of the four counties where the party enjoyed its strongest membership proportionally had been the location for these contests – Clare, Longford and Roscommon (Laffan, 1999: 187).

However, the Rising alone does not explain the extent of Sinn Féin's electoral success in 1917; the progress of the war was equally important. When conscription was introduced to Great Britain in 1916, Ireland was exempted, but as casualty figures continued to rise the threat of its extension loomed. During the by-elections, and especially in the Longford contest, Sinn Féin was successful in convincing voters that it was the only party that could defend Ireland from compulsory military service. While the IPP had been instrumental in preventing the extension of conscription to Ireland, it was tainted by its support for voluntary recruitment; Sinn Féin effectively blurred the distinction between both issues, creating the misleading impression that the IPP supported conscription. This issue had particular resonance in rural constituencies, such as Longford, Roscommon and Clare, where Irish farmers were benefiting from the war-time economy and fearful of the prospect that their sons would be forced to join the army. A third factor that determined the outcome of the 1917 by-elections was the spectre of partition. After 1914 it was clear that at least part of Ulster would be excluded in some form from home rule when it came into effect. This reality was strengthened during the abortive 1916 home rule negotiations.

The cumulative effect of the by-election victories was to forge Sinn Féin into a cohesive political party. At the start of 1917 it was still a loose coalition of advanced nationalists and many republicans were still wary of Griffith's earlier support for a dual monarchy in Britain and Ireland, along the lines of Austria and Hungary. Opinion had also been strongly divided on whether or not imprisoned 1916 rebels should contest elections under the party's banner. The close result in contests like Longford indicated that the IPP was not dead yet, and a defeat might have been interpreted as a repudiation of the Rising. However, the four successive victories vindicated the strategy of contesting elections and by the time Sinn Féin held its first *ard fheis* in October 1917, at which de Valera was elected president and the pledge to achieve an 'independent Irish Republic' was adopted, it was well placed to challenge the IPP for the political leadership of nationalist Ireland.

ard fheis: Annual national convention of Sinn Féin.

The defeat of Sinn Féin by the IPP in three successive by-elections early in 1918 suggested that the previous year's trend was being reversed in part. However, this was merely illusory. Two of these contests (Armagh South in February and Tyrone East in April) took place in Ulster constituencies, where the home rule movement benefited from a stronger grass roots organisation because of the strength of the Ancient Order of Hibernians, which owed much to the controlling influence of the Belfast MP, Joe Devlin. The strength of unionism as a political opponent of nationalism also meant that the home rule movement remained stronger in Ulster than much of the rest of the country.

The third seat held by the IPP was in Waterford City in March, where the vacancy was occasioned by the death of its leader John Redmond. The seat was held comfortably by his son, William Archer Redmond. The younger Redmond was already an MP for Tyrone East and had to resign this seat on his transfer to Waterford; the party held onto his old seat, though by a small margin. The Waterford City by-election was also notable for being the first contest held in Ireland after the passing of the **Representation of the People Act (1918)**, which made it the first Irish parliamentary election in which women were entitled to vote (Laffan, 1999: 112–28).

Representation of the People Act (1918): Legislation extending the vote to women over 30 and widening the franchise generally.

THE POST-RISING VOLUNTEERS

The arrests that followed the Rising did further damage to Eoin MacNeill's rump Irish Volunteers. Martial law prohibited all public gatherings and meetings with the result that there was very little organised republican activity for the remainder of the year. However, a recovery was noticeable in early 1917 as republicanism began to gain a new stimulus from Sinn Féin's by-election victories. In Clare a new county brigade and a number of battalions were formed in February 1917 under the guidance of the county's three leading republican families – the O'Donnells, Brennans and Barretts (Fitzpatrick, 1977: 205). The re-emergence of the Volunteers was especially noticeable in areas of the country where Sinn Féin was growing on the back of its electoral successes. In Longford, a small Volunteer company was formed in Ballinalee at Easter 1917, around the time of the Longford by-election and the organisation continued to spread throughout the county in the second half of the year (Coleman, 2003: 78). Frequently, branches of both Sinn Féin and the Volunteers were formed at the same time in the same locations and consisting largely of the same personnel. There was very little distinction between both organisations at local level at this stage in 1917, which was partly deliberate as meetings of Sinn Féin clubs were often used as cover for Volunteer activity. This was also the case at national level where the Volunteer convention took place secretly in October 1917 at the same time as the Sinn Féin *ard fheis*.

Much of the reorganisation was carried out by 1916 veterans who had been released at Christmas. The communal experience of prison camps, such as **Frongoch** in north Wales, had provided them with an important opportunity to forge networks and make plans for reorganisation which were duly acted upon after their release. The release of the remaining internees from the Rising in June 1917 was a further fillip to the Volunteers. A third republican organisation to undergo a post-Rising recovery at this time was the IRB, with the re-establishment of a permanent Supreme Council under the presidency of Thomas Ashe after the prisoners' release in June (Hart, 2005: 141). Many of those who were travelling around the country setting up Volunteer corps, including Collins, Ashe and Mulcahy, were leading figures in the IRB and its recovery also had an impact on the continuing progress of the Volunteers.

Frongoch: Prison camp in north Wales where many of the 1916 prisoners were interned.

Alarmed at the rising tide of republicanism the authorities began to apply the war-time Defence of the Realm Regulations more thoroughly and this new policy resulted in the arrest of Ashe for making what was deemed to be a seditious speech at Ballinalee in County Longford in August. His death the following month – as a result of force-feeding in Dublin's Mountjoy Prison where he had undertaken a hunger strike in an effort to receive recognition as a political prisoner – was another landmark in the re-establishment of the Volunteers. His funeral was the first opportunity for the Volunteers to stage a large militant display since the Rising and afterwards drilling and marching by local units became much more widespread (Augusteijn, 1996: 65).

The recovery of the Volunteers throughout 1917 was epitomised by the staging of a convention on 27 October 1917 at which a new executive was elected that included Richard Mulcahy as Director of Training and Michael Collins as Director of Organisation (Valiulis, 1992: 24–5). By the end of 1917 the Volunteers were beginning to recover from the devastation of the Rising. National and local structures had been re-established, a new leadership was in place and the country was moving noticeably in a more republican direction.

THE IRISH CONVENTION

Following the failure of the 1916 home rule negotiations the British Government was still seeking a solution to the Irish question. It was now hoped that the Irish could produce a solution themselves and this led to the establishment of an Irish Convention that sat for nine months between July 1917 and April 1918. The convention was chaired by Sir Horace Plunkett, a one-time constructive unionist who had come around to supporting dominion home rule and still hoped that a home rule solution which did not encompass partition could be achieved. Its 95 members had a slim nationalist majority and included members of the IPP, unionists, members of local government bodies, clergymen from the Roman Catholic Church and the Church of Ireland as well as prominent individuals in Irish society including the Provost of Trinity College Dublin, where the convention's meetings took place. Sinn Féin boycotted its proceedings and only a small number of individuals with advanced nationalist opinions attended, including Erskine Childers, Edward MacLysaght, an independent nationalist from Clare, and the writer George Russell (Æ).

Sinn Féin's participation was not initially seen as essential to the convention's success; by June 1917 it still had a long way to go in establishing itself as the main nationalist political party in Ireland. Even without the input of republicans, the convention suffered terminal internal divisions, from an early stage. The main point of contention was the level of fiscal autonomy that would be conceded to Ireland under a home rule settlement. This had already proved to be a controversial aspect of the third home rule bill. On the unionist side, Ulster and southern unionists were divided, with the southern unionist leader Lord Midleton arguing for a compromise under which a home rule parliament would have control over internal taxation and excise duties, with the imperial parliament retaining the privilege of imposing customs duties, whereas Ulster unionists wanted Westminster to control both customs and excise.

The IPP's influence at the convention was hampered by the ill-health of John Redmond, who died on 6 March 1918. He was replaced as party leader by John Dillon. A month after Redmond's death a minority report was passed by 44 members of the Irish Convention, with 29 voting against. Two dissenting minority reports were also published. In hindsight the convention was often viewed as having been doomed from the outset by Sinn Féin's boycott, but this ignored the fact that a settlement was close to being agreed by all the parties as late as January 1918 but was scuppered by hardline unionist insistence on a partitionist outcome. The Irish Convention was yet another failed attempt to solve the Irish home rule question while the war was in progress, and by the time of its conclusion in April 1918 it had been overshadowed by political developments in Westminster, where the Prime Minister had finally bowed to pressure to extend conscription to Ireland (O'Day, 1998: 280–5; Jackson, 2003: 177–83).

THE CONSCRIPTION CRISIS

In March 1918 the German Army launched its last effort to win the war. The British Army now required more manpower to deal with this new threat and Lloyd George began to consider the option of conscripting Irishmen. He did so in spite of advice to the contrary from his Irish advisers, including Sir Edward Carson and the Chief Secretary for Ireland, H. E. Duke, who warned that Britain might as well conscript Germans. Lloyd George ignored this counsel and sought to sweeten the pill for the Irish by promising to introduce home rule simultaneously. However, having been duped by Lloyd George during the negotiations on home rule that took place after the Rising, IPP leaders were justifiably distrustful of the Prime Minister on this occasion. When the Military Service Act was passed in the House of Commons on 16 April 1918 John Dillon led his members out of the chamber in protest and returned to Ireland to join the efforts to prevent its implementation [**Doc. 8**].

In view of the extent of opposition to extending conscription to Ireland the question of why the Prime Minister persisted with such a counter-productive policy must be addressed. Opposition to conscription in Ireland and among Lloyd George's Irish advisers was counter-balanced by strong support for the move within British society, the military and political establishment and Britain's war-time allies. Public opinion in Britain, where most men between the ages of 18 and 41 had been subject to the draft since 1916, held a very poor opinion of Irish 'shirkers' and felt that Ireland should play its part in the war effort in the same way as the rest of the United Kingdom. Prominent politicians and senior military leaders encouraged the Prime Minister to draw on the excess manpower available in Ireland. The French, who were suffering crippling casualty figures, could not understand why a part of the United Kingdom remained exempt from conscription (aan de Wiel, 2003: 205–9).

The enormity of Lloyd George's mistake became apparent immediately as all sections of political opinion, apart from unionism, united in an unprecedented show of unity to prevent conscription from being put into effect. Political rivals from Sinn Féin and the IPP came together on platforms at public meetings to voice their shared opposition to the measure. A meeting of Irish political leaders, including Dillon, Griffith and de Valera, was convened at the Mansion House in Dublin, at which a pledge was adopted 'Denying the right of the British Government to enforce compulsory service in this country', and promising 'to resist conscription by the most effective means at our disposal'. The Labour Party and trade union movement also played a central role in the campaign, calling a general strike on 23 April, which was widely observed outside of Belfast (Laffan, 1999: 133–8).

One of the most striking features of the conscription crisis was the leadership role adopted by the Roman Catholic Church. A week before the enactment of the conscription bill, the Irish bishops issued a statement warning the government against the proposed measure [**Doc. 9**]. Local Catholic churches became the focus for much of the campaign of opposition. On Sunday, 21 April, almost two million people signed the anti-conscription pledge outside church gates. On the same day special masses were held in churches where congregations prayed 'to avert the scourge of conscription', and parish priests spoke out vehemently against the action of the government. Some even went so far as to incite violence; Father Gaffney, parish priest of Virginia in County Cavan, held that people were justified in shooting those who tried to enforce conscription, and Dr McGinley of Letterkenny in County Donegal felt that passive resistance was a last resort (Travers, 1983: 173).

Many Irish church leaders had initially supported the British war effort, in sympathy with the Belgian Catholic population. However, by mid-1916 they were becoming alienated by British rule in Ireland and felt that the imposition of conscription without public support was unjust. This was compounded by Lloyd George's initial failure to exempt priests and clerical students, a position which was later reversed but not before the damage had been done. The principal reason why church leaders took such a strong guiding role in the campaign against conscription was to ensure that the movement stayed under their control and did not descend into violence and bloodshed. An immediate result of the passing of the Conscription Act was a massive influx of members to the Irish Volunteers, along with the other republican bodies Sinn Féin and Cumann na mBan. Without some form of moderate leadership to channel nationalist anger, the Irish hierarchy feared an armed uprising in Ireland and a repeat of 1916 (aan de Wiel, 2003: 224–30; Travers, 1983).

The extent of opposition made conscription unenforceable in Ireland. Yet, the government never repealed the legislation and the threat remained there until the end of the war in November 1918, though realistically by May it was clear that it could never be applied. The defeat of conscription was a major embarrassment for Lloyd George and his government's Irish policy. The conscription crisis cemented the rise of Sinn Féin, with the party's membership increasing by almost one-third by mid-1918. The close association between the party's leaders and the Catholic hierarchy added an important aspect of legitimacy to it.

While the IPP had also played a prominent role in the campaign against the enforcement of conscription, it received very little credit from an electorate which criticised it for failing to defeat the passage of the bill in Parliament in the first place. In order to defeat the application of conscription it was forced into an uncomfortable alliance with Sinn Féin. This nationalist unity was short-lived, with Arthur Griffith winning another important by-election for Sinn Féin against the IPP in Cavan East in June 1918. This was the last by-election held before the end of the war and the general election that followed it in December 1918, a contest that would complete the process of Sinn Féin's replacement of the IPP as the largest nationalist party in Ireland (Laffan, 1999: 146–9).

The conscription crisis consolidated further the progress made during 1917 in re-establishing Sinn Féin and the Irish Volunteers after the Rising. All republican organisations, including Cumann na mBan, experienced a massive surge in membership and activity. In Cork most Volunteer companies 'doubled in size almost overnight' (Hart, 1998: 239). Many of these proved to be fair weather republicans and by the summer of 1918 had faded away along with any serious threat of conscription. Nevertheless the conscription crisis was an important stage in the radicalisation of the military wing of the republican movement, which had begun to arm itself to defend the country against conscription and became more dedicated to resorting to violence in pursuit of Irish independence (Augusteijn, 1996: 85).

Not long after the effective defeat of conscription a former soldier, who had been a prisoner of war in Germany and recruited to Casement's unsuccessful Irish brigade, was arrested in County Clare, sparking wild rumours of a German conspiracy involving Irish republicans. Despite very flimsy evidence of a German plot the British Government ordered the arrest of senior Sinn Féin members, 73 of whom were seized on 17–18 May, including de Valera and Griffith, but not the up-and-coming leaders such as Michael Collins, Richard Mulcahy and Harry Boland. Collins's mole within the British intelligence system had forewarned him, but de Valera chose imprisonment for its propaganda value (Ward, 1974: 118–19).

The effect of the German plot arrests on Sinn Féin has been equated with the party having been 'beheaded'. Most of its senior leaders were interned, including the moderate wing represented by Griffith. Effective control of the party now fell to the more radical republican cadre of Collins, Mulcahy and Boland, who were closely connected to the Irish Volunteers and the IRB. As the military men gained the upper hand, the likelihood of the revolution taking on more of a military than a political form increased (Laffan, 1999: 145–6). If the German plot arrests represented an act of revenge by the government on Sinn Féin for the humiliation of conscription, the long-term effect was counter-productive.

THE 1918 GENERAL ELECTION

The incarceration of Sinn Féin's leaders failed to prevent the party from completing its takeover of Irish nationalist politics at the general election which eventually took place in December 1918. Sinn Féin had been preparing for the election since July and spent the latter half of the year recruiting suitable candidates. The standing committee of the party controlled nominations and in the absence of the more moderate leaders, Collins and Boland appear to have exerted influence in ensuring the choice of IRB members in some cases. Three women were selected – Constance Markievicz in the St Patrick's Division of Dublin, Winifred Carney (Belfast Victoria) and Hanna Sheehy-Skeffington, although the latter declined the offer. By the end of the war in November 1918 a full slate of candidates had been decided upon (Laffan, 1999: 153–5).

An important part of Sinn Féin's preparations for the election was the compilation of a manifesto and once again the radical republican influence of Boland, Collins and Father O'Flanagan was visible [Doc. 10]. It dedicated the party to achieving an independent 'Irish Republic'. This was to be achieved by withdrawing from Westminster and establishing in its stead in Ireland 'a constituent assembly comprising persons chosen by the Irish constituencies'. It also included a commitment to pursue Ireland's claim for independence at the post-war peace conference. The most significant phrase in the document was the commitment to use 'any and every means available to render impotent the power of England to hold Ireland in subjection by military force or otherwise'. This was a deliberately vague wording that could later be construed as representing a mandate to pursue independence by military as well as political means.

The 1918 general election was 'one of the greatest electoral landslides in western Europe in the twentieth century' (Coakley, 1995: 31). The result – 73 seats for Sinn Féin, 6 for the IPP and 26 for the Unionists (mostly in Ulster) – signalled the completion of the process whereby Sinn Féin replaced the Irish Party as the political representative of nationalist Ireland. This trend was personified by the defeat of the IPP's leader, John Dillon, by de Valera in

Mayo East, where the latter took two-thirds of the votes cast in a constituency represented by Dillon since 1885, and in which he was only opposed on one previous occasion in the acrimonious 1892 election than followed the Parnell split. Indeed the IPP's performance was even weaker than its six seats would suggest. Only two of those – Joe Devlin in Belfast Falls (who soundly defeated de Valera, winning 72 per cent of the vote) and William Redmond in Waterford City – were won in outright contests with Sinn Féin. Devlin had one of the strongest personal political machines in the country and Redmond was defending the seat held for many years by his late father and party leader, John Redmond, and while there was still residual Redmondism there he had less than 500 votes to spare over his Sinn Féin opponent. The remaining four seats were effectively ceded to the party in Ulster constituencies where a pact was agreed with the assistance of local Catholic bishops to ensure that the nationalist vote would not split and gift seats to unionists (Laffan, 1999: 160–8). The election of the veteran T. P. O'Connor in Liverpool, the only IPP MP elected outside Ireland, brought its parliamentary representation to seven.

The fact that the IPP was in a position to nominate candidates in many Ulster constituencies was an indication that the party retained a stronger hold on nationalist political sentiment there and that Sinn Féin had failed to make the same inroads in the north as it had in the south during the previous two years. The electoral pact between Sinn Féin and the IPP in Ulster makes it difficult to gauge the true electoral strength of either party; however, in constituencies where the pact did not operate and unionists were returned, the Irish Party tended to gain the greater portion of the nationalist vote. In the only constituency where voters failed to abide by the terms of the pact, Down East, the IPP candidate came second ahead of the Sinn Féin representative (Hepburn, 2008: 199). This constituency provided a good example of why the bishops and some nationalist politicians agreed the electoral pact. The combined nationalist vote was 8,238, but because it was split the seat was ceded to a unionist who polled 6,007.

The resilience of the Irish Party in Ulster can be explained in part by the fact that it faced serious political competition in the form of organised unionism, so had not become lazy and apathetic as it had in the southern constituencies where it had not faced any serious electoral opposition since the Parnell split. Unlike the United Irish League (the party's local organisation in the south), the Ancient Order of Hibernians had remained strong and active in the north under the tutelage of Devlin, whose *Irish News* was also an important source of support for the party within the Ulster nationalist community. Sinn Féin's policy of abstention from Westminster also concerned many nationalist voters, who feared the prospect of an imperial Parliament legislating for Ireland in which the only serious Irish political representation would be unionist.

Sinn Féin's resounding victory is usually seen as the most significant outcome of the 1918 general election. However, the contest was also important in consolidating unionist political dominance in Ulster. Of the 30 seats in the six counties that would become Northern Ireland, 23 were won by unionists, including three Labour Unionists. Devlin was the only nationalist to be returned among the nine Belfast City MPs. The confinement of unionism to Ulster was also confirmed by the fact that only two unionists were returned for southern constituencies, the University of Dublin (Trinity College) and the Rathmines division of Dublin City, where the combined nationalist vote was only 54 votes behind the successful unionist candidate, Maurice Dockrell.

Proportional representation by single transferable vote (PRSTV): An electoral system based on multiple-seat constituencies, in which voters vote numerically in order of preference (1, 2, 3 . . .), and votes are allocated accordingly until all seats are filled. Favours smaller parties.

The resounding success of Sinn Féin can be explained by a number of factors. First, the election was held under the first-past-the-post electoral system; **proportional representation by single transferable vote** favours smaller parties and could have helped the IPP. The fact that Sinn Féin only won 47 per cent of the votes cast is sometimes cited as detracting from the extent of its victory. However, this does not take into account the large number of southern constituencies that were uncontested because the IPP was simply unable to field candidates. Twenty-five Sinn Féin candidates were returned unopposed in republican strongholds like counties Kerry and Cork. Had these constituencies been contested it is likely that Sinn Féin would have enjoyed substantial majorities. In contests in the 26 counties that would become the Irish Free State, Sinn Féin's share of the vote rose to almost 65 per cent. Therefore, the number of uncontested seats meant that the figure for Sinn Féin's proportion of the vote distorted the party's true level of support. While 25 might appear to be a significant number of seats to have been conceded without a contest, the 1918 general election was in fact one of the most hotly contested since the Parnell split and in fact a higher number of seats were contested than in any election since 1892; in the preceding general election in December 1910, 63 of the 101 Irish constituencies had not been contested and only 19 of the 44 by-elections held in the meantime were contested.

Between 1910 and 1918 there had been a major reform of the franchise which benefited Sinn Féin and which explains also the dominance of unionists in Ulster. The Representation of the People Act (1918) extended voting rights to all adult males (not just householders) over the age of 21 and women over 30 if they or their husbands were on the electoral register for local elections, resulting in the Irish electorate almost trebling from 698,000 in 1910 to 1,931,000 in 1918. Because of the unusually long time between the general elections a significant number of voters from 1910 had passed away and it is estimated that about 70 per cent of the 1918 electorate were first-time voters. As such the IPP had probably lost some of its traditional voters and many of the new young voters had no existing affiliation. The by-election campaigns of 1917 and 1918 also showed that Sinn Féin was more likely to attract support from the youth. The franchise extension necessitated a redistribution of seats. In Belfast, where the number of seats rose from four to nine, this was seen as favouring unionists (Laffan, 1999: 151; Hepburn, 2008: 198).

The Irish Party suffered from having little new to offer. It ran on its record of having achieved land reform, advancing home rule and having the old age pension introduced to Ireland in 1908, a platform that offered little to new youthful voters who had a dim memory of such events. What they did remember was that the IPP had agreed to a partitionist settlement, and this, along with recent government folly in the shape of conscription, all contributed to the annihilation of Irish constitutional nationalism in 1918. Finally, Sinn Féin appears to have resorted to personation and intimidation to ensure its success (Laffan, 1999: 162–4).

The extent of Sinn Féin's victory can also be explained by the abstention of the Labour Party from the election. Labour had initially intended to contest the election, although it promised to join Sinn Féin in abstaining from Westminster afterwards, though not necessarily agreeing to sit in Sinn Féin's alternative constituent assembly. Sinn Féin was very concerned at the prospect of Labour participating in the election, fearing it could win up to 20 seats, many in the highly desirable Dublin City divisions. This resulted in efforts either to persuade Labour to withdraw or, if not, to agree to an electoral pact. By November 1918 Labour was having such great difficulty in finding suitable candidates – many, like Markievicz, who could have stood in the Labour interest, were already committed to Sinn Féin – that the party decided by a large majority (96 to 23) to withdraw from the election (Mitchell, 1974: 95–102).

Labour's decision not to contest the election also took into account its nature as an all-island party that had to consider its supporters in Ulster, many of whom would not have been happy with the alternative options of competing with Sinn Féin by offering an advanced nationalist manifesto or agreeing an electoral pact. To placate its northern wing by contesting the election and trying to avoid taking up a position on the national question would have resulted in losing considerable ground to Sinn Féin and possibly even to the remnants of the IPP (Gallagher, 1977: 99–100).

Historians have debated the impact of abstention on the subsequent political fortunes of the Labour Party, with some arguing that its failure to participate in the election that laid the foundations of the modern Irish state handicapped the party from the outset making it impossible for it subsequently to challenge the hegemony of the two main parties (**Fianna Fáil** and Fine Gael) that were the offspring of revolutionary Sinn Féin. However, an analysis of subsequent electoral contests suggests that Labour was not so terminally damaged; it won a quarter of the seats in the January 1920

Fianna Fáil: Political party formed by Eamon de Valera in 1926 following a split in Sinn Féin.

Government of Ireland Act (1920): Legislation partitioning Ireland into the six counties of Northern Ireland and the 26 counties of Southern Ireland that later became the Irish Free State.

Dáil Éireann: Irish Parliament, established by Sinn Féin in January 1919.

local elections for urban councils and 17 seats in the first election for the 26-county state in 1922 (having abstained again in the elections held in Southern Ireland in 1921 under the **Government of Ireland Act (1920)** (Laffan, 1985: 214–17).

The failure of Labour to emerge as one of the two main parties in Ireland until the twenty-first century probably owes more to the conservatism of Irish society, the absence of the largest industrial section of Ireland after partition, the divisiveness of Jim Larkin, the Roman Catholic Church's hostility to socialism and Fianna Fáil's historic success in attracting the urban and rural labour vote than to the party's decision not to contest the 1918 general election. However, had Labour contested the election and taken seats in **Dáil Éireann**, it might have been able to steer that assembly towards a more radical social and economic policy.

GUIDE TO FURTHER READING

The role of Collins and Griffith in reorganising Sinn Féin and the Irish Volunteers in the regions is illustrated well in A. T. Q. Stewart's, *Michael Collins: The Secret File* (Blackstaff, 1997), containing extracts from the RIC's intelligence file on Collins from 1916 to 1920.

The rise of Sinn Féin after the Rising, its transformation into a republican party and replacement of the IPP as the leading nationalist party in Ireland is chronicled in detail in Michael Laffan's, *The Resurrection of Ireland: The Sinn Féin Party, 1916–1923* (Cambridge University Press, 1999). The demise of the IPP from the home rule perspective is treated in the standard works on home rule by Jackson and O'Day (see Chapter 1).

The conscription crisis and the 1918 general election are examined by Pauric Travers in 'The priest in politics: the case of conscription', in Oliver MacDonagh, W. F. Mandle and Pauric Travers (eds), *Irish Culture and Nationalism, 1750–1950* (Gill and MacMillan, 1983), and in Jérôme aan de Wiel's, *The Catholic Church in Ireland, 1914–1918: War and Politics* (Irish Academic Press, 2003), both of which focus on the role of the Roman Catholic Church in marshalling opposition to conscription. John Coakley's, 'The election that made the First Dáil', in B. Farrell (ed.), *The Creation of the Dáil* (Blackwater, 1994) and Brian Farrell's *The Founding of Dáil Éireann: Parliament and Nation Building* (Gill and Macmillan, 1971) provide a good explanation of the results of the 1918 election, the full results of which for Ireland can be found online at www.ark.ac.uk/elections/h1918.htm.

4

The Political Campaign for Independence, 1919–21

THE FIRST DÁIL ÉIREANN

Sinn Féin's electoral promises to withdraw from Westminster and establish an alternative constituent assembly in Ireland were put into force on 21 January 1919 when the First Dáil Éireann was convened in Dublin's Mansion House (the official residence of the city's Lord Mayor). Only 27 of the party's elected members attended as many were still in prison as a result of the German plot arrests of the previous year. The proceedings of the First Dáil's inaugural sitting, held in public, were largely ceremonial. In de Valera's absence, Cathal Brugha was elected president and an interim cabinet was elected. The four foundation documents of the assembly were also issued. The constitution of Dáil Éireann was a short document comprising only five articles and declared the legislative supremacy of the Dáil: 'all legislative powers shall be vested in Dáil Éireann' [**Doc. 11**]. An executive was to be formed consisting of five departments (President, Finance, Home Affairs, Foreign Affairs and National Defence). The ministers who held these posts were appointed and could also be dismissed by the Dáil. The Dáil had ultimate responsibility for finance and the constitution could only be altered by the Dáil.

Although a short document that is often overlooked by historians and overshadowed by the better-known documents issued on that day, the Dáil constitution is a significant document in Irish constitutional and political history. It enshrined the principle of popular sovereignty as the powers of the Dáil were ultimately based on its electoral mandate, and established the model of British cabinet government that survives in Ireland to this day. Many of the features of the Republic of Ireland's modern parliamentary and democratic institutions have their origins in this document, such as the **Ceann Comhairle** and an independent Comptroller and Auditor General.

Ceann Comhairle: Chairman or Speaker of Dáil Éireann.

It is also notable as the first modern Irish constitution and acted as the legal basis of the state until the adoption of a more detailed constitution for the Irish Free State in 1922 (Farrell, 1988: 21–2).

The Declaration of Independence, its title copying that of the American colonies in the late eighteenth century, was a direct descendant of the 1916 Proclamation and asserted that the result of the 1918 general election constituted a democratic mandate to establish an independent republic in Ireland [**Doc. 12**]. Rhetorically, it contained much of the Anglophobia common to Irish republican discourse, repudiating 'seven hundred years' of 'foreign usurpation' and condemning 'English' rule in Ireland as being 'based upon force and fraud and maintained by military occupation against the declared will of the people'. It reiterated the intentionally vague threat of Sinn Féin's 1918 election manifesto to utilise 'every means at our command' in pursuit of the goal of establishing the republic. The document was read first in Irish, then French and finally in English.

The use of French indicated that the proceedings of the new revolutionary assembly were designed for foreign press and political consumption. This was most evident with the 'Message to the Free Nations of the World', essentially an appeal to the world powers convening at Versailles to draw up a post-war settlement to recognise Ireland's independence [**Doc. 13**]. Its principal target was the American President Woodrow Wilson and its language mirrored much of that used by Wilson in his famous Fourteen Points, including the right to self-determination, freedom of the seas and anti-imperialism. It was the precursor to the Dáil Department of Foreign Affairs's efforts to seek a hearing at the Paris Peace Conference.

The social and economic vision of the Dáil was espoused in the final document, the Democratic Programme [**Doc. 6**]. It was largely the work of the Labour Party leader Thomas Johnson, and was a reward for Labour having stood aside in the 1918 general election, as well as reflecting the lack of serious thinkers on social and economic issues within Sinn Féin (Laffan, 1999: 259; Mitchell, 1974: 107). Johnson's initial draft was a very radical document subordinating private property to the public good – 'no private right to property is good against the public right of the nation' – and asserting the state's right to appropriate its resources if not properly used – 'the nation must ever retain the right to resume possession of such soil or wealth whenever the trust is abused or the trustee fails to give faithful service' (Lynch, 1966: 46). This was unacceptable to Sinn Féin and it was redrafted by Seán T. O'Kelly, who removed the most strident socialist rhetoric.

Nevertheless, the document read in the Dáil contained ideas (described by some as 'communistic') that many of the more socially conservative members of Sinn Féin would have been uncomfortable with, declaring that 'the nation's sovereignty extends not only to all men and women of the Nation, but to all its material possessions, the Nation's soil and all its resources, all the wealth and all the wealth-producing process within the Nation'. Labour's opposition to private property remained, though it was toned down: 'we reaffirm that all right to private property must be subordinated to the public right and welfare'. It contained some specific policy aspirations, such as the plan to abolish the poor law, exploit natural resources such as peat bogs and fisheries and promote foreign trade.

In places there were distinct similarities with the 1916 Proclamation [**Doc. 5**], which was invoked in the opening paragraph of the Democratic Programme. Both used language that recognised gender equality; the proclamation addressed itself to 'Irishmen and Irishwomen', while the Democratic Programme claimed the allegiance of 'every man and woman'. It also promised 'to make provision for the physical, mental and spiritual well-being of the children', protect them from hunger and cold, and provide shelter and education, which could be read as a more detailed espousal of the proclamation's pledge to 'pursue the happiness and prosperity of the whole nation and of all its parts, cherishing all the children of the nation equally'. The only policy in the Democratic Programme that was acted upon by the Dáil was the abolition of the Poor Law, which was finally achieved by the new Irish Free State Government in 1925.

Irish governments since independence abandoned both the sentiments and content of the Democratic Programme and it is questionable whether the members of the First Dáil were ever serious about its implementation. Piaras Béaslaí, a Sinn Féin **Teachta Dála (TD)** who read the Democratic Programme in Irish to the Dáil, later wrote: 'It is doubtful whether the majority of members would have voted for it without amendment had there been any immediate prospect of putting it into force.' Its passage was no doubt helped by the absence in prison of some of the most socially conservative Sinn Féiners, such as Griffith and de Valera, and by 1922 it was dismissed by the Free State's Minister for Home Affairs, Kevin O'Higgins, as 'largely poetry' (Mitchell, 1974: 109–10).

Teachta Dála (TD): Member of Dáil Éireann.

Following the first ceremonial meeting in January the Dáil did not reconvene until 1 April, sitting for four days. The attendance of 52 TDs was the largest number ever to attend a session of the revolutionary assembly. Many of the leaders who had been in prison in January were in attendance and the interim cabinet was replaced with a permanent one, presided over by de Valera. Ministerial posts were allocated to Arthur Griffith (Home Affairs), Count Plunkett (Foreign Affairs), Cathal Brugha (Defence) and Michael Collins (Finance). New posts of Industries and Labour, not mentioned in the Dáil constitution, were created and given to Eoin MacNeill and Constance Markievicz respectively. Markievicz was only the second woman to hold a cabinet post at the time, alongside Alexandra Kollantai in the USSR; there would not be another woman minister in Ireland until Dehra Parker was made Northern Ireland's Minister for Health in 1949, while the Republic of Ireland had to wait for the appointment of Máire Geoghegan-Quinn as Minister for the Gaeltacht in 1979. Departments of Fisheries and National Language were added later in the year. In addition there were non-cabinet directorships for Propaganda, Agriculture and Industry and Trade (Mitchell, 1995: 33).

FOREIGN POLICY

The Declaration of Independence and the Message to the Free Nations indicated that foreign recognition of the republic was one of the Dáil's highest priorities. Both of these documents also highlighted the significance that the Dáil attached to making Ireland's case for independence to the post-war Paris Peace Conference. Early in February Seán T. O'Kelly arrived in Paris to begin the campaign for recognition. O'Kelly was accompanied by his wife and a Dáil civil servant, Michael MacWhite, all of whom spoke French. On 22 February O'Kelly wrote to the French Prime Minister Georges Clemenceau, who was hosting the conference, stating that he was the accredited representative of the Provisional Government of the Irish Republic and requesting a seat for Ireland. The result of the 1918 general election was cited as the democratic mandate underpinning these demands (Mitchell, 1995: 26–7).

When no reply was forthcoming from the French Prime Minister, O'Kelly switched the focus of his lobbying to US President Woodrow Wilson. With his Ulster-Scot's family background and admiration for British politics, Wilson was not personally inclined to support the Irish claims. Furthermore, he was anxious to secure British support for his Fourteen Points and the League of Nations. Nevertheless, he was coming under pressure from Irish-American elements within his own Democratic Party to be seen to make some representations about Ireland. This resulted in him sending a close adviser, George Creel, to Ireland in February 1919 to meet with Dáil leaders, including Collins and Boland. Creel offered them little hope of American support in public, pointing out that the main aim of the Paris Peace Conference was to impose peace terms on the defeated powers and highlighting the way in which Wilson's League of Nations could become a forum for Ireland to pursue its claim for independence. In private, however, he reported to Wilson that Britain should grant **dominion status** immediately in order to avoid republican sentiment hardening (Mitchell, 1995: 28–9; Carroll, 1978: 124; Whelan, 2006: 203–4).

Dominion status: The sovereignty granted to the Irish Free State under the Anglo-Irish Treaty, under which the King remained as head of state, similarly to Australia, New Zealand, Canada and South Africa.

Support for Ireland was growing elsewhere in the USA. On 4 March the House of Representatives passed the Gallagher Resolution calling on the peace conference to recognise Ireland's right to self-determination. The wording was a watered-down version of the original which sought support for Irish 'freedom' and 'independence' as well. It was not considered by the Senate, and most historians agree that it was little more than a gesture (Carroll, 1978: 125–6). Similar resolutions were passed at state and municipal level and by the powerful trade union the American Federation of Labor, to equally insignificant effect (Mitchell, 1995: 28).

The most prominent American support for Ireland came in April 1919, when the American Commission on Irish Independence, comprising three influential Irish-American politicians, was formed to travel to Ireland and Paris to press Ireland's case with the President. The chairman, Frank P. Walsh, was a labour lawyer from Kansas City; Michael J. Ryan had been President of the United Irish League of America until his pro-German views during the war led John Redmond and the IPP to distance themselves from him; and Edward F. Dunne was a former Mayor of Chicago and Governor of Illinois.

At a meeting with Wilson in Paris in April they received assurances that he would raise the Irish situation with Lloyd George and were hopeful that a Sinn Féin delegation consisting of de Valera, Griffith and Count Plunkett would be granted passports to travel to Paris, although not address the peace conference. The commission proceeded to Ireland for a 10-day visit, during which they addressed a meeting of the Dáil. Outside Dublin they met nationalist leaders, visited prisons and received the freedom of Limerick City. Their close association with the republican movement and criticism of both British and American policy towards Ireland annoyed both the British and American Governments and destroyed any chance of the Sinn Féin delegation being received in Paris. The London *Times* adjudged them to 'have done more political harm in one week than British statesmanship can expect to undo in many months'.

The commission's partisan behaviour had clearly resulted in the failure of its aim to secure passage to Paris for the Irish delegation, and its members, Walsh in particular, were accused of undertaking the mission to further their own political careers. However, certain aspects of their trip were successful. It generated useful publicity for the Irish cause. On returning to the USA, they appeared before the powerful Senate Foreign Relations Committee and in June the Senate passed a resolution of 'sympathy with the aspirations of the Irish people for a government of its own choice' (Carroll, 1978: 131–9; Carroll, 1985: 116–18; Whelan, 2006: 204–17).

The Dáil enjoyed some success in achieving recognition from international socialist organisations. In addition to the American Federation of Labor, noted above, the Irish labour representatives attending the post-war international socialist conference in Berne in February 1919 were treated as the representatives of a distinct nation. Furthermore, the conference passed resolutions supporting Irish self-determination and the right to have Ireland's case heard at the Paris Peace Conference. These were minor victories and fell well below the level of recognition the Dáil was aiming at, yet this was the first body to recognise the claims of the Dáil to be the legitimate government of an independent Irish Republic and the credit for this success belongs to the Irish Labour Party's representatives at the conference, Thomas Johnson and Cathal O'Shannon (Mitchell, 1995: 25–6).

There were also signs that another revolutionary government – the Soviet Union – was willing to recognise Irish independence. In June 1920 the Dáil decided to send a mission to Moscow to make a formal request for recognition. However, timing was a crucial factor; they were reluctant to receive such recognition from the USSR prior to making formal requests from other countries, lest Soviet recognition be considered a disadvantage as many countries were still unwilling to recognise the Bolshevik revolution. This decision to delay the request was fatal. By the time Dr Patrick McCartan arrived in the USSR in February 1921 the situation had changed. The Soviet Union was beginning to build cordial relations with Britain, resulting in the signing of a trade agreement in March 1921. The Soviet Government's representative, Maxim Litvinoff, made it clear to McCartan that the Irish had left it too late (Mitchell, 1995: 192).

Despite the conclusion of the Paris Peace Conference and the Dáil's failure to secure a hearing at it, the campaign for recognition in Europe continued. In addition to the Paris delegation, there were representatives in London, Switzerland, Genoa and Rome. The latter was significant from an Irish point of view as the location of the Vatican. In 1920 the British Foreign Secretary, Lord Curzon, sought to convince the Vatican to condemn the actions of Irish nationalists. The work of influential Rome-based Irish clerics, such as the Rector of the Irish College Father John Hagan and the Superior-General of the Carmelite order Peter Magennis, helped to head off any interference by the Vatican in Irish affairs on this occasion (Keogh, 1986: 40–4).

By 1921 Irish diplomatic representation had spread outside Europe to Commonwealth countries including Australia, New Zealand and Canada as well as South American countries with notable Irish links, such as Chile and Argentina. One of the more important missions was that to South Africa where Colonel Maurice Moore and P. J. Little were sent in 1921 to enlist support from Prime Minister Smuts to pressure the British Government into making concessions to Ireland. Although not prepared to go as far as supporting a republic, Smuts relayed his opposition to British policy in Ireland directly to Lloyd George at a Commonwealth conference in May 1921 and tried to convince all sides of the benefits of dominion status (Mitchell, 1995: 256–9, 296–7). Thus, by the time of the truce a nascent Irish diplomatic service had been established, marking another important achievement of the First Dáil's foreign policy.

After the failure of efforts to gain a hearing in Paris, the focus of the Dáil's foreign policy shifted to the USA, where it was hoped that the popularity of Ireland's cause would lead the US Government to giving some support to Irish self-determination. By concentrating on the USA it was also hoped to achieve another aim of the Dáil's foreign policy – raising sufficient funds to bankroll the revolutionary government at home and its various foreign missions. The most important aspect of the American campaign was the prolonged visit of de Valera to the land of his birth between June 1919 and December 1920.

De Valera's trip was a massive logistical effort for the infant Department of Foreign Affairs. Soon after his arrival he addressed an enthusiastic crowd of more than 50,000 in Boston's Fenway Park baseball ground. From his base at New York's Waldorf-Astoria Hotel he spent much of 1919 visiting cities with important Irish connections including Washington DC, Chicago, San Francisco, Detroit, Philadelphia, Pittsburgh, Butte (Montana), and Newport (Rhode Island), in addition to states that were less well-known for their Irish connections including Ohio, Kentucky, Indiana, Wisconsin (where he was made a chief of the Chippewa Indians), Missouri, Kansas, Nebraska, Colorado and Washington (Hannigan, 2008).

1920 was a presidential election year in the USA and one of the principal aims of the Dáil's mission was to have one of the main parties adopt a resolution supporting Irish independence at their selection conventions. Diplomatic representation was extended with the posting of personnel to Chicago, New Orleans, San Francisco and Boston, to bolster de Valera's New York-based mission. The work of the Dáil mission in the USA in 1920 also expanded considerably with the launch of the first bond drive, headed by James O'Mara, to raise funds for the revolutionary Irish Government. Supported enthusiastically by Irish expatriates and the descendants of Irish immigrants, it raised US$5.5 million in its first year (Mitchell, 1995: 194).

Apart from this success in raising money, the rest of de Valera's ambitious plan for 1920 was a failure. Neither the Republican nor Democratic Parties supported Ireland's cause at their conventions. The latter chose to bolster support for Woodrow Wilson at a time when he was facing fierce domestic opposition to the League of Nations that would result in the USA rejecting the Treaty of Versailles, refusing to join the league and electing a Republican President in November 1920. In March 1920 the US Senate voted to include a reservation supporting Irish self-determination in the Treaty of Versailles, but this was nullified by the Senate's eventual rejection of the overall treaty (Mitchell, 1995: 192–7).

The mission was hampered by divisions within the Irish-American political groups that were exacerbated by de Valera's arrival. The most important body agitating for Irish independence in the USA was Clan na Gael, the American

Friends of Irish Freedom (FOIF): Irish-American organisation led by John Devoy and Daniel Cohalan that supported Irish independence and split with de Valera's American Association for the Recognition of the Irish Republic (AARIR) in October 1920.

wing of the IRB, which supported military action and had provided finance and weapons for the Rising. Like its fraternal organisation in Ireland, Clan na Gael was a secret oath-bound society. In 1916 an off-shoot of the Clan, the **Friends of Irish Freedom (FOIF)** was formed, which was more open than the Clan and stated its intention to support 'any movement that will tend to bring about the National Independence of Ireland' (Carroll, 1978: 52).

By the middle of 1920 two distinct warring factions existed within the Clan and the FOIF. On one side was the head of the FOIF, Daniel F. Cohalan, the son of Irish immigrants who was a judge of the New York state Supreme Court and a prominent figure in the Democratic Party. By the time of de Valera's arrival in the USA in 1919 Cohalan was the most influential Irish-American politician and was supported by the veteran Fenian John Devoy and Diarmuid Lynch, a Cork TD. The rival group, based in Philadelphia, was led by the Tyrone-born Joseph McGarrity and supported by the Dáil's special envoy Dr Patrick McCartan.

Personality clashes and power struggles were some of the reasons for the discord between both groups. However, there were also significant differences of opinion about the best strategy to adopt in seeking American recognition of Irish independence. McGarrity's faction was solely concerned with the Irish cause, whereas Cohalan also had an eye on his own political advancement in the USA. Cohalan believed that lobbying American politicians and using diplomatic pressure was the method most likely to achieve success, whereas McGarrity and McCartan were proponents of more direct action such as raising funds and acquiring arms to support the revolution underway in Ireland. Specific events, such as O'Mara's bond drive, which Cohalan opposed, deepened the divisions between both sides. Soon after de Valera's arrival in 1919, Harry Boland sought unsuccessfully to heal the divisions and it was inevitable that de Valera would have to choose between the two sides.

In February 1920 in an interview with the *Westminster Gazette* de Valera controversially asserted that an independent Ireland would accept a version of America's Monroe Doctrine (which prohibited European interference in the American hemisphere) as a reassurance to Britain that Ireland would not be used as a base from which to attack it. This controversial 'Cuban analogy' was widely criticised in the USA and at home. McCartan was forced to return to Ireland to explain de Valera's position even though he did not agree with it. Cohalan objected to it and it led to the eventual sundering of relations between him and de Valera. De Valera and Boland sided with McGarrity and formed the American Association for the Recognition of the Irish Republic (AARIR) as a breakaway from the FOIF (Mitchell, 1995: 194–5; Carroll, 1978: 159–60).

By the time the AARIR was established towards the end of 1920, de Valera's mission had run its course and he returned to Ireland in December.

He had failed to achieve any serious political recognition for an independent Irish republic, though he had been successful in heading off any American statement of support for Ireland remaining an integral part of the UK. He contributed to the divisions among the Irish-Americans, although they were well established before his arrival. The money raised from the bond drive looked impressive at face value but very little of it made its way back to Ireland and was later tapped into by de Valera in the 1930s to set up Fianna Fáil's newspaper *The Irish Press* (Carroll, 2002: 90). Critics accused him of abandoning Ireland during some of the most crucial months of the revolution; was it acceptable for the President of the Dáil to be totally absent from the country for 18 months between June 1919 and December 1920? Overall, his trip was most successful as a propaganda exercise for the First Dáil, which was in itself a very important aspect of the Dáil's foreign policy.

The creation of a distinct Department of Publicity in March 1919 signified the importance the Dáil attached to publicising its activities, especially outside Ireland. The first Minister for Publicity was Laurence Ginnell but following his imprisonment he was replaced by Desmond FitzGerald, a 1916 veteran. The cosmopolitan FitzGerald was successful in making contact with foreign journalists and encouraging them to publicise the work of the Dáil as well as highlighting the 'acts of aggression' by the police and military in Ireland. The medium through which the revolutionary message was distributed was a news sheet initially called the *Weekly Summary*, which was replaced by the **Irish Bulletin** in November 1919. The matter-of-fact style adopted by the *Irish Bulletin* was central to the impact of its message, as seen in the following stark report of the killing of an elderly labourer:

Irish Bulletin: Propaganda newspaper of Dáil Éireann.

> *Murders*: Richard Lumley, a day-labourer, aged 60 of Rearcross, Co. Tipperary was shot dead without warning by a British military and police patrol, whilst on his way home from a wake at Abbey Hotel, Rearcross on the morning of July 4th.
>
> (Walsh, 2008: 113)

Emotive headlines such as 'Eighteen Innocent Men Murdered in Twenty-one Days' added to its effectiveness **[Doc. 14]**.

The *Bulletin's* first issue had a circulation of only 30, which was said to have risen to 2,000 (although this figure was produced by the Dáil's propaganda department and might not be reliable) by 1921 when five issues were produced each week. By 1921 foreign language editions were being published to cater for its popularity in Europe. It was popular in countries like India and Egypt that were also seeking to break away from British rule. Excerpts were published in reputable and influential foreign newspapers, such as the London *Times*. A copy appeared in the House of Commons in

November 1920 and the British propagandists in Ireland even tried to produce bogus issues to undermine its success, a ploy that backfired because the imitations were so unconvincing (Walsh, 2008: 113; Mitchell, 1995: 103–5, 250–2; Inoue, 2002: 89).

Even IRA guerrillas, who were often contemptuous of the politicians and administrators, were conscious of the important contribution of the *Irish Bulletin* to the success of the revolution; the Dublin volunteer Todd Andrews equated its worth to that of

Flying Column: Mobile active service unit formed by the IRA during the War of Independence to wage guerrilla warfare.

several **Flying Columns** . . . Had it not been for the exposures of the *Bulletin* the British campaign of terror could have been conducted relatively quietly and the measure of resistance of the IRA would never be known to the outside world.

(Andrews, 1979: 176)

The *Bulletin*'s success is even greater when seen in the context of the harsh press controls that were in place. Both the Defence of the Realm Act and the Restoration of Order in Ireland Act contained provisions to censor reports of events in Ireland during the First World War and the revolution, including the power to suppress newspapers deemed as seditious. The success of the *Bulletin* pierced this 'paper wall' erected around Ireland by British censorship restrictions (Kenneally, 2008).

When FitzGerald was arrested in February 1921 he was replaced by Erskine Childers, an English-born republican sympathiser who had also served as a British intelligence officer during the First World War. Childers had been an active member of the Dáil's publicity staff since settling in Ireland permanently in March 1919, publicising Ireland's cause in Paris during the Peace Conference and contributing to the *Irish Bulletin*. Under his steward-ship the foreign editions of the *Bulletin* were launched, there was greater

An tÓglach: Journal of the Irish Volunteers/IRA, edited by Piaras Béaslaí.

co-ordination with the IRA's publicity organ *An tÓglach* [*The Volunteer*], edited by Piaras Béaslaí, and questions about the government's Irish policy were planted with sympathetic MPs to be asked in the House of Commons in order to embarrass the government (Mitchell, 1995: 250). The activities of the IRA also received wider coverage in the *Bulletin* under Childers' editorship (Inoue, 2002: 92). Childers was also responsible for a number of pamphlets including *The Constructive Work of Dáil Éireann*, which highlighted the success of Dáil policies such as the arbitration courts, and *Military Rule in Ireland*, an account of British reprisals.

Propaganda was also an important function of the Dáil's foreign missions. In addition to its various foreign representatives mentioned above, by June 1921 there were also official press bureaux in Paris, Berlin, Rome, Madrid, Geneva and throughout the USA, and Dáil propaganda was circulated further afield to Denmark, Canada, Australia and South America (Inoue, 2002: 88). In Great Britain, an important centre for publicising events in Ireland, especially the impact of crown force reprisals, much of the propaganda work was undertaken by the Irish Self-Determination League, which played an important role in distributing the *Irish Bulletin* and circumventing censorship restrictions to keep British journalists informed about Ireland (Inoue, 1998: 48). By contrast to this extensive, sophisticated and effective foreign propaganda machinery, the Dáil's record on domestic publicity was poor, due to the focus on getting its message heard abroad and the impact of censorship on both the local and national press (Inoue, 2002: 97–8).

DOMESTIC POLICY

Much of the Dáil's early work was taken up with foreign policy because of the timing of the Paris Peace Conference. However, by mid-1919 it had begun to work on domestic issues in an effort to give effect to the existence of a separate government in Ireland. The Dáil Government faced a number of obstacles. Few of its ministers had any serious political experience, other than W. T. Cosgrave, who had served as a member of Dublin Corporation since 1908, making him the obvious choice for the local government portfolio. The constant harassment of the Dáil and its members, especially after it was outlawed in September 1919, also hampered its ability to work coherently. Many of its ministers also had other commitments, both in revolutionary and civilian life. In addition to serving as Minister for Finance, Michael Collins was at various times the IRA's Director of Organisation and Intelligence, while Defence Minister Cathal Brugha continued to be employed as a salesman for Lalor's candles.

The survival, continuity and success of the revolutionary Dáil owed much to the ability of its few permanent civil servants, in particular Diarmuid Ó hÉigeartuigh (O'Hegarty), the secretary to the Dáil cabinet and clerk of the Dáil. Ó hÉigeartuigh was on the Supreme Council of the IRB and the executive of the IRA, and had fought in the Rising. In addition to his republican credentials, he was an experienced civil servant, having worked for the Department of Agriculture and Technical Instruction from 1910 until his dismissal in 1918 for refusing to take an oath of allegiance. He was responsible for taking the minutes of Dáil sittings and cabinet meetings, organising its secret meetings, handling its correspondence and facilitating communication between ministers, earning him a reputation as 'the civil servant of the revolution' (Pakenham, 1972: 102).

The first priority of the Dáil's domestic agenda was to raise funds to finance its ambitious foreign activities and to run the bureaucracy at home.

The choice of Michael Collins as Finance Minister owed much to his experience working for the accountancy firm Craig Gardner prior to the Rising, and as secretary to the National Aid Association that handled fundraising for the families of republican prisoners afterwards. As such, he had more experience of financial administration than most other TDs, although this was still relatively slight for a finance minister. He was also a senior figure in both the IRA and the IRB, so his appointment also appeased the military wing of the movement, as Finance was possibly the most important post in the government (Hart, 2005: 188).

The Dáil considered levying an income tax but was unable to draw up a suitable plan for it. Therefore, the main method of raising funds was a national loan, which it was hoped would raise £250,000, half of it expected to come from Ireland. In fact the final total for the domestic subscription was £370,000, £171,000 of which came from the province of Munster alone (Hart, 2005: 189; Fanning, 1978: 21). The bond drive launched in the USA in January 1920 was expected to raise most of the foreign contributions. By November 1920, over US$5 million had been pledged, most of it from New York and Massachusetts, and had it not been for the in-fighting among the Irish-Americans a significantly larger amount could have been raised. In spite of the success in raising money in the USA, the Dáil would never see the full benefit of it; only £58,000 had been repatriated by mid-1920 and eventually only about half of the sum raised ever made its way to Ireland (Hart, 2005: 191–2).

Collins hid the money and bonds in banks whose managers were sympathetic to the republican cause and in a variety of locations around Dublin, including in a child's coffin hidden under the floor of Batt O'Connor's home in Donnybrook. O'Connor, a builder and close ally of Collins, modified other buildings used by Sinn Féin to provide safe hiding places for the precious funds (O'Connor, 1929: 116–18). British intelligence tried hard to confiscate the Dáil funds in an effort to cripple the revolutionary government. In 1920 a former RIC officer and magistrate, Alan Bell, who had investigated Land League funds during the 1880s, was tasked with locating the republican purse. On 26 March

Squad: A death squad controlled by Michael Collins that targeted British intelligence agents and was responsible for high-profile killings such as Bloody Sunday.

1920 he was assassinated by members of Collins's hit unit, the **Squad**, while travelling by tram from his home in Monkstown to Dublin Castle (Foy, 2006: 81–2). His death was a significant setback for British intelligence and eliminating a man who was getting uncomfortably close to discovering his secret stash of funds was an important strategic victory for Collins. British Intelligence only succeeded in confiscating a total of £23,000 (Mitchell, 2002: 79). From 1920, when the War of Independence began in earnest, much of the Dáil's budget was spent on the Department of Defence – over £150,000 from mid-1920 until the end of 1921. The Department of Foreign Affairs accounted for a further £36,529 in the same period (Carroll, 2002: 11).

A significant amount of the money – at least £200,000 – was spent by the Dáil's National Land Bank, which was set up to finance the purchase of land by tenants in an effort to curtail the re-emergence of land agitation. In spite of the series of Land Acts passed by the British Government between 1870 and 1909 that broke up many of the large landed estates and advanced loans to tenants to purchase their holdings, serious land problems remained into the 1910s and 1920s, especially in the west of Ireland. Many farms were small in size and uneconomic; land in the west of Ireland was often of poor quality; the new class of peasant-proprietor did not possess the money to expand or improve their holdings; and there was still insufficient land available to meet the demand of those who sought to make a livelihood from agriculture. These landless men looked enviously at large grassland farms used for grazing livestock and were frustrated in their efforts to increase their holdings by the inefficiency of the Land Commission, the body tasked with overseeing land redistribution. This situation was exacerbated by the outbreak of the First World War. The increased wartime demand for food was a boon to Irish tillage farmers and increased further the demand for land, while the curtailment of emigration meant that many who would otherwise have left the country joined the queue for it (Dooley, 2004: 26–32; Campbell, 2003: 161).

The fear that social unrest such as this would detract from the national question and initiate class conflict led Sinn Féin to take control of the situation by setting up a system of arbitration courts to settle the problem. The establishment of these courts, where disputes would be settled by compromise rather than confrontation, was first suggested by Griffith in his pamphlet *The Sinn Féin Policy* in 1906 and was based on the ideas of the Young Irelanders of the 1840s and courts used by the Land League in the 1880s [**Doc. 15**]. In 1917 Sinn Féin began to establish arbitration courts to settle land disputes, beginning in County Clare. In 1919 they were brought under the jurisdiction of the Dáil and extended beyond land to deal with all legal matters in an effort to supplant the existing crown courts with a domestic judicial system controlled by the revolutionary administration (Laffan, 1999: 311–13).

The Dáil courts consisted of four tiers. At the lowest level were the three-member parish courts that were empowered to deal with claims involving property that did not exceed £10 in value, evictions from low-rent dwellings and other minor crimes. Its members were not required to have any legal qualifications and one member could be a clergyman. The area covered by these courts corresponded to the local Roman Catholic parish. More serious claims for damage (from £10–£100) were dealt with by district courts, which corresponded to electoral constituencies and also heard cases dealing with land title, trade union rights and workmen's compensation as well as hearing appeals against judgments of the lower parish courts. There were five arbitrators on the district courts, two of whom could be clergymen and none of whom required a legal qualification. Appeals against the judgments of the district courts were heard three times a year by a circuit court judge, who was a qualified barrister (Davitt, 1968: 113–18; Kotsonouris, 1994: 30–1). The two men appointed to these posts were Cahir Davitt, the son of Land League founder Michael Davitt, and Diarmuid Crowley. The highest court in the land was the Supreme Court, the two members appointed to which were experienced barristers, James Creed Meredith, a Protestant with nationalist sympathies, and Arthur Clery, a Professor of Law at University College Dublin (Casey, 1970: 325–6).

The lower courts which did not require members to be lawyers often contained senior figures in the republican movement locally and nationally. For example, in Dublin, court members included Erskine Childers, Darrell Figgis, Hanna Sheehy-Skeffington and Maud Gonne MacBride, and in Limerick Mary Spring-Rice, the daughter of Lord Monteagle and a prominent republican supporter, sat on her local parish court in Shanagolden (Casey, 1970: 327–8). Parish courts often included the local parish priest or prominent local members of Sinn Féin, the IRA (as the Volunteers were more commonly known after 1919) or Cumann na mBan. Similarly, the administrative staff, the most important of which was the local registrar, usually had a record of activity in the independence movement (Fitzpatrick: 1977, 179).

The establishment of the Dáil courts coincided with the decline of the RIC as an effective police force as the IRA's campaign of intimidation and assault began to take effect. At the end of 1919 the police closed many of their small rural barracks and became increasingly unable to prosecute crimes or enforce decrees and judgments of the crown courts. The republican courts, along with the Irish Republican Police wing of the IRA, played an important role in ensuring the maintenance of law and order at this time, reflecting Sinn Féin's fear that social unrest could derail the independence campaign, and in the process winning many compliments from those who were not traditional supporters of the republican movement. The courts made the Dáil Government a reality in the lives of many and proved that it was capable of governing the country effectively, indeed more effectively than the beleaguered RIC and crown courts.

The courts were at the height of their success in the summer of 1920; Erskine Childers claimed that they were working effectively in 27 counties and were 'never busier' (Childers, 1921: 27–8). In Longford, one of the counties where the courts operated best throughout the War of Independence, the district court held three sittings in the north of the county in June and a further three in July (Coleman, 2003: 103). The public's willingness to bring their cases before the courts and abide by their rulings underlay much of this success and was in part a consequence of the ineffectiveness of the RIC and crown courts, as one correspondent explained to the unionist Walter Long:

> The fact is that everybody is going over to Sinn Féin, not because they believe in it, but because it is the only authority in the County; and they realize that if their lives and property are to be secured, they must act with Sinn Féin.
>
> (Costello, 1990: 49)

Even some unionists were prepared to bring their cases to the Dáil courts. One measure of the Dáil courts' success was the virtual cessation of business at the crown courts in many counties. The inability of the RIC to bring prosecutions was part of this, but it was also clear that litigants were defecting to the new courts (Coleman, 2003: 104–8; Kotsonouris, 1994: 33). The only area of the country where the courts either failed to operate or operated in a very small way was Ulster, especially the six most unionist counties that later constituted **Northern Ireland** (Casey, 1970: 335–6).

The cases brought before the courts give an insight into the mundane aspects of life that continued in spite of the revolutionary atmosphere of the time. In rural areas the subjects were usually related to property – land ownership disputes, allegations of trespass, rights of way and claims for damage. There were fewer criminal cases such as debt, assault, slander or intimidation. Social and family issues, such as child maintenance, were also dealt with on occasion (Coleman, 2003: 225). Judgments were based on the law in operation on 21 January 1919 and citations from ancient Irish Brehon law, Roman and French law were permitted, but British legal texts were prohibited. The courts earned a reputation for conservative judgments, reflecting their origins in an attempt to quell social unrest. Common punishments included the exclusion of an offender from an area for a period of time, the confiscation of illicit alcohol, the destruction of *poitín* (illicit whiskey) stills and fines (Laffan, 1999: 314).

Such conservative judgments were most noticeable in the distinct land tribunals that operated in parallel to the Dáil courts, staffed by Kevin O'Shiel, Conor Maguire and Art O'Connor. The judgments of the land courts often favoured the landowner or established tenant. In a case in Ballinrobe, County Mayo in May 1920, O'Shiel pronounced in favour of two tenants of a 120-acre grazing farm, against the claims of a number of labourers who wanted the estate in question divided among them. The dissatisfied claimants rejected the decision and occupied the land in defiance of O'Shiel's judgment, forcing him to employ the local IRA to arrest and imprison the men in question (Campbell, 2003: 168).

Northern Ireland: Six-county home rule entity created by the Government of Ireland Act (1920) comprising Counties Antrim, Armagh, Derry, Down, Fermanagh and Tyrone.

The scheme for the land courts, drawn up by O'Connor, was based on the principle that only untenanted land would be redistributed. The Dáil's National Land Bank, financed with the proceeds of the national loan, provided £340,000 in loans to allow 850 people to purchase 16,000 acres of land (Dooley, 2004: 47–9). The experiment was successful in keeping a lid on potentially explosive land agitation for the duration of the War of Independence. However, the re-emergence of land disputes during the Civil War indicated that it had solved neither the land question nor the class conflicts of the revolutionary period.

Initially the authorities adopted a tolerant approach to the courts, another factor responsible for their early success. However, by the summer of 1920 the British were clearly losing the battle for law and order on both the political and military fronts and the decision was taken to suppress the courts. The assault on the courts had mixed success. While Lloyd George claimed in April 1921 that they had 'vanished', there is evidence that the courts continued to operate effectively in some parts of the country; between March and July 1921 Cahir Davitt held circuit courts in Longford, Clare, Limerick and Cork and after the truce the Minister for Home Affairs, Austin Stack, praised these counties, along with Dublin City, for continuing to function throughout the repression. All of these were areas where the IRA was strong. Judges such as Maguire and O'Shiel believed that the government had waited too long and allowed the courts to become too well established to destroy them completely [**Doc. 16**]. The courts might not have been as successful from autumn 1920 onwards, but their survival in these key areas until the truce represents one of the greatest successes of the Dáil's domestic policy (Coleman, 2003: 105–6).

The Dáil courts were permitted to operate openly after the truce and enjoyed their most effective period in the six months from the truce to the treaty. From November 1921 until July 1922 the Supreme Court alone heard 150 cases (Casey, 1970: 332–3). However, when the republican movement split on the treaty in early 1921 the courts became a victim of their success. Anti-treaty republicans began to have recourse to the courts in an effort to embarrass the Provisional Government and when Count Plunkett applied to the courts for a writ of *Habeas Corpus* following the capture of his son George in the surrender of the Four Courts in June 1922, the government hastily rescinded the original decree of the First Dáil that set up the courts, on the dubious grounds that the then Minister for Home Affairs, Austin Stack, had acted outside his jurisdiction. A winding-up commission was established to dispense with the outstanding business of the Dáil courts before their eventual demise in 1925 (Kotsonouris, 2004).

The Dáil had more limited success in another key area of domestic policy – local government. The 1898 Local Government Act had introduced a very significant reform of Irish local government, replacing the old unrepresentative grand jury system, which was the preserve of the landed elite, with democratically elected county and district councils. Since the first local elections under the new Act in 1899, local government in most of Ireland, outside the unionist-controlled areas of the north, was dominated by the IPP. After the 1918 general election this was the only political power retained by the party but its hold on it was limited, with local elections due to be held in 1920.

The first set of elections for urban district councils was held in January 1920 and resulted in Sinn Féin taking the largest number of seats nationally (550), followed by Labour (394), Unionists (355), Nationalists (238), independents (161) and municipal reformers (108). The overall results gave Sinn Féin control of 72 of the country's 127 urban councils. The main reason why Sinn Féin won fewer than one-third of the seats was the use of proportional representation by single transferable vote (PRSTV), rather than first-past-the-post, which had helped the party to a massive landslide in the 1918 general election. The new system was first tried in a special local election in Sligo the previous year, in which Sinn Féin came second, taking only seven of the 24 seats on offer; the government had found a way to curtail the electoral success of Sinn Féin (Laffan, 1999: 323–7; Daly, 1997: 50).

However, PR was less successful in stemming the Sinn Féin tide six months later, when the more important county council elections took place, as well as those for rural district councils. In the intervening period, the republican movement had asserted a stronger hold on the country with the successful establishment of the Dáil courts and the routing of the RIC from large parts of the country. Determined to be more successful on this occasion, local Sinn Féin organisers also brought considerable pressure to bear on potential opponents for the nationalist vote, including Labour and constitutional nationalists, resulting in many of them refusing to contest vacancies leaving the field open for Sinn Féin. As a result the party took control of 28 of the country's 33 county councils (each of the 32 counties had one county council except Tipperary, which had two – North Tipperary and South Tipperary). Intimidation was one of the most significant factors explaining the result (Laffan, 1999: 328–9; Daly, 1997: 52).

After the January elections the Dáil requested that the new local authorities pledge allegiance to it and repudiate the existing Local Government Board (LGB). Very few councils did so initially, preferring not to act unilaterally without support from county and rural councils. The Dáil did not pursue the issue either, for fear that the more important June elections might be postponed. However, once Sinn Féin had taken control of such a large proportion of councils in mid-1920, the majority of these councils acted fast to declare their allegiance to the revolutionary government, a move that was of great symbolic significance in bolstering the Dáil's claim to be the legitimate government of Ireland (Daly, 1997: 50–2).

The patriotic fervour of the new councils was also to be seen in some of the motions passed at their early meetings, such as adopting resolutions on supporting the Dáil courts, refusing to co-operate with British tax collection, purchasing only Irish manufactured goods and reserving public service appointments for 'loyal citizens of the Republic with a knowledge of Irish'. Offending motions passed by outgoing councils, in particular those condemning the Rising, were rescinded; in the case of Longford Rural District Council one such motion was cut out of the minute book and burned by the chairman (Coleman, 2003: 91–2).

Councils that transferred their loyalties from the LGB to the Dáil soon felt the financial effects of their actions; one-fifth of the local authorities' income (£1.6 million) came from the LGB, in addition to various other infrastructural grants for housing and road maintenance. Dublin Corporation was brought to the brink of bankruptcy in August 1920 as a result. Dáil Éireann did not have the resources to compensate councils for the loss of such a significant portion of their income; alternative income sources, such as increased rates would be needed, and councils would also have to cut back on their services (Daly, 1997: 58–60; Coleman, 2003: 93).

Defection from the LGB also affected rate collection, with local rate collectors facing demands for the return of rates from both the LGB and the Dáil Department of Local Government and many rate-payers exploiting the dispute to avoid paying (Coleman, 2003: 94). Added to this was the fact that by 1920 and 1921, income from rates was more badly needed than ever because of the damage to roads and bridges caused by the fighting during the War of Independence. The significant increase in damage to property and personal injury during the fighting was a further financial burden as local authorities were expected to provide the compensation. When Sinn Féin-controlled councils refused, the British Government passed legislation to compel the banks which acted as the councils' treasurers to make these payments. As a result many councils removed the banks as their treasurers, resulting in the loss of overdraft facilities. Many councils were so close to bankruptcy in 1921 that they were forced to reinstate the banks (Daly, 1997: 59–61).

Financial troubles were not the only difficulties faced by the Dáil-controlled councils. Their day-to-day operations were hindered by the confiscation of important documents in raids by the crown forces. Many Sinn Féin councillors, some of whom were also active in the IRA, were arrested or forced to go on the run resulting in their absence from numerous meetings. Some of the personnel employed by the Dáil, such as rate or rent collectors, were incompetent or corrupt. Interference by local IRA units in the running of councils was also a problem in some areas (Coleman, 2003: 99–100; Daly, 1997: 71–2).

One side-effect of these financial troubles was the opportunity to implement one of the aims of the Democratic Programme – abolition of the poor law system. In many counties poor law unions were amalgamated initially and finally replaced by county homes and hospitals after 1922. In doing so the hated spectre of the workhouse, so strongly associated with the failures of British rule in Ireland during the famine, disappeared from Irish welfare provision, although the Poor Law System remained in Northern Ireland until it was replaced by the National Health Service after the Second World War (Daly, 1997: 75–8).

The scheme leading to the abolition of the workhouses is one of the best examples of how the Dáil-controlled local authorities made the alternative state created by the revolutionary Dáil a reality in the lives of many, similar to the Dáil courts. For many reasons, principally financial, the Dáil had less success in running local government than in establishing its own judicial system. Nonetheless, the local elections of 1920 put Sinn Féin firmly in control of local as well as national politics, and by the time of the truce the Dáil's Department of Local Government had established a permanent hold on local government throughout the country.

SOCIAL CONFLICT IN REVOLUTIONARY IRELAND

The establishment of the Dáil courts, and especially the land courts, illustrated that there was a strong undercurrent of social tension in revolutionary Ireland. Until recently the received wisdom had been that there was no social aspect to Ireland's political revolution because Ireland already had its social revolution in the shape of the transformation of land ownership from landlords to peasant-proprietors between 1870 and 1909. It was believed that by the late 1910s 'in rural Ireland thoughts of social revolution were held only by a minority', as a result of land purchase, the financial benefits accruing from the introduction of the old age pension in 1908 and the prosperity enjoyed by Irish agriculture during the First World War (Lynch, 1966: 41). However, more recent research has shown that the Land Acts had not solved the problem entirely and the level of land agitation emerging in the west towards the end of the war had the potential to cause serious social unrest (Campbell, 2003: 170–1).

The labour and trade union movement was also a significant factor in urban Ireland during these years. The 1913 Dublin lock-out was a significant defeat for organised trade unionism in Ireland. The temporary emigration of

James Larkin to the USA in its aftermath, and the execution of James Connolly for his role in the Rising further depleted the Irish labour movement by removing its most effective and charismatic leaders. The Rising also took its toll on the Irish Citizen Army, which suffered the loss of a number of key figures including Sean Connolly, Richard O'Carroll, William Partridge and Peadar Macken, all of whom died in the fighting and Michael Mallin, who was executed. While the Irish Volunteers revived in the aftermath of the Rising, the Irish Citizen Army did not. The trade union movement's headquarters at Liberty Hall had been destroyed along with its newspaper *The Workers' Republic* (Mitchell, 1974: 70–1).

The new labour leaders who emerged after the Rising, including the Labour Party leader, Thomas Johnson, and the General Secretary of the ITGWU, William O'Brien, prioritised trade union organisation over political activity (Mitchell, 1974: 78). The First World War provided a significant boost for the trade union movement in Ireland; in 1918 the ITGWU trebled in size and expanded further during 1919 and 1920. As a result strike activity increased steadily during and immediately after the war (Fitzpatrick, 1980: 28–30).

The trade union movement used strikes as a tactic to assist the revolutionary movement during the period 1918–21, when four important strikes linked to the revolution were held. On 23 April 1918 a general strike against conscription was very successful outside of Ulster. A general strike in Limerick a year later, somewhat grandiosely dubbed the Limerick Soviet, was a response to harsh government measures that proclaimed Limerick City as a special military area, requiring permits for those wishing to enter or leave the city, and resulted in the eventual withdrawal of the offending proclamation. In April 1920, a two-day general strike called by Sinn Féin in support of political prisoners helped to secure their release (Mitchell, 1974: 88, 117–20).

The most important action by the labour movement in support of the independence campaign was the railway-munitions strike that lasted from May until December 1920. It was initiated by Dublin dockers who refused to handle war materials intended for use by the crown forces [**Doc. 17**]. Soldiers were forced to unload the equipment themselves but were then faced with the difficulty of transporting it as the boycott spread to the railways as transport workers refused to load or drive trains carrying munitions, armed soldiers or policemen, actions which resulted in the dismissal of approximately 1,000 rail employees. The strike had a detrimental effect on the Irish railway system in the latter half of 1920. In some areas train services were suspended completely. No passenger services operated into Galway and the west of Ireland was serviced by only one daily goods train from Athlone. By the end of 1920 the side-effects the strike was having on the general public, which was suffering from the absence of both passenger and goods transit, resulted in it being called off, but not before it had caused serious embarrassment to the British authorities in Ireland and disruption to the crown forces' ability to counter the guerrilla campaign of the IRA (Townshend: 1979a).

The activity of land agitators in rural Ireland and trade unionists in the cities and towns provides ample evidence of the potential for social upheaval in revolutionary Ireland. That there was no such revolution owes more to the actions of Sinn Féin and the Dáil in acting to supress it at an early stage through the use of the republican courts, the nationalism of many within the labour movement who were prepared to use strikes for national rather than social reasons, the insurmountable problem of creating a united and effective labour movement out of a nationalist-minded proletariat in Dublin and Cork and a staunchly unionist one in the country's industrial heartland of Belfast, and the failure of Labour's political leaders to position their party to benefit from the political vacuum caused by the demise of the IPP.

GUIDE TO FURTHER READING

The proceedings and debates of the First Dáil Éireann can be accessed online at www.historical-debates.oireachtas.ie/index.htm. A detailed documentary account of the foreign policy of the Dáil is contained in *Documents on Irish Foreign Policy, Volume I: 1919–1922* (Royal Irish Academy, 1998), which is also available online at www.difp.ie.

The most comprehensive account of the workings of the First Dáil is Arthur Mitchell's, *Revolutionary Government in Ireland: Dáil Éireann 1919–22* (Gill and Macmillan, 1995). The work of individual departments is dealt with in their official histories, including Ronan Fanning's, *The Irish Department of Finance, 1922–58* (Institute of Public Administration, 1978) and Mary E. Daly's, *The Buffer State: The Historical Roots of the Department of the Environment* (Institute of Public Administration, 1997). Michael Collins's tenure as Minister for Finance is explored thoroughly in Peter Hart's biography, *Mick: The Real Michael Collins* (Macmillan, 2005). The Dáil courts are examined by Mary Kotsonouris in *Retreat from Revolution: the Dáil Courts, 1920–24* (Four Courts Press, 1992).

The best account of the Dáil's efforts to achieve recognition in the USA is Francis M. Carroll's, *American Opinion and the Irish Question, 1910–23* (Gill and Macmillan, 1978). Keiko Inoue's work on the *Irish Bulletin* in 'Propaganda of Dáil Éireann', in Joost Augusteijn (ed.), *The Irish Revolution, 1913–1923* (Palgrave, 2002), along with Ian Kenneally's, *The Paper Wall: Newspapers and Propaganda in Ireland, 1919–21* (Collins Press, 2008) and Maurice Walsh's, *The News from Ireland: Foreign Correspondents and the Irish Revolution* (I. B. Tauris, 2008) show how the Dáil publicised Ireland's cause internationally.

Social unrest in revolutionary Ireland has been highlighted in a rural context by Terence Dooley in *The Land for the People: The Land Question in Independent Ireland* (UCD Press, 2004), and in urban areas by David Fitzpatrick in 'Strikes in Ireland, 1914–21', *Saothar*, 6 (1980): 26–39 and Charles Townshend in 'The Irish railway strike of 1920: industrial action and civil resistance in the struggle for independence', *Irish Historical Studies*, 21: 83 (1979).

5

The Military Campaign for Independence, 1919–21

THE IRISH WAR OF INDEPENDENCE

At the same time that the First Dáil was convening in the Mansion House on 21 January 1919, a group of IRA men from Tipperary, including Dan Breen, Seán Treacy and Seamus Robinson, ambushed an RIC convoy at Soloheadbeg in an attempt to capture a consignment of gelignite that the police were escorting from the military barracks in Tipperary town to a local quarry. The aim of the action was to use the gelignite for the manufacture of explosives and to strike a symbolic blow against the RIC. The ambush resulted in the deaths of two police constables, James McDonnell and Patrick O'Connell, making them the first casualties of what became known variously as the Irish War of Independence, the Anglo-Irish War or, more colloquially in Ireland, the Tan War (Abbott, 2000: 30–3).

While the Soloheadbeg ambush is generally seen as representing the start of the war, it was purely coincidental that it took place on the same day as the Dáil opened; it was an isolated incident and did not spark off an immediate military confrontation between the IRA and the crown forces. The escalation of military activity during 1919 was gradual; indeed many volunteers were more occupied with the work of the Dáil, such as collecting for the national loan. Nevertheless there was a noticeable increase in what the police referred to as outrages, including raids for arms, threatening letters, assaults on police and civilians and resisting arrest.

Many of these were attacks on police. On 10 April 1919 the Dáil decreed a peaceful boycott of the RIC decreeing that people should avoid all forms of social and commercial interaction with them and their families. There is evidence that the social ostracisation of the police, a tactic popularised in Ireland during the Land War, was well underway before this decree; in Clare '[b]y April 1918 most barracks were no longer supplied locally with turf, butter, eggs or milk', and attacks on police by the Volunteers were growing in West Cork throughout 1918 and early 1919 (Fitzpatrick, 1977: 7; Hart, 1998: 62). An editorial in the IRA's journal *An tÓglach* on 31 January 1919 was seen as legitimising the use of violence against the RIC:

> Every Volunteer is entitled, morally and legally, when in the execution of his military duties, to use all legitimate methods of warfare against the soldiers and policemen of the English usurper and to slay them if it is necessary to overcome their resistance.
>
> (Valiulis, 1992: 40)

The police were targeted not only because they were the face of British rule in every locality, but also because their local knowledge of republican activities and activists made them a valuable source of intelligence and as an armed force they were also an obvious target for arms raids by the IRA as it sought to increase its own arsenal.

The assaults on the police became more violent as 1919 progressed and eventually resulted in more fatalities; in April Constable Martin O'Brien was shot dead while guarding a hunger-striking IRA prisoner being held at the hospital in Limerick City's workhouse, while Sergeant Peter Wallace and Constable Michael Enright died during the IRA's rescue of Seán Hogan at Knocklong railway station in County Limerick the following month. Ten more policemen, members of both the RIC and **Dublin Metropolitan Police (DMP)**, were to die in 1919 as the violence increased in the latter half of the year (Abbott, 2000: 33–50).

Dublin Metropolitan Police (DMP): Police force for Dublin until 1925.

The assault on the RIC was one of the reasons for the intensification of violence in 1919. The apparent failure of the Dáil's political initiatives, including the failure to gain a hearing at the Paris Peace Conference and the suppression of the Dáil in September 1919, were also factors in convincing some volunteers that military action might achieve more. British actions, such as the suppression of the Dáil, along with the outlawing of Sinn Féin, the Volunteers (IRA) and the Gaelic League in July, led to a further militarisation of the conflict. Even the head of the British Army in Ireland, Sir Nevil Macready, later admitted that the banning of Sinn Féin 'was not tactically a sound move' because it turned many moderate politicians into 'extremists' (Macready, 1924: 437).

Two incidents in the last third of the year indicated that the IRA's campaign was intensifying significantly. On Sunday, 7 September, in Fermoy, County Cork, an IRA party commanded by Liam Lynch ambushed 18 soldiers of the Shropshire Light Infantry on their way into the town's Methodist church; one soldier died, four were injured and the IRA made a valuable capture of 13 rifles. When a local coroner's jury refused to return a verdict of murder on the grounds that the aim of the raid was to seize arms rather than to kill, the soldiers destroyed business premises in the town that belonged to members of the jury. This was the first incident of the crown forces resorting to reprisals, a tactic that would become increasingly widespread as the conflict progressed (Townshend, 1975: 30).

The second incident that highlighted the intensification of the IRA's campaign was the failed attempt to assassinate the **Lord Lieutenant**, Field Marshal Viscount French, in the Phoenix Park in December (Townshend, 1975: 48). The end of the year 1919 saw the conclusion of the first phase of the War of Independence. Violence had increased gradually throughout the year, the IRA had begun to arm itself more effectively and the crown forces had exhibited their intention to use reprisals in revenge for IRA assaults. The scene was set for 18 months of full-scale guerrilla war.

1920 marked the start of the second phase of the War of Independence and was characterised by a sustained assault by the IRA on RIC barracks throughout the country. This new strategy, sanctioned by the IRA's executive, was in part a response to a change in police tactics. At the end of 1919 the RIC closed approximately 500 of its smaller rural posts and withdrew to quarters in larger towns to reduce the number of easy targets for the IRA, which in turn was forced to find new methods of attacking the police (Townshend, 1984: 335; Augusteijn, 1996: 96). The withdrawal of the police from large parts of rural Ireland was a symbolic victory for the IRA and demoralised further the already beleaguered RIC as well as removing a valuable source of local intelligence for the government.

In Cork, one of the counties where the IRA was most active, 10 barracks were attacked in the first three months of 1920 (Hart, 1998: 72). The most daring and successful action was the co-ordinated arson attack on evacuated barracks, courthouses and local taxation offices at Easter 1920 which resulted in the destruction of nearly 350 buildings. In the first six months of the year the IRA destroyed 30 courthouses, 343 vacated RIC barracks, 12 occupied RIC barracks and caused damage to a further 104 vacated and 24 occupied police barracks. Such assaults continued for the remainder of the war but never with same intensity as during the first half of 1920 (Mitchell, 1995: 128–9, Townshend, 1975: 214).

The IRA's campaign against the RIC had reached its peak in mid-1920. Coinciding with the success of the republican courts, it was clear that British law and order was under sustained threat and a viable republican alternative was being established in its place. Another side-effect of the IRA's campaign was a dramatic decline in recruitment to the RIC. Fear, intimidation, a lack of appetite for the tactics necessary to defeat the IRA and support for the independence movement resulted in over 50 constables leaving every week in the summer of 1920. Recruitment did not match retirements or resignations

Lord Lieutenant: The King's representative in Ireland under the Act of Union.

with the result that the force suffered a net loss of 1,300 men between July and September 1920 (Leeson, 2011: 20–2). The realisation that the war was being lost forced the British Government to resort to harsher tactics to curtail the success of the republican movement both politically and militarily.

The first such action had already been taken in January 1920 with the decision to recruit unemployed ex-servicemen from Britain to bolster the depleting ranks of the RIC. Dubbed the **Black and Tans** because of their combination of khaki and dark green uniforms, about 100 were recruited every month from January to June 1920, and as the IRA's campaign intensified in the latter half of 1920 so too did recruitment of Black and Tans, who were attracted by the prospect of employment that was proving so elusive at home and the generous remuneration on offer (Leeson, 2011: 24–5, 77).

The government's counter-attack in the summer of 1920 was characterised by two actions. The first was the introduction of a second force to assist the RIC and Black and Tans. The **Auxiliaries** were a paramilitary force also recruited from ex-soldiers but primarily from officer level, whereas the Black and Tans were more likely to have served in lower army ranks. Reflecting their higher rank they were paid at the same rate as RIC sergeants. The Auxiliaries became known as 'Tudor's Toughs', after the new police adviser in Ireland, Hugh Tudor, and in recognition of the rough treatment they meted out to their opponents. Approximately 10,000 Black and Tans and Auxiliaries served in Ireland during the 18 months from January 1920 to the truce (Leeson, 2011: 30, 37, 1). The reputation which they earned for brutality, drunkenness and unrestrained violence gained for them a notoriety that remains strong in Ireland almost 100 years later.

The government also resorted to new coercive legislation in an effort to quell the republican insurgency, with the hurried passing of the Restoration of Order in Ireland Act (ROIA) in August 1920 [**Doc. 18**]. Many of the provisions in this legislation, including internment, were carried over from the wartime Defence of the Realm Act. One specific aim of the new legislation was to deal with the crisis in the crown and coroners' courts. By mid-1920 the police were effectively unable to prosecute any crimes in the crown courts and many coroners' juries refused to return verdicts of murder in cases where crown forces were killed in conflicts involving the IRA. Therefore, some of the most important provisions of the ROIA were those dealing with the courts. The jurisdiction of courts martial (military courts) was extended to 'virtually all types of crime' and they were empowered to impose the death penalty for a wider variety of offences. Coroners' juries were also increasingly replaced by courts martial after September 1920. The Act also contained provisions for the imposition of curfews and restrictions on the use of motor transport (Campbell, 1994: 24–9). The provisions of the ROIA were also aimed at suppressing the Dáil courts.

Black and Tans: Paramilitary police force recruited largely from ex-soldiers and introduced to Ireland in January 1920.

Auxiliaries (Auxiliary Division of the RIC): Paramilitary police force recruited largely from ex-soldiers brought to Ireland in August 1920 to bolster the RIC.

The impact of the new government strategy was noticeable by the end of September 1920 as the number of IRA actions began to decline. The new measures forced the IRA to adapt its tactics and its principal unit of action became the flying column or active service unit. Rather than an entire brigade or battalion carrying out large-scale actions like attacks on RIC barracks, which had been the standard method of operation in the first half of 1920, IRA activists now went on the run and formed themselves into smaller more mobile units which focused on ambushing crown force units as they travelled around the countryside (Townshend, 1984: 335–6). The conflict had now become an outright guerrilla war.

The mobilisation of the IRA into flying columns ushered in the final and most violent phase of the war during which some of the most renowned ambushes of the conflict, producing some of the highest casualty figures, took place. November 1920 proved to be one of the bloodiest months of the war. Tensions in Ireland were running high at the time following the death of the Sinn Féin Lord Mayor of Cork, Terence MacSwiney, in Brixton Prison on 25 October on the seventy-fifth day of a hunger strike and the execution on 1 November of the 18-year-old Dublin medical student, Kevin Barry, for his part in an IRA ambush in Dublin City in September that had resulted in the deaths of three soldiers. Four policemen were killed in an ambush at Inches Cross in County Tipperary on 13 November and 17 Auxiliaries died in controversial circumstances when they were waylaid by Tom Barry's west Cork flying column at Kilmichael, near Macroom, on 28 November. Barry subsequently claimed that half of these were killed after tricking the IRA with a false surrender, claims that were disputed by Peter Hart in the 1990s occasioning a heated debate about **revisionism** among historians of the revolution. There were also allegations that the Auxiliaries' bodies were mutilated after their deaths (Abbott, 2000: 149–50, 156–63; Hart, 1998: 21–38).

The most infamous deaths of the War of Independence took place on Sunday, 21 November, or **Bloody Sunday** as it later became known. Thirteen British personnel, most of them intelligence officers, and two civilians, were shot dead in their lodgings early that morning by Michael Collins's Squad. Later that day 14 unarmed civilians, including two boys and a woman, were killed when police opened fire on the crowd attending a Gaelic football match at Croke Park stadium in Dublin City, possibly in reprisal for the previous killings. This was followed by the killing of two senior figures in the Dublin Brigade of the IRA, Dick McKee and Peadar Clancy, and an innocent Gaelic League activist from County Clare, Conor Clune, shot while in custody in Dublin Castle [**Doc. 19**]. The fourth person to die in Dublin Castle that day was an Auxiliary who died of a self-inflicted wound. The cumulative death toll for the day was 41, including three RIC officers shot dead by the IRA in Cork, Down and Waterford, four civilians killed by crown forces in Dublin,

Revisionism: A term used to describe a critical re-evaluation of history that emerged in Ireland from the 1930s. In the context of the Irish revolution it is often a pejorative term applied to historians seen as critical of the traditional nationalist interpretation of the period.

Bloody Sunday: 21 November 1920. Forty-one people were killed including British Intelligence agents, civilians attending a football match at Croke Park and senior IRA prisoners in Dublin Castle. Not to be confused with Bloody Sunday in Derry in January 1972.

Mayo and Meath, and one soldier, whose death in Dublin remains unexplained (Carey and de Búrca, 2003; Leeson, 2003; Leonard, 2012: 139–40).

Ambushes continued into 1921. Four Auxiliaries died in a well-planned ambush by the Longford IRA at Clonfin on 2 February. On the following day 11 RIC and Black and Tans were killed in an ambush by the East- and Mid-Limerick IRA Brigades at Dromkeen. Two major ambushes in County Mayo, at Tourmakeady in May and Carrowkennedy in June, resulted in the deaths of four and seven police officers respectively. Two more ambushes resulting in multiple police fatalities took place in Castlemaine (Kerry) and Kellegbeg Cross (Tipperary) on consecutive days in June. Incidents in which individual police or police travelling in pairs were attacked and killed by the IRA also became much more common during 1921; between January 1921 and the truce there were 118 incidents that resulted in the death of an individual policeman (Abbott, 2000).

One of the few examples of the IRA laying an ambush for the army (rather than the police) was the Battle of Crossbarry, in County Cork in March 1921, where Tom Barry's column attacked a detachment of the Essex Regiment, killing nine soldiers and one Auxiliary (Kautt, 2010: 146). While the IRA usually inflicted heavier casualties on the crown forces in these engagements, the Battle of Clonmult, near Midleton in County Cork, in February 1921 was an example of the IRA coming off worst; 12 members of the east Cork flying column were killed and eight captured effectively destroying the active service unit (O'Neill, 2006). Similarly, the burning of the Custom House in Dublin on 25 May, while successful from the point of view of causing serious damage to the headquarters of British local government in Ireland, was a logistical disaster that resulted in the arrest of between 80 and 130 men; the IRA had inadvisedly, probably at the prompting of de Valera, resorted to an unusual 1916-style assault that left little room for retreat (Hopkinson, 2002: 103).

From January 1921 IRA general headquarters (GHQ) encouraged local units to undertake smaller operations including digging up and blocking roads to hamper the movement of crown forces, raiding mail trains to capture documents that would assist the IRA's intelligence gathering, disrupting communications (such as cutting telephone and telegraph wires) and sniping at police. The change in tactics was designed to allow the IRA to carry out a greater number of actions as these smaller operations required fewer personnel than the large-scale ambushes (Townshend, 1979b: 342).

It also reflected the realties of the war. IRA manpower was always much more limited than that of the police or army and was further depleted by deaths and arrests, examples of which included the deaths of three IRA men at Kilmichael, the decimation of the east Cork flying column at Clonmult and the capture of the Longford IRA leader, Seán MacEoin, in March 1921.

The strength of the IRA was estimated to be 5,000 in May 1921, the vast majority of whom (3,386) were based in Munster (Townshend, 1975: 179). Firepower was in equally short supply. It was estimated that the IRA had approximately 3,000 rifles, 4,600 revolvers, 1,200 automatic pistols and 15,000 shotguns at the time of the truce in addition to approximately 50 machine guns of various types (Comerford, 1978: 839). Ammunition was in even shorter supply than arms; according to Tom Barry, the Cork IRA had 310 rifles at the time of the truce, but only 50 rounds of ammunition for each (Barry, 1981: 207).

The IRA's new strategy was also an admission that the police and army were becoming more effective in dealing with guerrilla warfare. They no longer made themselves an easy target for ambush, ensuring their motorised transport was more heavily fortified and often carrying civilians with them to ensure safe passage. The Clare IRA leader, Michael Brennan, complained that 'there seemed no possibility of finding any British parties in the open where we could attack them on more or less equal terms' (Brennan, 1980: 86). In Cork the IRA found it equally hard to engage either the Auxiliaries or the army (Barry, 1981: 154). The army also began to receive special instruction in dealing with guerrilla warfare and from early 1921 greater use was made of the military in conducting large-scale round-ups in parts of the country where the IRA was most active, often resulting in the arrest of prominent local IRA fighters (Coleman, 2003: 131–2).

The declining manpower and firepower of the IRA, combined with the sense that the British forces were starting to cope better with the guerrilla conflict, has resulted in an inconclusive debate about whether the war could have continued much longer had the truce not been agreed in July 1921. Parts of the country that had been active, such as Longford, had practically ceased to play any serious role in the fighting and the IRA was dealt a serious blow with the large number of arrests that followed the burning of the Custom House. In addition the fine weather conditions of July 1921 made it difficult to carry out successful guerrilla operations; it was much easier for the crown forces to mend roads and travel more quickly, while long hours of daylight forced the IRA to stay hidden for longer (O'Donoghue, 1954: 173).

On the other hand, areas of the country that had been slow to get off the mark in 1919 and 1920 were becoming very active, such as Mayo. The number of IRA actions continued to increase, especially in June 1921 (Costello, 2003: 144). There appeared to be no reduction in the IRA's ability to inflict casualties on its enemy; 17 policemen were killed in the last 11 days of the war between 1 and 11 July (Abbott, 2000: 261–6). Many IRA leaders themselves felt they possessed the ability to continue. Florence O'Donoghue believed the force had overcome many of its difficulties adjusting to the

hardship of being on the run, gaining greater combat experience and manufacturing effective mines and grenades (O'Donoghue, 1954: 176). The Mayo
IRA leader, Tom Maguire, also believed that the IRA campaign could have
gone on after July 1921 (Murphy, 1991: 324). Agreement among historians
is also divided and perhaps the best conclusion is that of David Fitzpatrick
and Peter Hart that the war had reached a stalemate by mid-July 1921 and
that victory for either side 'was a very distant prospect' (Fitzpatrick, 1977: 230;
Hart, 1998: 108).

THE SOCIAL COMPOSITION AND MOTIVATION OF THE IRA

Contemporary depictions from hostile British sources portrayed the
revolutionary IRA as comprising 'a horde of proletarians, grocers, curates,
farm labourers, porters, stable boys, car-conductors and what not', or
'unmistakably of the rabble class to be found in every large town', complemented by 'intellectuals . . . young men with high foreheads and thin
lips' (Hart, 2003: 117, 131). Much recent research on the revolution has
focused on the men who made up the guerrilla army and a reasonably
clear picture of the typical volunteer has emerged, disproving much of the
above characterisation.

Volunteers were young – most were aged in their late teens or early twenties
and had been born in the decade of the 1890s – although officers tended
to be slightly older. They were literate, educated (most possessing at least
primary school education) and skilled. Very few were married, an absence of
responsibility and obligation that made it easier for them to engage in IRA
activities. The overwhelming majority were Roman Catholic – Peter Hart could
only find three Protestants who were in the IRA – and there is ample evidence that they were devout practitioners of their religion, with many seeking
blessings or absolution in advance of ambushes (Coleman, 2003: 148–50;
Hart, 1998: 129–64; Hart, 2003: 110–38). Aside from a handful of well-known
Protestants like Sam Maguire, Erskine Childers and Ernest Blythe, a couple of
Jews, including Robert Briscoe and the republican lawyer Michael Noyk and
a maverick Presbyterian clergyman, Reverend J. A. H. Irwin, the republican
movement was almost exclusively composed of Roman Catholics.

The IRA was successful in recruiting from a variety of social classes,
particularly from those involved in the building trade, drapers' assistants,
creamery workers, teachers and medical students. In rural areas guerrilla
fighters not surprisingly came largely from agricultural backgrounds, although
the proportion of volunteers who came from farming backgrounds did not
correspond to the high proportion of young men of that age group involved

in agriculture in the country as a whole. This recent finding of historians such as Peter Hart is at odds with the IRA's conception of itself as having a strong rural base (Hart, 2003: 113–20). The title of the Cork IRA activist Micheál Ó Suilleabháin's memoir of the revolution, *Where Mountainy Men Have Sown*, highlights the perception that the War of Independence was waged from isolated rural outposts: 'he and his comrades were destined to fight a guerilla war on their native mountainsides, that was to become an important part of the pattern of the nation-wide fight for freedom' (Ó Suilleabháin, 1965). Another prominent Cork IRA man, who later became a respected writer on the subject, Florence O'Donoghue, similarly described the IRA in which he fought as 'predominantly a product of the country' (Hart, 2003: 116).

The social background of volunteers helps to explain in part their reasons for joining a revolutionary organisation and subsequently taking part in armed uprising against British rule in Ireland. Family circumstances often influenced men to join the IRA or their sisters to join Cumann na mBan. Some came from families with republican traditions stretching back to the United Irish revolt of 1798 and taking in involvement with the Fenians or the Land War. There had not been a violent revolt against British rule in Ireland between the Fenian uprising of 1867 and the Easter Rising in 1916; therefore some young volunteers felt their parents' generation had let them down and had a desire to rekindle the revolutionary spirit (Augusteijn, 1990: 26). Family circumstances also appear to have been important in cases where fathers were absent and unable to exert a restraining influence. Prominent IRA leaders, including Seán Treacy and Dan Breen in Tipperary, and Seán MacEoin in Longford, fell into this category (Augusteijn, 1990: 33–4).

As well as taking their example from their ancestors, Volunteers followed along with their friends and the decision to join was often more of a collective than an individual one. The core of a local IRA company was often composed of a group of friends of a similar age who had been at school together, worked together or were members of the same social or sporting club (Hart, 1998: 208). In this way recruitment to the IRA mirrored much of the voluntary recruitment to the British Army during the First World War, when members of the same social organisations often joined up together forming the so-called pals' battalions.

The failure to implement conscription in Ireland during the First World War resulted in a surplus of young men especially in rural areas and the restrictions on emigration closed off a traditional exit route for them. In the same way that this phenomenon contributed to the recurrence of land agitation in the west of Ireland, it also appears to have been a factor in some of these disaffected youths finding vent for their frustrations through politicisation and revolutionary violence (Garvin, 1981: 110).

Christian Brothers: An
Irish Catholic teaching
order founded in the
nineteenth century.

Many volunteers believed that their education influenced their subsequent participation in revolutionary organisations. This is especially true
in regard to the **Christian Brothers**. According to the Dublin volunteer,
Todd Andrews, who attended the Christian Brothers' school in Dublin's
Synge Street: 'Without the groundwork of the Christian Brothers' schooling
it is improbable that there would ever have been a 1916 Rising and certain
that the subsequent fight for independence would not have been successfully
carried through' (Andrews, 1979: 74). Eamon Price, another Dubliner who
fought in the Rising, considered the Christian Brothers to have played an
important role in his political formation (McGarry, 2010: 34). A Christian
Brothers education certainly appears to have been a predominant feature of
the backgrounds of Irish revolutionaries in the 1910s; seven of the 14 men
executed in Dublin after the Rising and a very significant proportion of the
members of the Sinn Féin executive elected in October 1917 were products
of these schools (Laffan, 1999: 193; McGarry, 2010: 34).

However, it is too simplistic to see Christian Brothers' schools (CBSs)
simply as factories of revolution. From his study of Ernie O'Malley, one
of the Christian Brothers' more renowned revolutionary alumni, Richard
English, has concluded that 'the impact of the Brothers' schools involved
the intensification and reinforcement of Catholic values rather than their
creation' (English, 1998: 124–5). This echoes the first-hand experience of
Todd Andrews, for whom the importance of the Christian Brothers came
from the way in which they taught religion and religious history. Rather than
indoctrinating 'their pupils with Irish nationalism or hostility to Britain',
the Anglophobia of a CBS education was the product of 'the teachings of the
Catholic Faith which it was the basic objective of the Brothers to inculcate.
The persecution of the Catholics rather than the persecution of the Irish
as such was the burden of the Brothers' history teaching'. All of this was
underpinned by a broad nationalist curriculum, with a strong emphasis on
Irish history and Gaelic civilisation (Andrews, 1979: 73).

In rural areas nationalist-minded teachers in national schools were equally
if not more influential. Denis Lyons and James Santry infused Michael Collins
with 'a pride of the Irish as a race' in Lisavaird National School (Coogan,
1990: 10). In Garryshane, County Tipperary, Charlie Walshe departed from
the official curriculum to provide his students – who included Dan Breen,
Seán Treacy, Dinny Lacey and Seán Hogan – with 'the naked facts about
the English conquest of Ireland and the manner in which our country was
held in bondage. We learned about the Penal Laws, the systematic ruining
of Irish trade, the elimination of our native language' (Breen, 1981: 21).

Education outside the confines of a classroom also appears to have played
an important role in the formation of Irish revolutionaries. Gaelic League
classes were a particular source of politicisation by 'promoting an awareness

of the importance of national identity and the baleful impact of "Anglicization" '. William Daly, a London-born 1916 rebel of Irish ancestry, admitted that he 'knew nothing of Ireland . . . until I joined the Gaelic League' (McGarry, 2010: 18, 108). The League's emphasis on the distinctiveness of the Irish language and Gaelic culture underpinned the development of a belief in Irish separatism in the minds of many aspiring revolutionaries. Senior figures in the pre-Rising Volunteers, including Pearse and MacNeill, also held leadership roles in the Gaelic League. By 1916 the League had fallen strongly under the influence of the IRB, especially in Dublin where the Keating Branch of the League was effectively a front for the Teeling circle of the brotherhood.

This sense of cultural distinction was reinforced by the Gaelic Athletic Association (GAA), which had been founded in 1884 to revive and codify traditional Irish sports such as hurling and Gaelic football. Involvement in the administrative structures of the organisation was a significant factor in the development of leadership skills that would serve many of these young men well and help then to achieve leadership roles within the IRA. This was particularly noticeable in the revolutionary careers of Michael Collins (secretary of the Geraldines Gaelic Athletic Association club in London from 1908 to 1915), Harry Boland (chairman of the Dublin County Committee) and Eoin O'Duffy (secretary of the Ulster Council) among others (Fitzpatrick, 2003: 33; Hart, 2005: 44; McGarry, 2005: 26–9). The significance of cultural nationalist organisations raises the question of how important political ideology was as a factor in the conditioning of republicans and revolutionaries in the Ireland of the 1910s. Ideological inclinations were often reinforced by specific events. In this regard the Rising appears to have galvanised many young men into joining the Volunteers in 1917 and 1918. For Florence O'Donoghue, a draper's apprentice in Cork, 'the Rising was an illumination' and he joined the Volunteers in 1917 (Borgonovo, 2006: 25).

Many historians consider ideology to be less important in the formation of revolutionaries than social circumstances or personal experience. After the 1918 general election, the Sinn Féin activist, Father Michael O'Flanagan, felt the party now had to explain 'what Sinn Féin is' to those who had voted for it, and according to Michael Laffan, 'People joined Sinn Féin in their tens of thousands because they were attracted by its image, not because they believed in its ideology' (Laffan, 1999: 214). Florence O'Donogue believed that 'Republicanism, as a form of Government, had no more than an academic interest for Volunteers' and 'republic' was a by-word for freedom from British rule rather than a political ideology (O'Donoghue, 1954: 43).

Apart from Griffith, there were few ideologues in the movement. While a commitment to achieving a republic became an article of faith after the Rising, very few appeared to have a clear idea of what it would entail. There were certainly very few signs of the secularism or anti-clericalism of

European republicanism, or even of nineteenth-century Fenianism, present in the version of republicanism promoted by Sinn Féin and the IRA. Eamon de Valera is well known for his disavowal of 'doctrinaire' republicanism and initially at least appears to have had an open mind on what form of government an independent Ireland would have, even allowing for the possibility of 'an Irish monarch', and while Michael Collins was 'one of the more vociferous republicans', his republicanism was 'nationalistic rather than ideological' (Laffan, 1999: 214, 241–2). Thus, it is ironic that while ideology does not appear to have ben a primary factor in the motivation of revolutionaries, it would later emerge as the main cause of the split in 1922.

THE GEOGRAPHY OF WAR

The question of why certain young men joined the IRA is linked to the question of why the IRA was more active in certain areas of the country than others at various times during the course of fighting from the Rising until the end of the Civil War. The War of Independence was a series of small localised campaigns, rather than a nation-wide struggle, with little co-ordination between brigades or overall control by IRA GHQ, in spite of its efforts to impose some form of uniformity. The scale and extent of IRA violence varied widely over the course of the war and the most active areas of the country changed. In certain areas of the country, such as Munster (and especially Cork) and Dublin City, the IRA remained active throughout the conflict. Other counties, such as Longford between November 1920 and February 1921, were active for a sustained period but then faded. Longford was the only midland county to experience a high level of IRA activity that was not matched by surrounding counties such as Westmeath, Cavan, Leitrim or Roscommon.

Some counties which had a proud tradition of fighting in 1916, in particular Wexford, were inexplicably dormant during the guerrilla campaign, and some slow starters (Mayo) had made up ground by the time of the truce. Even within individual counties and brigades the levels of activity and violence varied dramatically. In the small county of Longford, IRA activity was confined to an enclave in the north of the county around the towns of Ballinalee and Granard, while the south of the county saw very little action at all. In Cork, the contrast between west and north Cork was striking.

Historians have suggested numerous theories to explain this regional disparity in IRA activity. In the same way that some youths joined the IRA because they came from families with a tradition of political activism, the IRA might have emerged more naturally in parts of the country that had seen radicalism and political violence previously, a good example of which was the Land War. IRA veterans, such as Florence O'Donogue, also considered it important to have good local leaders – 'The success of IRA operations depended very largely upon the initiative of local Commanders particularly at brigade and battalion level' – although more recent historians, in particular David Fitzpatrick, dispute this.

Local socio-economic circumstances also appear to have been influential. Neither the most prosperous areas of the east coast or the richer farming areas of Munster, nor the poorest regions along the western seaboard were among the areas where the IRA was most active, suggesting that a certain level of economic comfort was a prerequisite for involvement in revolutionary activity. Conversely, the better off had too much of a stake in society to seek the overthrow of the status quo.

The guerrilla nature of the conflict also determined activity to some extent. Although Peter Hart is sceptical that physical terrain had much effect on whether or not the IRA was active in certain areas, mountainous terrain in Tipperary, the remoteness of west Cork and the system of small inter-connected fields in Longford made it much easier for the IRA, with the benefit of local knowledge, to move about undetected and plan ambushes of unsuspecting crown forces. Guerrillas also needed guns and the absence of these in the first place is often cited as a reason why some local IRA units remained largely inactive. On the other hand, other IRA units displayed sufficient initiative to raid for arms, thus equipping themselves to carry out further arms seizures and attacks upon their enemies, so a lack of arms might have been an indication of lethargy on the part of IRA units that also affected their performance during the war.

Guns were of little use without a target to shoot at and the presence of an enemy or hostile element was at times a factor instigating IRA violence. The most obvious targets were crown forces. The presence of a large contingent of crown forces in a given area was usually the result of IRA activity to begin with but the arrival of the crown forces often set off cycles of violence whereby the IRA attacked the police, who responded with reprisals that occasioned further attacks by the IRA. However, the presence of the army was often a deterrent towards IRA activity, with so-called garrison towns, whose local economy traditionally depended heavily on the army barracks, showing little enthusiasm for the revolution.

The importance of IRA GHQ in either directing or co-ordinating the war is also openly disputed by both veterans and historians. Two Mayo IRA leaders, Tom Maguire and Tom Heavey, gave completely different interpretations of GHQ's role. According to Maguire 'the war effort was directed, and well directed by a chain of command from Dublin which centred around Brugha, as Minister for Defence, and Mulcahy, as Chief of Staff of the IRA', whereas Heavey asserted that 'Of course there was no such thing as centralised command'.

Tom Garvin has noted that many of the areas where the IRA was most active were characterised by being far away from Dublin, yet the IRA in Longford appears to have benefited from its proximity to Dublin and the close personal links that Michael Collins developed there during the conflict. Many members of IRA GHQ were also in the IRB, and while this organisation does not appear to have permeated the rank and file of the IRA it could be argued to have played an important role in influencing local officers, many of whom were in the brotherhood (Coleman, 2003: 159–78; Fitzpatrick, 1978: 117–18; Garvin, 1981: 123–6; Hart, 2003: 30–61; O'Donoghue, 1954: 72–3).

The IRA was least effective in the province of Ulster. The most active IRA units there were under the command of Frank Aiken in Armagh, south Down and north Louth (which became the Fourth Northern Division when the IRA introduced a divisional structure in 1921) and Eoin O'Duffy in Monaghan (McGarry, 2005: 47–73). Apart from these areas and the city of Belfast, the northern IRA was largely 'disorganised and inactive' (Lynch, 2006: 42). Belfast was an exception to this trend. From 1920 to 1922 it was one of the most violent places on the island; in the space of these two years 557 people were killed (Hennessey, 1997: 11). However, the conflict there could be seen as a distinct one from that which was taking place in the rest of Ireland between 1919 and the truce. While the IRA was the protagonist on the nationalist side, its motivation and its enemies were different to those of the southern IRA. The Black and Tans and Auxiliaries had a minimal presence in the city (Leeson, 2011: 26). Instead, the majority of armed confrontations were between the IRA and the third supplementary police force to operate in Ireland during the period, the **Ulster Special Constabulary (USC)**.

The increasing violence of the IRA's campaign throughout the island sparked the beginning of serious communal and sectarian violence in Belfast in July 1920 when Catholic shipyard workers were attacked by Protestant vigilantes and expelled from the city's two main shipyards, Harland and Wolff and Workman, Clark and Company. In response the Dáil imposed the **Belfast boycott**, which only intensified anti-Catholic actions. The situation soon spiralled into a tit-for-tat conflict as the IRA responded to a perceived need to protect the city's Catholic population. In an effort to quell the violence the government recruited the new USC, consisting of full-time armed 'A' Specials, part-time, armed and paid 'B' Specials and an emergency reserve of 'C' Specials. By the end of 1920 these categories contained approximately 3,500, 16,000 and 1,000 men respectively. Unlike the Black and Tans and Auxiliaries, the Specials were recruited locally and in effect were composed largely of members of the UVF, which only served to heighten the sectarian conflict further as Catholics interpreted this as state-sanctioned targeting of their community, while Protestants viewed the Specials as defending them against the revolutionary violence of the IRA (Hennessey, 1997: 15).

Ulster Special Constabulary (USC): Special constabulary formed to deal with violence in Ulster in 1920 that contained a large number of Ulster Volunteer Force (UVF) members and was associated with high-profile sectarian attacks and killings of Catholics.

Belfast boycott: Boycott of Ulster businesses introduced by Dáil Éireann in protest at partition and sectarian attacks on Catholics in Ulster.

Sectarian violence also erupted in the predominantly Protestant towns of Lisburn, County Antrim and Banbridge and Dromore, County Down in August 1920 following the IRA's killing of RIC District Inspector Oswald Swanzy, who had been implicated in the shooting dead of the Sinn Féin Lord Mayor of Cork, Tomás MacCurtain, the previous March. Rioting ensued that resulted in considerable damage to property in the Catholic areas of these towns. It then spread to Belfast where it was estimated that 18 people were killed in a single week (Abbott, 2000: 114; Hennessey, 1997: 13).

GUERRILLA WARFARE AND VIOLENCE

During the War of Independence the IRA did not repeat the mistakes of 1916, with the exception of the attack on the Custom House. Rather than setting themselves up as easy targets by occupying buildings which could easily be besieged, IRA members evolved a form of guerrilla warfare that played to their strengths. Based in local areas, where they had a good knowledge of the terrain and a certain level of support from the community, they had the upper hand on the crown forces for much of the conflict. The IRA of 1919–21 exhibited only some of the characteristics of a successful guerrilla movement; there was a wide variation in activity across the country, certain areas of the country were inactive, there was poor co-ordination between brigades and an absence of coherent central control of the conflict from IRA GHQ (Townshend, 1979b).

In many ways the IRA was lucky rather than consciously successful in planning and executing a guerrilla campaign. Training in guerrilla warfare was limited. The Director of Training from November 1920, J. J. 'Ginger' O'Connell, who was one of the few professional soldiers on the GHQ staff having served briefly in the US Army in the early 1910s, published articles on training in the IRA journal *An tÓglach* [*The Volunteer*] and also delivered some lectures on the subject in Dublin that were attended by regional commanders. *An tÓglach* also published accounts of successful ambushes to provide examples of actions for other units to follow [**Doc. 20**].

Occasionally GHQ sent organisers who had military experience to train local units in the use of firearms (Coleman, 2003: 138). Some volunteers, most notably Tom Barry, had fought in the British Army during the First World War, bringing valuable experience to the organisation. However, the fighting in Mesopotamia in 1916 differed radically from that in rural west Cork in 1920 and Barry freely admitted that his unit had a 'complete ignorance of high explosives'. This often resulted in injuries or fatalities among volunteers as a result of carelessness stemming from simple lack of experience and training in the use of weaponry (Coleman, 2003: 138). The success of the IRA in holding out against the crown forces for two-and-half years, in light of its inexperience and rudimentary military training, was a significant achievement.

That the IRA managed to survive as long as it did is also surprising in light of the inadequacy of its arsenal. In early 1920 the IRA enjoyed a measure of success in arming itself through raids on RIC barracks to capture its enemies' weapons. By June 1920 'the Bandon Battalion had acquired 29 rifles, 44 revolvers, and 146 shotguns: almost as many weapons as the whole of Cork at the beginning of 1917' (Hart, 1998: 72). Prior to this the IRA had to content itself with the odd shotgun or hunting rifle pilfered from private homes, often of Protestants or unionists with army, hunting or Ulster Volunteer connections, and guns donated by soldiers home on leave (Hart, 1998: 67). Some high-profile ambushes also resulted in the acquisition of valuable hardware; the Longford IRA captured 18 rifles, 20 revolvers, a Lewis gun and a substantial cache of ammunition from the Auxiliaries at Clonfin in February 1921 (Coleman, 2003: 127).

One of GHQ's most important tasks during the conflict was the importation and distribution of guns. Irish people living in Britain and IRA units based there smuggled various types of weapons into Ireland. Guns were also sourced in Germany and the USA (Augusteijn, 1996: 148). While many of the individual consignments were small, it is estimated that the IRA smuggled 289 handguns, 53 rifles, 24,141 rounds of ammunition and 1,067 pounds of explosives from Liverpool to Dublin within the space of two years (Hart, 2003: 183–4). GHQ's most ambitious effort was the attempted importation of Thompson sub-machine guns (Tommy guns), a new type of rapid-fire machine gun developed in the USA at the end of the First World War. The IRA was the first organisation to place a substantial order for this gun, which was to become ubiquitous in twentieth-century warfare. In May 1921, Harry Boland, an IRB representative in the USA, placed an order for 653 guns, most of the cost of which was borne by wealthy American supporters of the Irish cause. Four hundred and ninety-five of these were seized by US customs officials in New Jersey but the remaining 158 were smuggled to Dublin via Liverpool. The guns arrived in the final two months of the conflict so were not widely used. They were employed, though with disappointing results, by both sides in the Civil War (Hart, 2003: 178–93).

The shortage of ammunition was an even greater problem. The Lewis gun captured by the Longford IRA at Clonfin was never used because there was not enough ammunition for it and Michael Brennan admitted that the IRA in Clare had an average of 30 rounds of ammunition per rifle (Brennan, 1980: 71; Coleman, 2003: 134). In order to avoid running out of ammunition the guerrillas had to ensure that their engagements with the enemy were of relatively short duration. During the defence of Ballinalee in County Longford in November 1920, the Black and Tans withdrew just as the IRA's guns ran out of ammunition (Coleman, 2003: 124).

Explosives were required to lay ambushes for the crown forces and the IRA's inexperience in handling such dangerous substances was also revealed. An attack on a police barracks in east Clare had to be abandoned because the gelignite had frozen. In west Cork three mines laid for the crown forces failed during one month alone because, as Tom Barry conceded, 'we were simply incapable of properly making a mine'. Obtaining gelignite does not appear to have been a problem, with county council workers, some of whom were IRA members, often obtaining supplies from local authority stores. Much of the IRA's gelignite appears to have originated in Glasgow and been smuggled through the same channels as guns. Some IRA units displayed ingenuity in manufacturing their own improvised explosive devices (Barry, 1981: 75; Coleman, 2003: 136–8; Kautt, 2010: 162).

Volunteers with expertise in engineering, metalwork and chemicals were a great asset. The Longford IRA leader, Seán MacEoin, who was a blacksmith, manufactured the 56lb mine containing concrete and scrap metal that was used in the successful ambush of Auxiliaries at Clonfin (Coleman, 2003: 137). James O'Donovan, a university chemistry student and successful amateur bomb-maker, invented highly explosive substances known as war flour (which proved to be too unstable) and Irish cheddar (composed of paraffin and potassium chlorate); his experiments led to him blowing off two fingers on his right hand in 1922 (Kautt, 2010: 162–3). Many local IRA units operated make-shift bomb factories, manufacturing improvised and often very volatile explosives and dangerous hand grenades (Breen, 1981: 37–8).

Successful guerrilla campaigns also depended on the support of the surrounding community. IRA men always attested to the support of civilians in regard to the provision of safe houses, contributions to arms funds, participating in the boycott of the RIC and providing useful information about the crown forces. The activities of the crown forces, especially the reprisals carried out by the Black and Tans and Auxiliaries, made civilians increasingly likely to provide tacit and practical support for the revolutionaries.

Yet, there is evidence that this support was by no means uniform. Garrison towns were seen as unhelpful. The number of civilians executed as suspected spies (a punishment that became more commonplace in 1921 as the conflict intensified) shows that the IRA itself was aware that elements of the population either did not support it or actively sought to undermine it. Longford was a county where the IRA was active and support from the community strong, yet the flying column commander, Seán MacEoin, was arrested as a result of information passed to the police when he was seen boarding a train at Longford railway station (Coleman, 2003: 151–4). It is difficult to say how many of the people executed on suspicion of spying had actually passed on information. In some cases the IRA produced definite evidence but in others there is strong speculation that some of these victims were dispatched because they were either perceived as threats or alien to the IRA; this is especially true of ex-soldiers, a considerable number of whom were executed by the IRA having been accused of spying (Leonard, 1990).

One important group within the civilian community that had an ambivalent attitude to the IRA was the Roman Catholic clergy. The hierarchy and individual clerics had shown support for earlier aspects of the political resistance, including supporting Sinn Féin in by-elections and spearheading the campaign against conscription. The Church distanced itself from republicanism after the conflict became more violent in 1919, as witnessed by the hierarchy's refusal to recognise officially the revolutionary Dáil Éireann. Violence by both sides was condemned and there was a strong sense of disappointment that British Government policy was largely responsible for the escalation of the war, resulting in a powerful and influential body in Irish society being alienated by the authorities. Cardinal Logue, the primate of Ireland who was well known for his antipathy to Sinn Féin, abhorred the activities of the Black and Tans and believed the crown forces carried the greatest share of the blame for the Bloody Sunday killings (Miller, 1973: 458–9).

Actions such as the murder of Canon Magner in Cork in December 1920 and Father Michael Griffin in Galway the previous month drove a deeper wedge between Church and State. One member of the hierarchy, Bishop Cohalan of Cork, issued a decree excommunicating anyone in his diocese guilty of taking part in ambushes, kidnappings or murders, although this appears to have had little effect (Miller, 1973: 456). Some priests continued to provide absolution for IRA men and of course Father Michael O'Flanagan remained active in Sinn Féin in spite of having been suspended by his bishop. Individual clerics, including Archbishop Clune of Perth, were active in seeking to arrange a peaceful settlement, though others, such as his Australian hierarchical counterpart, Archbishop Daniel Mannix of Melbourne (both men were born and trained in Ireland), heightened tensions to the extent that he was prohibited from travelling to Ireland in 1920 (Miller, 1973: 471–3).

The military wing of the revolutionary movement had an ambivalent relationship with the political side, in spite of the cross-over of personnel in many cases, including that of Collins who was Director of Intelligence and Organisation for the IRA and the Dáil's Minister for Finance. A number of guerrilla leaders exhibited clear contempt for their political counterparts. According to Ernie O'Malley 'the men had little use for anyone who was not of the physical force belief' and they 'sneered' at those who were not in the IRA. Liam Lynch viewed Sinn Féiners and republican members of local government bodies as 'a burden on the Army' (Hart, 1998: 229, 238).

This attitude was explicit at leadership level within the IRA. The civilian Minister for Defence, Cathal Brugha, struggled to bring the army under the authority of the Dáil, encountering stiff resistance from both Collins and Mulcahy, who were wary of Brugha's ulterior motive of seeking to weaken the influence of the IRB and, by extension, that of Collins. Bringing the army under the control of the democratically elected Dáil added substance to the republican claim that the independence campaign had a popular mandate. Eventually Brugha was successful in having the IRA adopt an oath of allegiance to the government of the republic in July 1920; however, the IRA continued to act independently for the duration of the war. This personal conflict between Brugha and the senior IRB men within the IRA foreshadowed the split that emerged in 1922 (Valiulis, 1992: 42).

It is difficult to state with certainty how many people died as a result of political violence in Ireland between the Easter Rising and the end of the Irish Civil War. One estimate for the four-year period from 1917 to 1921 recorded 2,141 such deaths, though this excludes the Rising, the violence in Northern Ireland in 1922 and the Irish Civil War. The IRA and the crown forces appear to have been responsible for a fairly similar proportion of these deaths, 46 per cent and 42 per cent respectively, and the proportion of civilian deaths (48 per cent, compared to 52 per cent combatant deaths) was quite high (O'Halpin, 2012: 152).

The levels of violence intensified in the last quarter of 1920 when the crown forces reacted to IRA attacks on police by carrying out reprisals which were not officially sanctioned by their superiors. As mentioned above the first of these revenge attacks took place in Fermoy in September 1919, but it was not for another year that they became more widespread following the introduction of the Auxiliaries and Black and Tans. Fermoy was attacked again by soldiers in June 1920 in response to the kidnapping of the army's General Lucas by the IRA. This was followed by raids on the towns of Upperchurch, Templemore and Thurles (Tipperary) and Limerick City in July and August. Attacks on isolated towns such as these did not generate much publicity or attention until the crown forces focused their vengeance closer to Dublin City with the sack of Balbriggan, which took place on 20 September 1920 in a quiet seaside town on the border of counties Dublin and Meath following an altercation between local IRA men and Black and Tans, both of which parties had been drinking in different pubs in the town, that led to the shooting dead of RIC Head Constable Peter Burke. When news of his death reached the nearby Gormanstown camp a contingent of Auxiliaries and Black and Tans descended on the town and by the following morning 'it was reported [that] twenty-five houses had been burned, fifty had

had windows broken, and four public houses, two groceries, a newsagency and the Deedes hosiery factory had been destroyed' and two republicans killed (O'Mahony, 2012: 62–6).

Between September 1920 and the truce a number of other towns suffered a fate similar to that of Balbriggan, including Ennistymon, Lahinch and Miltown Malbay (Clare) the following day; Trim (Meath) and Mallow (Cork) a week later; Boyle (Roscommon), Listowel and Tralee (Kerry), Tubbercurry (Leitrim) and Bandon (Cork), in October; and Templemore (Tipperary), Ballymote (Leitrim) and Granard (Longford) in November (Hopkinson, 2002: 80). The most notorious of all these attacks were undoubtedly the Croke Park shootings and the burning of large parts of Cork City, including City Hall and the Carnegie Library, on 11–12 December 1920 by Auxiliaries in reaction to the death of one of their comrades in an ambush by the IRA at Dillon's Cross earlier that day. The incendiarism of the crown forces was no doubt also an expression of their frustration at the recent success of the IRA at Kilmichael and the generally increased tensions in Cork City following the death of Terence MacSwiney (Hopkinson, 2002: 83).

These large-scale reprisals are the most infamous, but were also the least common. Most such revenge attacks consisted of relatively small-scale arson attacks on property or farm livestock and creameries which were valuable community facilities. Reprisals tended to be targeted against people involved in republicanism and their families, or communities seen as sympathetic to them, rather than being random acts. Some murders and personal assaults occurred during reprisals but tended to be much less common than attacks on property (Leeson, 2011: 157–65).

While these reprisals were considered to be unofficial in that they were not authorised or sanctioned by the government or the Irish administration, suspicion existed that there was a level of official connivance in them. Many of the properties targeted in Balbriggan belonged to prominent republicans, and newly arrived Auxiliaries and Black and Tans who did not live in the area would not have possessed this knowledge. Some senior British politicians, including Austen Chamberlain and Winston Churchill, saw the benefits of fighting terror with terror. The British press detected 'a directing influence' behind attacks such as Balbriggan (Hopkinson, 2002: 81–2). The Cabinet Secretary, Maurice Hankey, conceded that 'reprisals are more or less winked at by the Government'. The government, the Irish administration and the leadership of the crown forces in Ireland gave tacit support to reprisals because of their effectiveness in leading to the capture or death of prominent IRA leaders, like McKee and Clancy, or in scaring the civilian population sufficiently into refusing to co-operate with or assist the IRA. Eventually, the government accepted the reality of the situation and made certain reprisals against property official policy in late December 1920; it was estimated that approximately 150 official reprisals were carried out between then and the truce (Hopkinson, 2002: 81–2; Townshend, 1975: 149).

While reprisals might have been effective in the military campaign they were a disaster on the propaganda front. Balbriggan's proximity to Dublin City meant that the incident was covered widely by journalists based in the city, bringing the extent and impact of reprisals to a wider domestic and international audience. The extent to which the policy backfired on the British Government and strengthened Ireland's cause for independence raises the question of whether some of the actions which led to reprisals were deliberate provocation of the Tans and Auxiliaries by the IRA.

The actions of the crown forces in Ireland prompted the British Labour Party to send a delegation to Ireland, led by the party's chief whip, Arthur Henderson, to investigate and report on crown force reprisals. The commission collected much valuable evidence about the nature and extent of violence carried out by both sides in the conflict [Doc. 21]. The counter-productiveness of reprisals was being recognised in the lead up to the truce, and its continuation was not helping to achieve a peaceful settlement. Elements within the crown forces, especially the army, which were much less culpable in carrying out reprisals than the police, and many members of the government disliked the policy and the damage it had done to Britain's reputation. As a result the policy of official reprisals ceased on 3 June 1921 (Townshend, 1975: 184–5).

For decades it was popularly held in Ireland that the Black and Tans who carried out most of these reprisals were the sweepings of the English prisons, 'ex-convicts and psychopaths hardened by prison and crazed by war'. However, new research into the personnel of both the Tans and the Auxiliaries has shown that if anything the Auxiliaries 'behaved with even greater licence' than the Tans, and that Irish members of the RIC were much more involved in reprisals than previously believed and few had criminal records (Leeson, 2011: ix). The view held by historians for some time that the lawlessness of the Tans and Auxiliaries was explained largely by the traumatic effects of First World War has also been challenged; professional soldiers who had served in the army prior to 1914 – rather than those who entered for the war – were much more likely to carry out reprisals.

The motivation of these otherwise law-abiding men to resort to apparently uncharacteristic and unrestrained violence can be put down to a mixture of poor leadership, alienation, frustration and boredom. On arrival in Ireland the new recruits received cursory training that was wholly inadequate to prepare them for a guerrilla conflict in a hostile environment and very little effort was taken by their leaders to instil or ensure proper discipline. With the exception of some friendly elements within the loyalist community, the Tans and Auxiliaries had no connections with the local civilian population by whom they were despised, a feeling that intensified as their campaign of reprisals progressed. The psychological impact of the deaths of their comrades, the failure of coroners' inquests to return murder verdicts (as in Fermoy) and the sense that the IRA was winning often led to frustration boiling over into violence. The dangers involved in travelling outside barracks led to the effective incarceration of these forces in their quarters even during periods of leave, where there were very few recreational pursuits other than alcohol consumption, which was a prevalent factor in many instances of reprisals (Leeson, 2011).

INTELLIGENCE

A successful guerrilla campaign needed to be complemented by effective intelligence. Michael Collins's operation of the IRA's intelligence system is generally seen as one of the greatest successes of the republican campaign during the War of Independence. In March 1918 an IRA GHQ was formed under the leadership of Richard Mulcahy as Chief-of-Staff. The first Director of Intelligence was Eamon Duggan, though in practice Collins gradually assumed responsibility for this role as 1918 progressed and was eventually made Director of Intelligence in his own right in 1919.

During the first year of the war in 1919 he gradually put together the structure and personnel of his intelligence system. His first success was in recruiting spies from within the British system, including four relatively junior members of the G (Intelligence) Division of the Dublin Metropolitan Police – Ned Broy, James Kavanagh, James McNamara and David Neligan – all of whom had access to important documents which were passed to the IRA. In March 1918 Broy furnished Collins with a list of names of leading members of Sinn Féin and the IRA who were about to be arrested as part of the alleged German plot. The highest ranking spy from the British side was probably RIC Head Constable Peter Forlan, based in the Phoenix Park. (Foy, 2006: 14, 49–50).

Female clerical workers in government offices were also important informants. Nancy O'Brien, who was Collins's cousin, worked as a government typist and 'Many of her lunch hours were spent in the GPO lavatory copying out decoded messages which she then smuggled out to him [Collins] in her bodice' (Coogan, 1990: 82). Piaras Béaslaí's cousin, Lily Mernin (code-named the 'Little Gentleman'), worked in Dublin Castle, where she was able to discover and furnish Collins with the addresses of the intelligence officers targeted on Bloody Sunday (Foy, 2006: 145). From his own experience working in the Post Office in London, Collins was well aware of the significance of this agency as a conduit for official communications and established a dedicated postal section within his intelligence department that was aided by postal employees who passed confidential information and stolen RIC cyphers to help the IRA decode enemy correspondence (Foy, 2006: 50–1).

On 7 April 1919, Ned Broy smuggled Collins into the headquarters of the DMP's G Division in Great Brunswick (now Pearse) Street, allowing him access to the division's files and giving him a valuable insight into the workings of the enemy's intelligence network that he subsequently proceeded to replicate with the formation of his own Squad from mid-1919 (Foy, 2006: 21–5). Recruited from the IRA's Dublin Brigade and containing some of Collins's most trusted lieutenants – including Liam Tobin, Frank Thornton and Tom Cullen – the Sqaud became central to Collins's efforts to win the intelligence war against British agents in Dublin City. Rising in strength to 12 in 1920 and 21 at the height of the war in 1921, it operated on a full-time basis from September 1920 and carried out a number of cold-blooded assassinations often in broad daylight, such as that of Alan Bell (Foy, 2006: 53–4, 63).

While the Squad had some major coups, including Bloody Sunday, it was not an unqualified success. One of its early targets was the Lord Lieutenant, Lord French, but the failed ambush of his car at the Ashtown Gate of the Phoenix Park in December 1920 only resulted in the death of a Dublin volunteer, Martin Savage (Foy, 2006: 32–3). Personality clashes and intra-Squad rivalry created tensions within the unit that were exacerbated by the tedium and frustration of much waiting around for opportunities for action to present themselves (Foy, 2006: 60). Having received no formal training they were expected to execute the enemy at close range and be prepared for their own deaths if an operation went wrong, all of which exacted a psychological toll (Dolan, 2006: 808).

Even Bloody Sunday was not without its down sides. Collins had initially hoped to eliminate up to 60 agents. The deaths of Dick McKee and Peadar Clancy were a serious loss to the Dublin Brigade. Crucially, it left the British under no illusions about what they were dealing with and British policy towards Ireland changed putting greater pressure on the IRA. This was especially noticeable in Dublin City during 1921 as the Squad and the Dublin Brigade came under increasing pressure from constant raids that resulted in a significantly higher number of arrests (Foy, 2006: 175–7, 218–9).

Other parts of Collins's intelligence system had also fallen apart by the time of the truce. The removal of G Division from Brunswick Street to the safer confines of Dublin Castle negated much of the usefulness of his spies, who in any case were coming under suspicion by 1921. Joe Kavanagh died in September 1920, James McNamara went on the run to avoid being discovered and Broy was arrested in February 1921 and interned until after the truce, although the authorities were unable to find sufficient evidence to prosecute him (Foy, 2006: 188–91).

The Dublin-based intelligence organisation was complemented by a regional IRA one with each brigade having its own intelligence officers who were trained by and kept in constant contact with the GHQ Intelligence Directorate. The intelligence officer of the Longford Brigade, Michael Heslin, was brought to Dublin for instruction from Collins and Gearóid O'Sullivan on how to set up a secret service network. He cultivated sympathetic clerical staff in the local post offices and railway stations, who along with Cumann na mBan members, formed a vital part of his communications network. Collins provided the key to decoding British cyphers. Intercepting postal communications in this manner led to the unmasking of at least one local spy. Heslin also used his brother's friendship with a local RIC sergeant to glean useful information from the unsuspecting policeman. All of the information was gathered from Heslin's own agents and he never succeeded in recruiting a spy from the British side (http://www.bureauofmilitaryhistory.ie/reels/bmh/BMH.WS0662.pdf#page=1).

GENDER IN THE IRISH REVOLUTION

The War of Independence allowed Cumann na mBan to undertake military activities, although they were not involved in actual combat. Their military activities usually concerned the acquisition and movement of arms and ammunition. Cumann na mBan members attached to the country brigades, such as Brigid Lyons in Longford, often travelled to Dublin to obtain ammunition from IRA GHQ and carry it back home for use by local units. Within brigade areas the task of transporting arms and ammunition, from magazines to the sites of ambushes or to safe locations to avoid detection, often fell to women. These tasks were allocated to women because they were less likely to come under suspicion. The social mores of the time also resulted in the crown forces being less willing to search women, although by the end of the conflict they were becoming more aware of these surreptitious actions and female searchers were drafted in. Cumann na mBan also played a role in acquiring arms, including plying British soldiers with alcohol and offering to buy their guns.

Because women did not fall under suspicion as easily they were also trusted with some vital intelligence work. Cumann na mBan members were among the most important channels of communication between IRA brigades and between local units and GHQ. Written and verbal communications could largely be transported safely in this manner, with women often hiding messages in their underclothes to avoid detection. Simple intelligence-gathering, such as reporting on the movements of crown forces, was another way in which women assisted the campaign. One particular category of women who played a crucial role in IRA intelligence-gathering were postmistresses, many of whom were members of Cumann na mBan, and through whose post offices important crown force communications were relayed. Sympathetic postmistresses often copied these for the local IRA intelligence officer using Cumann na mBan couriers to transport them.

Cumann na mBan also supported both the military and political campaigns in a number of other ways. With the formation of flying columns and IRA men on the run, women played an important role in providing food, laundry and shelter. Volunteers who had not evaded capture were visited in prison and brought meals and news from their families. The emphasis on first aid paid off when trained Cumann na mBan members, some of whom were professional nurses, travelled with IRA ambush parties and provided essential first aid to wounded volunteers. Women often deputised for men attending ceremonies, including republican funerals and pilgrimages to Wolfe Tone's grave in Bodenstown (Coleman, 2003: 186–9; McCarthy, 2007: 123–54).

On the political side of the campaign, Cumann na mBan members were engaged in distributing republican propaganda. Prominent republican women were among the most important propagandists during the war. Following the controversial and high-profile death of Terence MacSwiney in October 1920, his sister and widow, Mary and Muriel, travelled to the USA in December 1920 to give evidence to the sympathetic American Commission on Conditions in Ireland. Mary remained until August 1921 undertaking a very successful lecture tour during which she addressed over 300 meetings in 58 cities (Mooney Eichacker, 2003: 92–137). Highlighting the plight of Ireland abroad, especially in the USA, resulted in success in raising funds to provide relief for the civilian population who were badly affected economically by the war, either through the loss of a bread-winner or destruction to property. Charitable activities such as raising and distributing these funds, through the mechanism of the Irish White Cross, also occupied the time of many Cumann na mBan women during the War of Independence (McCarthy, 2007: 151–3; Matthews, 2010: 255–60).

It is very difficult to estimate how many women took part in the revolution. In 1921 Cumann na mBan reported that it had 702 branches, over half of which (375) were in Munster. Leinster had the next highest concentration (188), whereas the organisation was relatively weak in Connacht (93) and Ulster (46) (McCarthy, 2007: 159). These figures show that Cumann na mBan was strongest where the IRA was also strongest. Local studies indicate that branches of Cumann na mBan tended to be formed in the same areas as IRA units (Coleman, 2003: 182). The strong links between the IRA and Cumann na mBan were also forged through republican families. Prominent Cumann na mBan women were often the relatives of senior Sinn Féin and IRA leaders. The women who undertook lecture tours of the USA were close relatives of republican martyrs. Brigid Lyons was a niece of the Sinn Féin TD Joseph McGuinness. Four of the six women elected unopposed to the Second Dáil in 1921 (Margaret Pearse, Mary MacSwiney, Kate O'Callaghan and Kathleen Clarke) were the mother, sister and widows respectively of men who had either been executed, died in prison or killed by crown forces.

The similarities between the IRA and Cumann na mBan extended to social backgrounds, which is not very surprising given the family ties between them. Similarly to the IRA, many of the most active members of Cumann na mBan were young, single women. Those who had previously been active and who married during the course of the conflict tended to fade very fast. Active women who were married and had families tended to have independent means or important domestic support to allow them to continue their activities; Constance Markievicz had family wealth and seven-year-old Owen Sheehy-Skeffington stayed in the homes of Irish-American political supporters while his widowed mother toured the USA (Mooney Eichacker, 2003: 65–70).

Violence against women during the revolution was physical, psychological and to a lesser extent sexual. There were very few deliberate killings of women. In Cork the IRA executed Mrs Mary Lindsay for informing on the volunteers responsible for the Dripsey ambush, and in Monaghan the intellectually challenged *poitín* maker, Kitty Carroll, was similarly dispatched on a convenient charge of spying. Incidental fatal attacks on women included the deaths in Galway of the pregnant Ellen Quinn in a drive-by shooting by police on 1 November 1920, and Lily Blake, the wife of an RIC district inspector whose vehicle was ambushed by the IRA in May 1921 (Leeson, 2011: 51, 62).

There is ample evidence attesting to assaults on women by the Black and Tans and Auxiliaries. Frequently this took the form of cutting off their hair. In September 1920 five members of Cumann na mBan in Galway were subjected to this unofficial punishment in reprisal for a similar attack carried out by the IRA on a woman who had given evidence to a military court. This incident indicates that the IRA was equally culpable for such attacks and there are likewise many instances of women who were friendly with the police or who worked for them being subjected to similar degradation (Coleman, 2003: 120; Leeson, 2011: 46, 176–8). Black and Tans and Auxiliaries also earned a reputation for rough treatment and threats against women, as evidenced by the report of the British Labour Commission [**Doc. 21**].

Women were also subjected to the psychological terror of seeing their male relatives assaulted or killed. Tomás MacCurtain's wife was restrained by her husband's assassins and suffered a miscarriage soon after his death. The mother and sisters of Richard and Abraham Pearson were in attendance when they were executed by the IRA at Coolacrease in County Offaly on 30 June 1921. The fatal shooting of William Frederick Newberry by the Squad on Bloody Sunday was witnessed by a female companion, probably his wife (Leonard, 2012: 108; Stanley, 2005: 21). In March 1921 the serving Mayor of Limerick, George Clancy, and his predecessor, Michael O'Callaghan, were shot dead in their homes in the presence of their wives by suspected Black and Tans (McCoole, 2003: 71).

Evidence of sexual assaults on women is more difficult to find, which is not to say it did not take place. The British Labour Commission explained that it was 'difficult to obtain direct evidence of incidents affecting females, for the women of Ireland are reticent on such subjects', but clearly suspected a sexual assault had taken place in a case where 'A young woman who was sleeping alone in premises which were raided by the crown forces was compelled to get out of bed and her nightdress was ripped open from top to bottom' [Doc. 21]. The *Irish Bulletin* carried two reports by a Mrs Healy and a Miss Nellie O'Mahony who claimed to have been raped and sexually assaulted respectively by members of the crown forces; the veracity of these reports is difficult to judge given the propaganda nature of the *Irish Bulletin* and lack of any other evidence (Ryan, 2000: 89).

SECTARIANISM

The most controversial topic in the historiography of the Irish revolution at present is the extent to which it was a sectarian conflict. Outside of the sectarian violence in Ulster between 1920 and 1922, there is some evidence of a sectarian element to the war in the south. The issue was highlighted by the Canadian historian, Peter Hart, in the late 1990s with the publication of his book *The IRA and Its Enemies* and an article on 'The Protestant experience of revolution in southern Ireland'. The former highlighted incidents such as 'the Bandon Valley massacre' of 18 Protestants on the nights of 27, 28 and 29 April 1922, while the latter produced revealing statistics about the disproportionate number of assaults on Protestants in Cork between 1920 and 1922; 36 per cent of civilians deliberately shot by the IRA were Protestants, five times the proportion of Protestants in the population, while only 15 per cent of the houses burned by republicans were owned by Catholics (Hart, 1998: 273–6; Hart, 2003: 234). Sectarian attacks by the IRA also took place in County Monaghan, although historians have found little or no evidence of a determined sectarian attitude in the IRA in other areas, including Longford and Limerick (Coleman, 2003: 156–7; Dooley, 2000: 43–50; O'Callaghan, 2010: 203). As with the regional variations in violence, sectarianism in the War of Independence appears to have been a response to local circumstances.

Hart believed that the intensity of sectarian attacks between 1920 and 1922 was the principal reason for the substantial decline of 34 per cent (from 248,635 to 164,215) in the Protestant population of the 26 counties that now make up the Republic of Ireland between 1911 and 1926 (Hart, 2003: 223). It is difficult to ascertain exactly when these people left because the political upheaval prevented a census of population being taken in the intervening years. The Protestant exodus is also explicable by a number of other reasons. The removal of the British state from Ireland, including civil and military personnel, accounted for some of the decline. The desire to remain under British rule either in Britain itself or in Northern Ireland also explains some of the movement, especially in border areas. The continuation of land purchase resulting in the final sale of entire estates, combat deaths during the First World War, the influence of Catholic teaching on legislation in the early years of the Free State (including a prohibition on introducing divorce and strict censorship of publications and films) and the effect of the Roman Catholic Church's *Ne Temere* decree of 1908, which required the children of a marriage between a Catholic and a non-Catholic to be raised as Catholics, all undoubtedly contributed to this significant change in the religious demography of the Irish Free State (Bowen, 1983: 20–46).

One event that has recently highlighted the controversy about sectarianism during the War of Independence was the botched execution of Richard and Abraham Pearson, members of a small Protestant sect known as Cooneyites, in Coolacrease, near Cadamstown in County Offaly a few days before the truce. Defenders of the IRA claim the Pearsons were spies and informers who deliberately antagonised and threatened the IRA and the local civilian population and that some of the girls in the family socialised with British soldiers. It has also been suggested that the local jealousy of the Pearsons' large farm, dissatisfaction with their compliance with a government compulsory tillage order during the First World War, the desire of the hitherto inactive Offaly Brigade to record a success before the truce and the perception of the Pearsons as an alien element within the community were factors responsible for their deaths (Hanley, 2008: 5–6).

GUIDE TO FURTHER READING

The Bureau of Military History witness statements (see Chapter 2) provide detailed accounts of the War of Independence from the perspective of the participants.

The only single-volume history of the war is Michael Hopkinson's, *The Irish War of Independence* (Gill and Macmillan, 2002). Studies of the war at regional level are quite plentiful and include Joost Augusteijn's, *From Public*

Defiance to Guerrilla Warfare: The Experience of Ordinary Volunteers in the Irish War of Independence, 1916–1921 (Irish Academic Press, 1996), Marie Coleman's, *County Longford and the Irish Revolution, 1910–1923* (Irish Academic Press, 2003), David Fitzpatrick's pioneering study of County Clare, *Politics and Irish Life: Provincial Experience of War and Revolution* (Gill and Macmillan, 1977), Peter Hart's, *The IRA and Its Enemies: Violence and Community in Cork, 1916–1923* (Oxford University Press, 1998) and John O'Callaghan's, *Revolutionary Limerick: The Republican Campaign for Independence, Limerick, 1913–1921* (Irish Academic Press, 2010).

The nature of the IRA's guerrilla campaign and the British response to it are the subject of Charles Townshend's, *The British Campaign in Ireland, 1919–1921: The Development of Political and Military Policies* (Oxford University Press, 1975) and *Political Violence in Ireland: Government and Resistance since 1848* (Oxford University Press, 1984). The British security response is also considered in D. M. Leeson's, *The Black and Tans: British Police and Auxiliaries in the Irish War of Independence* (Oxford University Press, 2011).

Plate 1 John Redmond delivering a speech on the third home rule bill,
April 1912.

(© Getty)

Plate 2 The destruction of the GPO after the Easter Rising, 1916.

(© Bibliothèque Nationale de France)

Plate 3 The Irish Citizen Army outside Liberty Hall.

(© Getty)

Plate 4 Arthur Griffith (1871–1922).

(© National Library of Ireland)

Plate 5 Eamon de Valera (1882–1975).

(© National Library of Ireland)

Plate 6 Constance Markievicz (1868–1927).

(© National Library of Ireland)

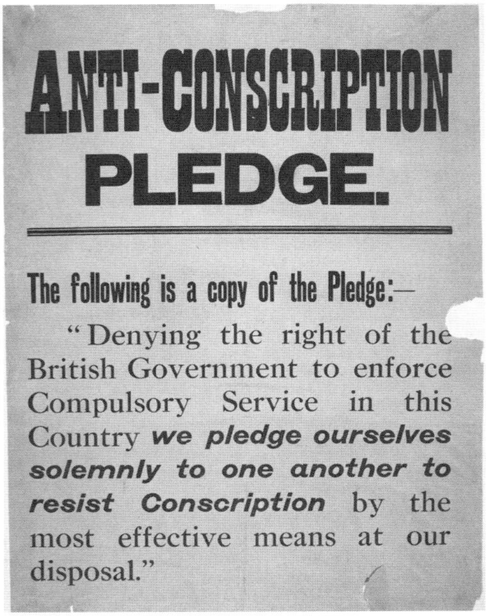
ANTI-CONSCRIPTION
PLEDGE.

The following is a copy of the Pledge:—

"Denying the right of the British Government to enforce Compulsory Service in this Country ***we pledge ourselves solemnly to one another to resist Conscription*** by the most effective means at our disposal."

Plate 7 Anti-conscription pledge poster.

(© National Library of Ireland)

Plate 8 Auxiliary recruits.

(© Getty)

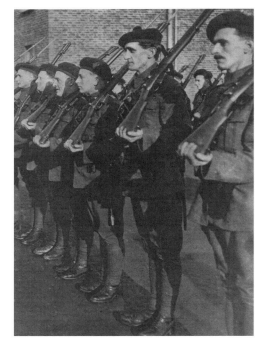

Plate 9 The Irish Army taking over Portobello Barracks, Dublin, in 1922.
(© Getty)

Plate 10 Sir James Craig, first prime minister of Northern Ireland at the opening of the Northern Ireland Parliament in City Hall, Belfast, June 1922.
(© Getty)

6

Peace and Civil War, 1921–3

BRITISH POLICY IN IRELAND, 1919–21

The two tasks facing the British Government in regard to Ireland during the years 1919–21 were restoring law and order and finding a political settlement. The Government of Ireland Act had been postponed for the duration of the First World War and was due to be implemented. Events in Ireland in the meantime meant that it could not be enforced in the form it had taken in 1914, so the government was tasked with drawing up yet another home rule bill for Ireland.

The government's ability to deal with the IRA insurgency was hampered by poor leadership. The Irish administration based in Dublin Castle was unprepared for dealing with the IRA's guerrilla campaign and Sinn Féin's usurpation of the powers of the state. The Lord Lieutenant for most of the period was the retired Field Marshal, Lord French, who was chosen because of his Irish family background and support for home rule. However, he was unsuitable for the circumstances that prevailed in Ireland during the War of Independence. He was neither a good administrator nor politician and fell too heavily under the sway of prominent unionists such as Walter Long. He failed to take republicans seriously and, as a former soldier, advocated suppression of the guerrilla campaign. His position was not helped by the role of his sister, Charlotte Despard, in the republican movement.

The Dublin Castle administration was also hamstrung by a succession of weak chief secretaries, who were effectively in charge of the Irish policy. Edward Shortt, who supported conscription and oversaw the German plot arrests, was frequently at odds with French and was replaced after less than a year. His successor, Ian MacPherson, who did not last much longer, was equally incapable of dealing with the Irish insurrection, failing to draw any distinction between the political and military wings of the republican movement and acquiescing with the hardline approach favoured by French and his unionist advisers, whose influence he was too weak to resist (O'Halpin, 1987: 180–95).

The weakness of the Irish administration was compounded by the IRA's assault on the RIC and the success of the Dáil courts. Recognising the problems in Ireland, the government appointed the head of the British Civil Service, Sir Warren Fisher, to investigate the operation of Dublin Castle. His subsequent report was damning, criticising the Irish executive's inability to administer and advise on or implement policy effectively. A major over-haul of senior administrative personnel ensued. MacPherson was replaced by Sir Hamar Greenwood and senior civil servants from Britain were brought over to set the Irish administration on a more effective footing. Sir John Anderson became the Joint Under Secretary, with Mark Sturgis and Alfred ('Andy') Cope as Assistant Under Secretaries. The latter was also charged by Lloyd George with the task of making contact with the Sinn Féin and IRA leaders with a view to achieving peace (Hopkinson, 1999: 4–7).

These administrative changes were accompanied by changes to the leadership of the military and the police. Sir Nevil Macready was appointed Commander-in-Chief of the British Army in Ireland in early 1920 and improved the army's morale, efficiency and effectiveness in countering the IRA. Sir Hugh Tudor, a decorated soldier with no policing experience, was appointed police adviser without any defined powers. As a result he assumed control of all policing functions and earned a reputation for condoning the worst excesses of the paramilitary police forces introduced in 1920, over which he was both unable and unwilling to impose any authority or discipline.

While the armed response to the IRA became more effective during late 1920 and 1921, due in part to these reforms, one major drawback of the British campaign in Ireland was the failure to establish a unified command over the police and the army, partly because of Macready's refusal to assume such responsibility. The resulting failure to produce a coherent reaction to the IRA was also hindered by the British Government's indecision about whether to pursue a political rather than a military strategy in Ireland because of its unwillingness to admit that it was faced with a war, for fear of conferring legitimacy on the actions of the IRA and Sinn Féin (Jeffery, 1994: 163–76). Nevertheless, these changes to the British administration, army and policing in Ireland in 1920 were a recognition by the government of the seriousness of the Irish insurrection; and, as a result of the new leadership and a more organised policy, the counter-offensive against the IRA became much more effective in late 1920 and 1921.

THE PARTITION OF IRELAND, 1920–1

Meanwhile in Westminster legislation was being formulated to revive the Government of Ireland Act. The political position in Parliament had changed dramatically since the crisis over the third home rule bill. The Irish Party was reduced to a rump of seven MPs, and while the Liberal leader, Lloyd George, remained as Prime Minister, there was a Conservative majority in the government. This would ensure that the position of Ulster unionists was protected. The status of unionists was further enhanced by the fact that a former Unionist leader, Walter Long, was the Cabinet's chief Irish adviser and chairman of the committee charged with producing new legislation to determine the constitutional position of Ireland.

The Long committee reported in November 1919, recommending the repeal of the Government of Ireland Act that was passed in September 1914 and its replacement with a new one. Long's proposals envisaged two Home Rule Parliaments, one based in Belfast with jurisdiction over all nine counties of Ulster and one in Dublin that would govern the remaining 23 counties. An idea known as county option, which would have allowed individual counties to hold plebiscites to decide whether to opt in or out of home rule, was rejected as unworkable and likely to exacerbate sectarian sentiment in those Ulster counties such as Fermanagh and Tyrone that had Catholic majorities.

The suggestion of a separate Home Rule Parliament for a nine-county Ulster was significant. In the first place it was a recognition of how unionist opinion had changed since 1912. At the outset of the third home rule crisis unionists were implacably opposed to home rule for any part of Ireland, preferring to remain an integral part of the United Kingdom. Since then they had faced the reality that the British Government was prepared to break up the union by implementing Irish home rule. The changing political attitudes of nationalist Ireland also convinced them that they had no desire to remain part of the same political entity. In the eyes of unionists, nationalists' loyalty during the war was questionable, especially in view of their opposition to conscription, and the armed uprising against British rule was further testament to their treachery. By 1920, while most unionists would still have preferred to remain within the union, they had realised that the best chance of protecting their own interest lay in self-government for Ulster [Doc. 22].

However, the nine-county Ulster recommended by the Long Committee was not that favoured by Ulster unionists. In 1911, 43 per cent of the entire province of Ulster was Roman Catholic, whereas the Catholic population of the six counties with the largest Protestant populations was only 34 per cent (Buckland, 1973: 179–80). The third option for Ulster unionists would be to take control of only four counties – Antrim, Armagh, Derry and Down – excluding the most contentious counties of Tyrone and Fermanagh, which had Catholic majorities of around 55 per cent. However, such an entity would be too small to survive economically or politically. The Long Committee's choice of a nine-county Ulster was a deliberate effort to ensure that partition would be temporary and that eventual Irish reunification would be achieved. However, the opposition of the Ulster unionists and their influence with the Conservative-controlled Government ensured that a six-county Ulster was the solution adopted (Laffan, 1983: 61–8).

The Government of Ireland Act was passed on 23 December 1920 and partitioned Ireland into two home rule entities to be called Northern Ireland (comprising Counties Antrim, Armagh, Derry, Down, Fermanagh and Tyrone) and Southern Ireland which contained the remaining 26 counties [**Doc. 23**]. The powers of the legislatures of both jurisdictions were similar to those envisaged for the Irish Home Rule Parliament under the 1914 Act, and considerable powers over defence, finance and trade were reserved for Westminster. The lack of effective taxation powers would prove to be a serious problem for the Northern Ireland Government during the 1920s and 1930s. The inclusion of a plan to establish a Council of Ireland 'to make orders with respect to matters affecting interests both in Southern Ireland and Northern Ireland' (O'Day, 1998: 327), and a clause outlining how a Parliament for the whole of Ireland might be established, indicated that the government hoped partition would not be a permanent solution. The Northern Ireland Parliament was offered the alternatives of continuing to operate under the Government of Ireland Act or accept a form of home rule within the Irish Free State, set out in article 14 of the treaty. There was never any likelihood that this latter option would have been availed of.

A number of safeguards were inserted to protect both the Catholic minority in Northern Ireland and the Protestant minority in Southern Ireland. These included a prohibition on the endowment of religion or interfering with educational rights on religious grounds, clauses that had also been in the 1914 Act, and the use of proportional representation by single transferable vote (PRSTV) to elect the members of both Houses of Commons. This latter provision was designed to ensure that minority political parties would secure adequate parliamentary representation. The British Government did not intend a Sinn Féin-style landslide like 1918 to recur in Ireland. The provision remained in Northern Ireland until 1929 when it was repealed, in the face of Labour-Unionist opposition to the ruling **Ulster Unionist Party**. The abolition of PR in Northern Ireland reinforced unionist dominance and remained a grievance for nationalists. PRSTV remains the electoral system in the Republic of Ireland.

Ulster Unionist Party: The political party representing unionists in Ulster.

The Government of Ireland Act came into operation in May 1921. Elections for both Parliaments were held, although Sinn Féin refused to recognise the new notional political entity of Southern Ireland and deemed the election to be a contest for the Second Dáil. Neither Labour nor the remnant of the IPP contested the election and all 124 Sinn Féin candidates were returned unopposed. Four independent southern unionists were returned unopposed for the Dublin University (Trinity College) constituency. In Northern Ireland, 40 of the 52 seats in the House of Commons were taken by Unionists, with Sinn Féin and the Nationalists (effectively the old home rulers) taking six each. Sinn Féin's northern MPs, including Collins, de Valera and Griffith, did not take their seats in the new Northern Ireland Parliament which was opened by King George V in City Hall, Belfast on 22 June 1921. Home rule had finally been implemented in Ireland, but ironically it was the Ulster Unionists who had been so strongly opposed to the idea a decade previously upon whom it was conferred. The partition of Ireland was now a reality. The British Government had solved the Ulster part of the Irish question and could now concentrate on seeking a peaceful settlement with Sinn Féin in the south.

THE TRUCE AND THE TREATY

The first efforts to reach a peaceful settlement in the War of Independence started in autumn 1920. Plans to organise a meeting between Griffith, the acting Dáil president, and Sir John Anderson, foundered over the issue of recognition of the Dáil. In the absence of direct contact between Sinn Féin and the British Government, efforts were made for neutral figures to liaise between both sides. Between October and December 1920, Patrick Moylett, a businessman with a republican background, acted as a go-between for communications between Griffith and senior British civil servants. His mission was unsuccessful because of the British insistence that Sinn Féin abandon its demand for a republic and also because of contemporary events including Bloody Sunday and the arrest of Griffith on 25 November. Details of the secret mission were also leaked to the *Irish Independent* newspaper, by which time Moylett had lost Sinn Féin's trust (Hopkinson, 2002: 180–1).

The peace mission that came closest to success was that undertaken by the Irish-born Archbishop of Perth in Western Australia, Patrick Joseph Clune, whose personal motive sprang from the death of his nephew, Conor Clune, in Dublin Castle on Bloody Sunday. Acting with the support of Lloyd George between November 1920 and January 1921, Clune held meetings in Ireland with Griffith, Collins and other senior Sinn Féin members as well as Anderson and the other members of the administration in Dublin Castle. By December 1920, however, it was clear that the government was making demands that were unacceptable to Sinn Féin, especially the precondition of disarmament prior to a truce (Hopkinson, 1999: 93). The government appears to have felt that the republicans were desperate for a settlement and tried to impose as many demands as possible on them. Lloyd George was also coming under pressure from Conservatives, who now comprised the majority of his government, and senior military figures, to take a hardline approach. As a result, republican leaders became suspicious of Lloyd George's intentions and Clune's closeness to him, and the negotiations were abandoned. Various other efforts by prominent southern Unionists, religious leaders, literary figures (Shane Leslie and George Russell), Lady Greenwood (the Chief Secretary's wife), Mark Sturgis and the Tory peer, Lord Derby, all came to nothing (Hopkinson, 2002: 181–91).

These efforts indicate that there was a will on both sides to bring the conflict to a conclusion in the appropriate circumstances. By July 1921 circumstances were more amenable to a settlement for both sides. The military campaign had reached a stalemate and the republican advantages in areas such as intelligence and guerrilla warfare were not as strong as they had been. De Valera's return to Ireland in December 1920 was significant as the recognised leader of the republican movement was now back in the country and effectively allowed to function unmolested by the government in the hope that an agreement could be reached with him. From the government's point of view the enactment of the Government of Ireland Act and the establishment of a Home Rule Parliament in Belfast removed the thorny issue of Ulster from any subsequent negotiations with Sinn Féin. The provisions of the Government of Ireland Act also acted as a stopwatch for a peace settlement; if the southern Irish provisions were not enforced by 12 July 1921, the British Government faced the prospect of having to impose crown colony government with martial law, and many influential people, including Anderson and Macready, were opposed to resorting to further coercive measures. Politicians from the dominions, in particular the South African Prime Minister, Jan Smuts, were urging Lloyd George to concede dominion status to southern Ireland; this pressure was a testament to the work of the Sinn Féin envoy, Colonel Maurice Moore (Hopkinson, 2002: 194–5).

The truce of 11 July 1921 ended the War of Independence. It was followed by a series of four meetings and an exchange of over 50 letters and telegrams between de Valera and Lloyd George aimed at establishing the basis for formal peace negotiations. The biggest obstacle at this point was the status of the Irish delegation, with de Valera insisting that the delegates be recognised as the representatives of a sovereign nation, a request which Lloyd George was not prepared to concede. The negotiations were rescued by the judicious actions of the middlemen, Harry Boland and Joe McGrath, who disobeyed de Valera's more uncompromising instructions (Fitzpatrick, 2003: 232–4). On 30 September de Valera accepted Lloyd George's invitation to send a team of Irish negotiators to London 'with a view to ascertaining how the association of Ireland with the community of nations known as the British Empire may best be reconciled with Irish national aspiration' (Pakenham, 1972: 77).

The Irish delegation was headed by Griffith and also included a reluctant Collins, Eamonn Duggan, Robert Barton and George Gavan Duffy, with Erskine Childers as secretary. The most glaring omission was de Valera, who felt that Griffith and Collins provided good leadership without him and preferred to remain in reserve at home, providing an opportunity for the delegation to demur in agreeing to anything in haste without consulting him first. The decision was strongly opposed by Collins and Griffith who felt that it was a mistake to leave their most skilled negotiator behind. De Valera's absence from the treaty negotiations remains a polarising issue in Irish history, with his detractors arguing that he deliberately absented himself in the knowledge that Lloyd George would never concede a republic and thereby de Valera could avoid the taint of compromise, a view held at the time by Collins (Hopkinson, 1988: 25). There was also a possibility that the negotiations would fail and if de Valera was not part of them he could not be blamed for such an eventuality (Ferriter, 2007: 82–7; Pakenham, 1972: 83–4).

The opposing delegation was headed by Lloyd George, and included the Lord Chancellor, Lord Birkenhead (who, as F. E. Smith, had been a prominent supporter of the UVF in 1913), Austen Chamberlain (Conservative Party leader), Winston Churchill (Secretary of State for the Colonies), Sir Laming Worthington Evans (Secretary of State for War), Sir Hamar Greenwood (Irish Chief Secretary) and Gordon Hewart (Attorney General) (http://www.treaty.nationalarchives.ie/the-delegates).

The negotiations took place in London between 11 October and 6 December 1921. Sinn Féin's main aim was to achieve the greatest level of sovereignty possible. While a republic was the ideal goal, in reality the delegation knew that it was an unlikely outcome; instead they would seek as much independence as possible, preferably avoiding any reference to the King in the government of Ireland. Partition was not a major concern for the delegation. It had become a reality in June 1921 and there was little likelihood of any change in the status of Northern Ireland in the foreseeable future. They hoped for some indication of the British Government's commitment to eventual Irish unity. Sir James Craig, the Prime Minister of Northern Ireland, had been invited to attend the negotiations but refused. Partition was important to the delegation as a popular issue on which to break off the negotiations if they were not going well.

The constitutional position of the 26-county state and its relationship to Britain was the most important issue in the negotiations. The outcome was the creation of the Irish Free State, which would have the status of a dominion of the Commonwealth, similar to Canada, Australia, New Zealand and South Africa. While the state would be largely independent, enjoying a much greater level of self-government than Northern Ireland under home rule – including its own army, coinage, postage, central bank etc. – it was not a fully sovereign republic and the controversial trappings of the monarchy remained. The King was still head of state and members of the Free State Parliament had to take an oath of fealty to him and his successors. This clause, often mistakenly referred to as the oath of allegiance to the King (it was an oath of allegiance to the Constitution of the Free State and an oath of fealty to the King), would prove to be one of the core issues in the split that subsequently emerged [**Doc. 24**].

Partition figured in the debates in regard to the exact geographical boundary of the new Free State. On 12 November Griffith scuppered the Irish delegation's strategy of using Ulster as a convenient excuse to break off unsuccessful negotiations by agreeing to Lloyd George's suggestion that a **Boundary Commission** be established to delineate the border between the Free State and Northern Ireland (Hopkinson, 1988: 29). Lloyd George was also successful in convincing Collins that the Commission would grant the Free State 'large territories' and 'that Ulster, reduced to an uneconomic unit, would probably be "forced in" [to the Free State] before long' (Pakenham, 1972: 222). This appears to have been a decisive factor in convincing Collins to sign the treaty.

Boundary Commission: Commission established under the Anglo-Irish Treaty to delineate the border between Northern Ireland and the Irish Free State. Its 1925 report was suppressed and the border left unchanged.

The British delegation was concerned about the implications of Irish independence for British defence and demanded that a British naval presence be retained at three Irish ports – Berehaven and Cobh in County Cork and Lough Swilly in County Donegal. This was a further reminder that the Free State was not fully sovereign. The ports were eventually returned in 1938 enabling Éire to remain neutral during the Second World War. The fourth major issue at stake in the negotiations was the Free State's responsibility for a portion of British public debt, including war pensions and compensation to civil and public servants and policemen who were not retained by the new government or chose to resign rather than serve in the new state or seek a transfer to Northern Ireland. This was subsequently estimated to amount to between £6.25 million and £8.25 million annually, but much of this was waived by the British Government in 1925 following the conclusion of the Boundary Commission (Laffan, 1983: 104–5).

On 30 November Lloyd George produced a draft treaty that the Irish delegation brought back to Dublin for consultation with the Dáil Cabinet. The confused and acrimonious debate which ensued foreshadowed much of what would emerge in the subsequent Dáil debate on the treaty, with republican hardliners such as Austin Stack and Cathal Brugha criticising the content of the document and tactics of the Irish negotiators. The delegation returned to London with vague instructions about seeking re-wording of the oath and no written instructions about strategy or whether they needed to refer an amended treaty back again before signing it. After the British delegation made concessions on the oath and other minor issues, Lloyd

George dramatically demanded that the Irish delegates sign the modified treaty immediately without referring it back to Dublin, or risk an immediate resumption of war. He was undoubtedly calling the Irish delegates' bluff, but knew that any hesitation would allow the republican opponents of the agreement to prolong or possibly even destroy the negotiations at the eleventh hour. The **Anglo-Irish Treaty** was subsequently signed in 10 Downing Street in the early hours of Tuesday, 6 December 1921.

Anglo-Irish Treaty: Treaty signed in December 1921 between Britain and Southern Ireland that created the Irish Free State as a dominion of the Commonwealth.

There are a number of reasons why the Irish delegation agreed to sign the treaty. Griffith was the most moderate member of the delegation and therefore always likely to sign a document that conferred a considerable level of sovereignty, if not full independence. His agreement to a boundary commission also made it impossible for him to refuse. Lloyd George had been a most skilful negotiator. At an early stage he identified the fault-lines within the Irish camp, recognising that Collins and Griffith could be worked around while seeking to exclude the more recalcitrant Duffy and Duggan from some of the deliberations. He also used the Conservative majority in his government to his advantage, arguing that his hands were tied because of it, especially on the question of Ulster. Throughout the negotiations he raised the prospect that if the negotiations failed, his government would fall to be replaced by a Conservative government, possibly led by the Unionist stalwart Bonar Law, that would not be prepared to offer the Irish such a generous settlement.

Lloyd George's success in convincing Collins of the potential of the Boundary Commission to destroy Northern Ireland was significant in his decision to sign. Collins had also gained the support of the IRB supreme council for an amended oath, and by early December was aware that this was the best deal possible. As the only military man in the delegation he knew that the IRA had lost much of its valued anonymity during the truce and would be unable to resort to the successful covert guerrilla tactics it had practised prior to July 1921. With the two principal negotiators having decided to sign, the others followed reluctantly, aware of the divisive reaction that would ensue back in Ireland (Hopkinson, 1988: 31–3).

THE TREATY SPLIT

The first group to express an opinion on the Treaty was the Dáil Cabinet, which included three of the signatories (Griffith, Collins and Barton), in addition to de Valera, Brugha, Austin Stack and W. T. Cosgrave. The cabinet divided four to three, with the more republican-minded de Valera, Stack and Brugha voting against it. Robert Barton would subsequently recant his support but at this early stage the Treaty had passed its first hurdle. Its fate would now be decided in the Dáil debate, which took place between 14 December 1921 and 7 January 1922, with a break for Christmas.

The Dáil treaty debate was one of the most acrimonious ever to take place in the Irish Parliament [**Doc. 25**]. Much of the early debate centred on whether the delegates had acted outside their powers in signing the treaty, most likely a deliberate strategy by the treaty's opponents 'to personalize the debate, to put the delegation – Collins and Griffith, in particular – on the defensive' (Knirck, 2006: 118–19). Personal animosities that had been simmering throughout the War of Independence rose to the surface. Cathal Brugha, who, as Minister for Defence, had tried to bring the IRA under Dáil control in spite of opposition from Collins and the IRB, took exception to a comment that Collins 'was the man who won the war', pointing out that he was 'merely a subordinate in the Department of Defence', whose image as a romantic hero was manufactured by the press. Griffith, who was the target of many personalised attacks from anti-treatyites, reacted furiously to their verbal attack on him, referring cuttingly on one occasion to Erskine Childers as a 'damned Englishman'.

All six women TDs (Countess Markievicz, Ada English, Mary MacSwiney, Margaret Pearse, Kate O'Callaghan and Kathleen Clarke) opposed the treaty, with the last four invoking the republicanism of their male relatives who had died since 1916. In the longest speech of the debate, lasting over two-and-a-half hours, Mary MacSwiney delivered one of the most ardent republican arguments against any compromise short of complete sovereignty. The debate appears to have had little outcome on the result of the vote and was more of an opportunity for TDs to record their opinions and vent their frustration at former colleagues who had now become political enemies. Most TDs seem to have made their decisions well before the vote was taken, though the Christmas break might have been significant in some making their minds up as a result of pressure from their constituents, especially influential figures such as the largely pro-treaty Roman Catholic clergy.

The most influential opponent of the treaty was the Dáil's president, de Valera, who argued that it was incompatible with Sinn Féin's stated ambition of achieving a republic. As an alternative de Valera introduced **Document No. 2**, which outlined his idea of external association, an idea that was mooted during the treaty negotiations but did not receive any serious consideration at the time [**Doc. 26**]. External association envisaged a relationship between the Free State and the Commonwealth whereby the Irish Free State would be associated with the Commonwealth for matters relating to foreign affairs, war and defence and would recognise the King as head of the Commonwealth, though not as Irish head of state. It was a complicated and sophisticated arrangement that he would later put into operation under the External Relations Act in 1936, but was still too convoluted for the circumstances of 1922,

Document No. 2: De Valera's alternative to the treaty that envisaged an external association relationship between the Free State and Britain, under which the King would not be recognised as Irish head of state.

as Irish independence was in its fledgling stages and the relations between the dominions and Britain had yet to evolve in the way they did after the Statute of Westminster in 1929 that gave greater autonomy to the dominions. De Valera subsequently withdrew Document No. 2 before the Dáil had an opportunity to vote on it as an alternative to the treaty.

The treaty was put to a vote in the Dáil on 7 January 1922 where it was accepted by a slim margin of seven votes – 64 to 57 – a mere four votes could have swung the balance in the other direction. De Valera resigned as president of the Dáil and was replaced by Griffith. Critics of de Valera often see this as one of his greatest political mistakes, arguing that by rejecting the democratic decision of the Dáil he precipitated a split in the republican movement that spread from the Dáil to Sinn Féin and the IRA, eventually leading to civil war six months later. De Valera's defence was that as he considered the Irish delegates to have acted outside their authority in signing the treaty, he was not bound by the Dáil's decision. There were also a number of dedicated republicans within the IRA, such as Liam Lynch and Rory O'Connor, who would have rejected the treaty regardless of de Valera's position.

In the aftermath of the Dáil Cabinet, the Dáil, the IRB, Sinn Féin and Cumann na mBan (which voted 419 to 63 against the treaty), the final and most significant body to split was the IRA (Laffan, 1999: 365). The majority of the army was opposed to the settlement. Very few senior officers, apart from Seán MacEoin in Longford and Michael Brennan in Clare, and some prominent members of GHQ including Mulcahy, Collins and J. J. O'Connell, took the pro-treaty side. The rank-and-file members tended to follow the lead given by their officers. The division within the IRA was exacerbated by the hasty withdrawal of the crown forces from Ireland in early 1922. Dublin Castle was handed over on 16 January, the disbandment of the RIC was put in place and most barracks were evacuated of troops by the end of March. Empty barracks were then taken over by the local IRA, regardless of whether they were pro- or anti-treaty. As a result a large number of vacated barracks were under the control of those opposed to the treaty settlement.

In the period immediately following the political split efforts were made to maintain the unity of the IRA. Plans were formulated to hold an army convention in March, an idea that was initially supported by Mulcahy, the chief-of-staff. However, due to increased tensions between both wings of the IRA, in particular over the contested occupation of vacated barracks in Limerick, Mulcahy grew wary of the divisive potential of the convention and prohibited it. Anti-treaty IRA leaders went ahead with it in defiance of his order and the convention reaffirmed the IRA's commitment to republicanism, withdrew recognition of the Dáil as the recognised government of the republic and established an alternative army executive, widening further the gulf between the pro- and anti-treaty factions (Laffan, 1999: 374).

While the debate about the army convention was taking place British soldiers withdrew from barracks in Limerick City. Pro-treaty forces were unwilling to allow the local anti-treaty IRA take control of these barracks as they would provide an important strategic link between anti-treaty strongholds in Munster and Connaught, and isolate pro-treaty bases in Athlone and Clare. A stand-off ensued between pro-treaty forces and Ernie O'Malley's Second Southern Division (anti-treaty IRA) that was only resolved when the pro-treaty side agreed to a compromise, which was in effect a climb-down, allowing Limerick Corporation to take control of police barracks while a small force of anti-treaty IRA under Liam Lynch occupied the city's two military barracks. While a confrontation was narrowly avoided, the situation highlighted how the existence of two opposing armed factions held the potential for the treaty split to spread from being a political dispute to a military conflict.

On two further occasions in April 1922 there was potential for the split to become militarised. On 13 April an anti-treaty IRA faction led by Rory O'Connor occupied the Four Courts, the most important judicial building in Dublin, in open defiance of the pro-treaty government. The inability of the government or the pro-treaty IRA to remove them highlighted the weakness of the government to deal with the IRA's resistance to the treaty. Later that month the anti-treaty IRA tried to prevent Griffith from speaking in Sligo Town, and a serious confrontation was averted when the local IRA leader, Liam Pilkington, allowed the address to proceed. During May and June further talks were held between delegations from the pro- and anti-treaty IRA factions in a last ditch effort to preserve the force's unity, but the treaty remained a sticking point with the pro-treaty faction insisting that acceptance of the treaty was the basis for negotiation. When the talks broke down in June the hitherto peaceful co-existence of two opposing armed forces appeared to be doomed.

Contemporaneous political developments also increased the likelihood of a civil war. Following the Dáil's vote in favour of the treaty a Provisional Government, headed by Collins, was formed that would remain in place until the official creation of the Free State in December 1922, one year from the date of the signing of the treaty. However, the Dáil Government, headed by Griffith, also remained in place because the Second Dáil was still in existence, and many ministers held the same portfolio in both administrations. Gradually most governmental work was taken over by the Provisional Government and the Dáil Cabinet was marginalised.

Political opponents of the treaty were also becoming more vehement and the language of their public pronouncements was increasingly inflammatory. This was especially the case with de Valera, who made a number of strident speeches against the settlement, the most notable of which was delivered at

Thurles in County Tipperary where he spoke of having to 'wade through Irish blood, through the blood of the soldiers of the Irish Government, and through, perhaps, the blood of some of the members of the Government in order to get Irish freedom'. De Valera was the leader of the political opposition to the treaty, and was not active in the anti-treaty IRA. His defenders argue that these were warnings of what might happen, rather than a threat of violence. Nevertheless, in the tense atmosphere of the time, with two opposing militant wings of the IRA vying for control of territory, it is difficult to disagree with the assessment that his statements were 'at best incautious and at worst very wildly irresponsible' (Laffan, 1999: 381).

The divided Sinn Féin Party also had to come to terms with how best to contest the general election that was planned for June 1922, which would effectively be a referendum on the treaty. Unlike the previous two elections in 1918 and 1921, the field was much more open, with Labour, Independents and Farmers (comprising some former home rulers) contesting a number of constituencies. In May, Collins and de Valera agreed a pact whereby a panel of pro- and anti-treaty Sinn Féin candidates would be put forward based on the existing strength of both wings within the Second Dáil. The cabinet to be appointed after the election was to have five pro- and four anti-treaty members. The pact was extremely unpopular with the non-Sinn Féin parties as well as supporters of the treaty and the British Government, who saw it as robbing the electorate of a clear choice and making unjustified concessions to republicans, who were largely pleased with an agreement that seemed to guarantee them a decent allocation of seats (Laffan, 1999: 388–9; Regan, 1999: 59–61). The pact was another last-ditch effort to avoid the split descending into violence, especially before the election. It does not appear to have been honoured universally, especially not by supporters of the treaty. Even Collins appears to have been luke-warm about it, urging voters in Cork two days before polling to 'vote for the candidates you think best of', though this did not amount to the outright repudiation of the pact that it is sometimes interpreted as (Gallagher, 1979: 412–13).

The election, held using proportional representation, was the most strongly contested election since 1892, with only seven of the 28 constituencies returning deputies unopposed. The result was a triumph for the pro-treaty wing of Sinn Féin, which won 41 of the seats in contested constituencies, as opposed to 19 for the anti-treatyites (17 of each side were returned unopposed). Only seven pro-treaty candidates were defeated in contrast to 22 republicans, including prominent figures such as Liam Mellows and Erskine Childers, who, like his cousin, Robert Barton, had since repudiated the treaty. Four of the six women who had voted against the treaty – Kathleen Clarke, Margaret Pearse, Countess Markievicz and Dr Ada English – were also rejected. Kate O'Callaghan was returned unopposed and Mary MacSwiney was re-elected by a slim margin. Dan Breen, who could not decide between the pro- and anti-treaty factions, was also defeated, as was his fellow Tipperary IRA comrade, Seamus Robinson. The constituency of Sligo–East Mayo was the only one in which the anti-treaty side won a majority of the votes cast (Laffan, 1999: 403–7).

Labour was the other winner in the contest, returning 17 of its 18 candidates and proving that it had not been terminally damaged by abstaining from the two previous elections. Seven Farmers' Party TDs and 10 independents (including four returned opposed for Trinity College) made up the final result (O'Leary, 1979: 12). If the election is to be seen as a referendum on the treaty then it was a resounding endorsement of it by the electorate as all of the other parties – Labour, Farmers and independents – were supporters of it. However, the success of the Provisional Government in achieving this result was tempered somewhat by the artificiality of the pact, the fact that pro-treaty Sinn Féin only won 38.5 per cent of the votes cast and allegations of 'widespread and not fully reported intimidation of Farmers' and Independent candidates' (Regan, 1999: 66–7).

While there was serious potential for a civil war to break out before June 1922, the desire to await the outcome of political events, such as the general election, partly explains why it did not. Another significant process in this regard was the framing of the Irish Free State constitution. In January 1922 Collins appointed a committee to draw up a new constitution for the Free State. He appears to have hoped that by omitting reference to the most contentious aspects of the treaty – the oath, the Governor General (the King's representative) and the treaty ports – the Provisional Government could produce an essentially republican constitution that would satisfy many of the treaty's opponents. This attempted sleight-of-hand did not fool the British Government, which demanded many changes to the draft constitution submitted to it in May. It was especially chagrined by the assertion that 'Ireland is a free and sovereign nation', the omission of any reference to the oath and the description of the Governor General as a 'Commissioner of the British Commonwealth'. Combined with what they saw as unacceptable tolerance of the anti-treaty IRA's activities, the British Government was not prepared to accept any further efforts by the Provisional Government to temporise with the treaty and insisted on a new version that included references to the oath, the Governor General and the right of final judicial appeal to the British Privy Council (Farrell, 1988: 23–6). The revised draft, published in June, was unacceptable to republicans, ending yet another slim chance of retaining unity.

One final factor that preserved a tenuous unity within the IRA was Collins's northern offensive in early 1922. In his dual capacity as president of both the Provisional Government and the IRB, Collins pursued a contradictory policy towards Northern Ireland following the signing of the treaty. In January

1922 he agreed what was known as the Craig–Collins Pact with Sir James Craig, promising an immediate end to the Belfast boycott in return for the re-instatement of expelled Catholic shipyard workers. Parallel to this official policy Collins and the Provisional Government set about trying to undermine Northern Ireland by encouraging Catholics in their non-recognition of the Northern Government, including paying the salaries of teachers in Catholic schools in the north for six months between February and October 1922, a gesture that achieved 'little but draining the fledgling Southern government of much needed resources' (Lynch, 2006: 98–9).

    Collins's more sinister scheme for undermining Northern Ireland involved using the IRA to foment violence and unrest there, although it is unclear whether he was using the IRA to destabilise the north, or using the north to help stave off the split in the IRA; Northern Ireland was one issue around which the sundering republican army could unite. In January 1922 Collins formed an Ulster Council within the IRA, led by himself and the most senior IRA leader in the six counties, Frank Aiken. A co-ordinated effort by this body to kidnap prominent unionists in border areas of Monaghan, Tyrone and Fermanagh, in response to the imprisonment and threatened execution of a number of IRA men captured in Tyrone in January 1922, led to violent skirmishes between the IRA and the **B Specials**. Armed confrontations between the IRA and the Specials along the border continued during the first half of 1922, often leading to fatalities, including the deaths of four Specials and one IRA man at Clones railway station in County Monaghan on 11 February. The event reverberated in Belfast where another spate of inter-communal violence resulted in the deaths of 43 people (27 Catholics and 16 Protestants) during February.

B Specials: See *Ulster Special Constabulary.*

    Belfast's death toll rose to 59 (37 of whom were Catholics) in March, as attacks on police barracks, Orange Halls and individual Protestants, and bombing raids by the IRA intensified along the border provoking a violent backlash against the city's Catholic population. The most notorious of these incidents was the killing of a well-known Catholic publican, Owen MacMahon, who had no connections to the republican movement, along with three of his sons and an employee, by RIC and B Specials at the MacMahon family home on the Antrim Road in north Belfast on 24 March. The IRA's attempt to show its muscle along the border was ultimately counter-productive and resulted in a murderous backlash against many innocent Catholics in Belfast (Lynch, 2006: 107–26).

    The split in the IRA confirmed by the army convention in March heightened Collins's efforts to use the north as a ploy to retain republican unity and dam-age the Northern Government. While some significant northern IRA leaders joined the anti-treaty side the majority of the rank and file remained loyal to GHQ, while Frank Aiken tried to steer a neutral course. A joint offensive by both wings of the IRA, including the Provisional Government's new army that had evolved from the pro-treaty IRA, was planned for May 1922, in which an uprising against Northern Ireland would be carried out by the northern IRA using arms and equipment provided by the Provisional Government Army. However, due to poor co-ordination, divisions within the IRA over the treaty and the southern leaders' increasing preoccupation with the deterioration of the political and military situation in the south, the elaborate offensive never materialised and the attacks which did take place were quashed forcefully and brutally by the B Specials (Lynch, 2006: 129–47).

This failed offensive provided the backdrop to one of the worst atrocities of the period, on a par with the massacre of the MacMahons. On 17 June a contingent of the IRA's Fourth Northern Division, based in Dundalk, County Louth, crossed the border and attacked a number of Presbyterian farmers in the townlands of Altnaveigh and Lisdrumliska in County Armagh, shooting dead six Protestant civilians, injuring many others and causing extensive damage to their property. Altnaveigh was a well-planned sectarian attack on innocent Protestants, ostensibly carried out as a reprisal for the killing of two local Catholics three days previously. More recent research suggests that it had more complex roots and was a response to a raid by the USC on the public house and home belonging to a local republican, James McGuill, during which it is alleged that McGuill's heavily pregnant wife was raped, a reaction to what was perceived as a campaign of violence against local Catholics, and 'part of a wider escalation of violence in the region around Newry' in the summer of 1922 (Lynch, 2010: 184–210).

Five days after Altnaveigh, on 22 June, two London IRA members, Reginald Dunne and Joseph O'Sullivan, assassinated the Irish-born Sir Henry Wilson, the former Chief of the Imperial General Staff of the British Army, outside his home in London. Their action was a result of Wilson's role as a security adviser to the Northern Government during 1922 when the Specials carried out some of their most notorious attacks. Ironically, Wilson had urged the Northern Government to dispense with the Specials (Jeffery, 2006b: 281–4).

This was the last straw for the British Government, which had lost patience with the Provisional Government's toleration of the anti-treaty IRA and its efforts to subvert the treaty with a watered-down constitution. Believing Rory O'Connor's unit in the Four Courts to be responsible for Wilson's killing, the British Government demanded that the Provisional Government take action against the IRA, or face a British invasion to remove them. On 27 June, the kidnapping of the Provisional Government Army's Deputy Chief-of-Staff, Colonel J. J. 'Ginger' O'Connell, by the IRA in the Four Courts, provoked the Provisional Government further, although it is likely that it had already taken the decision to move against the IRA. On the morning of 28 June 1922 the Provisional Government Army attacked the Four Courts with heavy artillery, finally igniting the long-expected Irish Civil War (Hopkinson, 1988: 112–18.)

THE IRISH CIVIL WAR, 1922–3

The IRA held the advantage over the Provisional Government Army at the outset of the Civil War. The republican side had a significant manpower advantage with approximately 13,000 men, in contrast to the army's 8,000. The IRA also enjoyed the same advantage that it had held against the crown forces during the War of Independence of fighting a guerrilla campaign from its own localities against a regular army that had to force its way into hostile territory. However, these advantages would not last for long as the Provisional Government Army launched a recruitment campaign that would soon lead to it outstripping the IRA's superiority in personnel, and it also had access to ample supplies of arms and ammunition provided by the British Government (Hokpinson, 1988: 127).

The best chance the IRA had of winning the Civil War was in the first couple of months but this opportunity was lost by its adoption of a largely defensive strategy. The initial fighting took place in Dublin, where republicans had occupied a number of prominent buildings, including hotels, appearing not to have learned the lessons of 1916. The bombardment of the Four Courts continued for a week before the republicans evacuated it. In the process a number of leading republicans were captured, including Rory O'Connor, the ring-leader of the occupation, Liam Mellows and Tom Barry, and Cathal Brugha was shot dead, effectively removing an important part of the IRA's leadership cadre for the duration of the conflict. An unintended consequence of the fight for the Four Courts was the destruction of the Irish Public Record Office which was also housed there and which the IRA had used as an ammunition store; the bulk of Irish state papers dating back to the thirteenth century were obliterated. Having cleared the Four Courts, the Provisional Government Army soon regained control of Dublin City and the fighting moved to the countryside (Hopkinson, 1988: 123–5).

Republican resistance was strongest in Munster and Connaught, especially in Kerry, Tipperary, Mayo and Sligo. By August 1922, the army's manpower advantage (recruitment had increased its size to 35,000, and it would eventually reach 50,000) was beginning to tell as it drove southwards into republican territory, re-capturing significant urban centres in Kerry, Cork, Tipperary and Waterford. It also made effective use of coastal landings in Mayo and Kerry. By contrast, the IRA was disjointed and had difficulty maintaining communication channels between its disparate units.

Once more Cumann na mBan members were deployed as despatch carriers but the Provisional Government Army, well aware of how they had acted in a similar capacity in the War of Independence, took a much harder line against them. Over 500 women were imprisoned during the Civil War and many of them undertook hunger strikes at various times in protest against the conditions of their incarceration. One woman, Nan Hogan from Clare, died afterwards as a result of the weakened state of her health (McCoole, 2008: 98, 121). The Irish Government and its army treated republican women much more harshly than the British had during the War of Independence.

The IRA also lacked finance and had to resort to looting, commandeering goods and supplies and bank robberies, all of which made its campaign of resistance increasingly unpopular with the civilian population. The sense of the IRA as outlaws was reinforced by the strong opposition to them from the Roman Catholic Church. In October 1922 the hierarchy stated emphatically its support for the treaty settlement when it issued a pastoral letter recognising the legitimacy of the Provisional Government and declaring that the IRA's campaign lacked 'moral sanction' as a result of which the killing of soldiers of the Provisional Government's Army amounted to 'murder before God'. Republicans were threatened with excommunication and any priests suspected of supporting them would be suspended (Murray, 2000: 75–6).

August 1922 was a pivotal point in the Civil War. The death of Griffith from a brain haemorrhage on 12 August, followed by the killing of Collins in an IRA ambush in west Cork 10 days later, removed the most senior political and military figures on the Provisional Government side. It also ended any slim hope of a negotiated settlement that might still have been a possibility while Collins lived. The new Provisional Government leadership resorted to harsher policies that Collins might not have been prepared to adopt. The IRA's tactics also changed at this time. Recognising the overwhelming advantage held by the army in regard to manpower and munitions, it resorted to outright guerrilla warfare, retreating to rural outposts from which it was more difficult for the army to dislodge it. By September a stalemate had set in. The IRA had lost any chance of winning the war and at best could only hope to hold out long enough to force the Provisional Government to agree to a truce (Hopkinson, 1988: 172–3, 179).

Meanwhile, important political developments had also taken place. On 5 September the Third Dáil convened, but was not attended by the anti-treaty Sinn Féin TDs who continued to recognise the authority of the Second Dáil. In October the anti-treaty politicians established their own cabinet. The principal figures in the Provisional Government were now the President, W. T. Cosgrave, and the Minister for Home Affairs, Kevin O'Higgins. On 28 September 1922 the Dáil passed an emergency powers resolution that signalled its intent to take a tougher line with the IRA [**Doc. 27**]. It empowered the army to set up military courts 'with full powers of enquiring into charges and inflicting punishments on persons found guilty of acts calculated to interfere with or delay the effective establishment of the authority of the Government'. This covered offences such as attacks against the army, looting and unauthorised possession of arms and explosives, for which the military courts were given the authority to impose 'punishment of death or of penal servitude'.

This new policy resulted in the controversial execution of 77 republican prisoners between November 1922 and the end of the war. The first executions took place in Dublin on 17 November when five men who had been caught in possession of arms were shot. One of the highest profile victims was Erskine Childers, who was shot by a firing squad on 24 November after being arrested while in possession of a small automatic pistol that had originally been given to him by Collins. Childers was the publicity minister of the Republican Government and was not active in the IRA. Technically he was in breach of the emergency powers regulations because he was not authorised to carry the gun, though it is difficult to see how he posed any significant military threat to the Provisional Government (Hopkinson, 1988: 189–90). The most controversial executions were those of Rory O'Connor, Dick Barrett, Joe McKelvey and Liam Mellows, carried out in Mountjoy Prison on 8 December, in response to the killing the previous day of a pro-treaty TD, Seán Hales, by the IRA. Incidentally, Hales's brother, Tom, was a leading IRA figure in Cork, illustrating the extent to which the treaty split and the Civil War divided families.

If the executions policy was intended as a deterrent, then it appears to have been effective as no more TDs were targeted by the IRA. The army's Chief-of-Staff, Richard Mulcahy, argued for the executions on the grounds that if they were not official policy, it would be almost impossible to prevent the army from carrying out its own unofficial ones. The policy was also seen by its proponents as essential in protecting a democratically elected government. While the policy did not determine the outcome of the war, it does appear to have hastened its conclusion (Hopkinson, 1988: 191; Kissane, 2005: 87). Yet, this came at a price for the reputation of the government. The IRA was effectively defeated by December 1922, yet executions peaked early in 1923 and continued long after there was any apparent need for them. The choice of victims was also at times bizarre. John Maguire was executed in Mayo in April 1923, yet his older brother, the IRA leader, Tom Maguire, who had been in prison since October 1922 and was undoubtedly a bigger threat to the government, was never executed, suggesting that the authorities were wary of executing certain prominent republicans.

The government's reputation was damaged further by unauthorised atrocities carried out by its forces. The most infamous of these was the killing of eight republican prisoners at Ballyseedy in County Kerry in March 1923. Nine IRA men were tied to land mines and blown up, with only one surviving, having been blown clear of the blast. The killings were a reprisal for the deaths of five soldiers following an IRA booby-trap bomb at nearby Knocknagoshel. In another controversial incident four republicans, including Brian MacNeill, whose father Eoin MacNeill was a minister in the Provisional Government, were shot dead by the army on Benbulben Mountain in Sligo in September 1922. Republican allegations that they were shot after they surrendered are difficult to substantiate but appear to be supported by circumstantial evidence (Farry, 2012: 102; Hopkinson, 1988: 240–1;).

Many of the most controversial incidents carried out in the name of the government were undertaken by its **Criminal Investigation Department (CID)**, 'an armed plain-clothes force' that 'initially combined detective, security, and military and political intelligence functions'. CID's principal targets were republican opponents of the state in Dublin City and it was staffed by a number of Collins's old Squad. It soon earned a reputation for mistreating prisoners and killing republican suspects in controversial circumstances. The most notorious incident that the CID is suspected of involvement with was the killing of Noel Lemass in July 1923. The older brother of the future Fianna Fáil Taoiseach, Seán Lemass, was abducted by plain clothes men in Dublin City in July 1923 and his body was found some months later in the Wicklow Mountains with signs that he had been tortured. His killing was particularly controversial as it took place two months after the end of the Civil War (O'Halpin, 1999: 3–4, 11–14).

Republicans were also responsible for atrocities, including the killing of Dr Thomas O'Higgins, a medical doctor from County Laois, who had no involvement in politics or the Civil War but was targeted because he was the father of Kevin O'Higgins. Sometimes controversial deaths were the result of what was considered to be collateral damage, as in the case of seven-year-old Emmet McGarry, who died when republicans burned down the house of his father, Seán McGarry, who was a member of the Irish Free State Senate (Dolan, 2003: 143; Hopkinson, 1988: 195–6).

Although IRA resistance had effectively ended by early 1923, the war continued, largely because the IRA's Chief-of-Staff, Liam Lynch, refused to surrender. He was shot dead by Free State troops in the Knockmealdown Mountains in County Tipperary on 10 April 1923 and soon afterwards, on 24 May, his successor, Frank Aiken, ordered a ceasefire. The IRA did not surrender or give up its arms, but simply ended its campaign and melted away.

The most enduring legacy of the Irish Civil War is undoubtedly the cleavage in Irish politics. For the remainder of the twentieth century the two largest parties in the state were Fianna Fáil (formed after a split in anti-treaty Sinn Féin in 1926) and Fine Gael, the direct descendant of **Cumann na nGaedheal**

Criminal Investigation Department (CID): Free State intelligence unit that operated during the Civil War and earned a reputation for ill-treatment and controversial killings of republicans.

Cumann na nGaedheal: Political party formed in 1922 from pro-treaty Sinn Féin.

and pro-treaty Sinn Féin. This remained the case until the Irish general election of 2011, when Fianna Fáil was overtaken by Labour as the second largest party. The Civil War division continued to overshadow Irish politics until the 1970s, by which time the revolutionary generation had retired or died. The deaths of prominent revolutionaries during the Civil War deprived the fledgling state of the important political talent of people like Collins, Griffith, Childers, Brugha and Harry Boland (who was shot dead in July 1922). The bitterness that resulted from the atrocities carried out on both sides was one of the more tragic legacies of the short fratricidal conflict.

EPILOGUE: THE CONSOLIDATION OF THE TWO IRELANDS, 1923–5

Another legacy of the Civil War was the consolidation of democratic rule in the new state. The first serious threat to its existence had been overcome. This was followed in 1924 by the quashing of an army mutiny, precipitated by a small number of Free State soldiers who were unhappy with army demobilisation and reorganisation after the Civil War and who felt that the Cumann na nGaedheal Government had drifted too far from Collins's agenda for seeking an end to partition. By the end of 1924 the mutineers and their supporters in government had been purged and the principle of civilian control of the army established beyond doubt. While elements of the IRA survived in the south and had brief moments of activity, including the assassination of Kevin O'Higgins in 1927, skirmishes with the Blueshirts in the early 1930s, some dalliances with the Nazis during the 1940s and an ultimately unsuccessful border campaign between 1956 and 1962, the republican army never again posed a serious threat to the southern Irish state until the Northern Irish troubles in the 1970s.

Anti-treaty republicans began to lose their political influence as the resonance of the Civil War faded and their boycott of the Dáil exempted them from political power. In the general election of August 1923 they won 44 Dáil seats (out of 153) and 27.4 per cent of the vote, but support dropped off noticeably after this and they won only four of the 19 seats contested in by-elections held between 1923 and 1926. By this time de Valera was considering the circumstances under which Sinn Féin could enter the Dáil if the oath was removed. However, many in Sinn Féin remained opposed to this move in principle, irrespective of the oath, leading de Valera to initiate another split in Sinn Féin and establish the new Fianna Fáil Party in March 1926 (Murphy, 1991: 145–56).

Fianna Fáil attracted many republicans who felt that Sinn Féin's refusal to recognise the state was impractical, that the party had failed to develop a coherent economic and social policy to challenge the middle-class dominance of Cumann na nGaedheal, and also failed to protect the interests of republican supporters (Dunphy, 1995: 73). Its popularity was reflected in the June 1927 general election, where it won 44 seats in comparison to Cumann na nGaedheal's 47. The oath prevented the Fianna Fáil TDs from taking their seats but this was short-lived as legislation passed after the death of O'Higgins forced their hand on this issue. They took their seats in the Dáil on 27 August 1927, having previously gone through a convoluted process of signing a book with the oath rather than reciting it.

This symbolic action did little to damage the party's support and it won 57 seats in a second general election held the following month. Cumann na nGaedheal remained the largest party with 62 seats but the growth of Fianna Fáil boded ill for the government's future and culminated in the defeat of Cumann na nGaedheal by Fianna Fáil in the 1932 general election. The decision of Fianna Fáil to enter the Dáil in 1927 and provide constitutional republican opposition to the Cumann na nGaedheal Government, and its victory in 1932 accompanied by a peaceful handover of power, brought the majority of republicans into the political fold and further strengthened democratic government in the Irish Free State. De Valera subsequently embarked on a project of dismantling the objectionable aspects of the treaty, paving the way for effective independence for Ireland in 1937 and the eventual declaration of a republic in 1949.

At the same time that civil war was breaking out in southern Ireland the conflict in Northern Ireland was subsiding as the IRA faced up to the failure of its offensive against the Northern Government and the southern leaders on both sides of the split became more preoccupied with events in Dublin. The security arrangements put in place by Craig's government also proved effective in quashing nationalist violence. In addition to the Special Constabulary, a new permanent police force, the Royal Ulster Constabulary (RUC), was established in mid-1922 and its deployment forced the IRA to abandon much of its planned assault. It was originally intended that one-third of the new force would be Catholic but this level was never achieved, due in part to Catholic reluctance as well as the clear sense that they were not welcome (Hennessey, 1997: 33).

Improved policing was supported by draconian legislation with the enactment of the Civil Authority (Special Powers) Act in April 1922, which gave a very wide remit to the Northern Ireland Minister for Home Affairs to make regulations 'for the preservation of the peace and maintenance of order' and allowed for stiff punishments including internment, flogging and death. It was initially introduced for one year but was renewed every year until 1928 and eventually made permanent in 1933. It was used disproportionately against Catholics and became one of the major grievances of the nationalist population with the Unionist-dominated government of Northern Ireland. Demands for its abolition formed an integral part of the demands of the civil rights movement in the 1960s but it was not repealed until 1973 after the introduction of direct rule (Jackson, 1999: 338–9, 373).

The next threat to the survival of Northern Ireland came from the boundary commission. Negotiations on its establishment began in 1924 but Northern Ireland refused to appoint a representative. The British Government appointed a former barrister and journalist, J. R. Fisher, to represent Northern Ireland's interests, while the Irish Free State chose the Minister for Education, Eoin MacNeill, as its representative, and both governments agreed on a South African judge, Richard Feetham, as chairman. The treaty had set the delegates the task of determining the border between the two Irelands 'in accordance with the wishes of the inhabitants', while also ensuring that this was 'compatible with economic and geographic conditions'. The remit was vague and these conditions were also contradictory in many cases [**Doc. 24**].

The commission met and gathered evidence throughout 1924 and 1925 before writing its report in October 1925. The leaking of the report to the British *Morning Post* newspaper caused outrage in the Free State when it emerged that there would be only minor transfers of territory between both polities. Crucially, the nationalist enclaves of Newry, Derry City, South Down and parts of Fermanagh and Tyrone would all remain within Northern Ireland. The controversy resulted in a decision by the British and Irish Free State Governments to suppress the report and leave the existing 26–6 county border in tact. The failure of the Boundary Commission was the last chance the Free State had of using the treaty settlement to end partition and much of the blame fell on MacNeill, who subsequently resigned (Jackson, 1999: 342–3).

By the end of 1925 the settlement of the Irish question brought about by both the Government of Ireland Act and the Anglo-Irish Treaty was firmly in place. A unified Ireland that had begun the twentieth century as an integral part of the United Kingdom had been sundered by ethnic, political, religious and ideological divisions into two distinct polities – a home rule entity in Northern Ireland governing the six of Ulster's nine counties that contained the largest Protestant populations, and an effectively independent dominion in the Irish Free State that enjoyed a much greater level of sovereignty over the 26 counties it ruled. Both had seen off early threats to their existence and both were characterised by the dominance of one religious group to the detriment of the minority. From a British point of view the Irish question was largely solved but the solution contained the seeds of a later conflict.

GUIDE TO FURTHER READING

The full text of the Anglo-Irish Treaty and numerous other documents relating to it can be found on the website of the National Archives of Ireland www.treaty.nationalarchives.ie. The Dáil debate on the treaty is also online at www.historical-debates.oireachtas.ie/index.htm.

The weakness of the Dublin Castle administration is discussed in Eunan O'Halpin's, *The Decline of the Union: British Government in Ireland, 1892–1920* (Gill and Macmillan, 1987), while Michael Hopkinson's edited version of the Sturgis diaries – *The Last Days of Dublin Castle: The Diaries of Mark Sturgis* (Irish Academic Press, 1999) – highlights the changes resulting from the introduction of British civil servants in 1920.

Michael Laffan's, *The Partition of Ireland, 1911–1925* (Dundalgan Press, Dundalk) charts the evolution of the Government of Ireland Act of 1920 and Frank Pakenham's (Lord Longford), *Peace by Ordeal: The Negotiation of the Anglo-Irish Treaty, 1921* (Sidgwick and Jackson, 1972) remains the standard work on the treaty negotiations.

Michael Hopkinson's, *Green Against Green: The Irish Civil War* (Gill and Macmillan, 1988) is the best treatment of the Civil War, including the political and military split that led to it. Collins's abortive northern offensive of early 1922 is analysed in detail by Robert Lynch in *The Northern IRA and the Early Years of Partition, 1920–1922* (Irish Academic Press, 2006).

Part 3

DOCUMENTS

Document 1   THE THIRD HOME RULE BILL

The third home rule bill became law on 18 September 1914 but was suspended for the duration of the war. It was never implemented and was replaced by the Government of Ireland Act (1920). The following sections illustrate the limited jurisdiction of an Irish Home Rule Parliament and the provisions aimed at protecting the Protestant minority.

An Act to Provide for the Better Government of Ireland, 4 & 5 Geo. V, Ch. 90 (18 September 1914)

2. Subject to the provisions of this Act, the Irish Parliament shall have power to make laws for the peace, order, and good government of Ireland with the following limitations, namely, that they shall not have power to make laws except in respect of matters exclusively relating to Ireland or some part thereof, and (without prejudice to the general limitation) they shall not have power to make laws in respect of the following matters in particular, or any of them, namely:

(1) The Crown, or succession to the Crown, or a Regency . . .
(2) The making of peace or war or matters arising from a state of war . . .
(3) The navy, the army, the territorial force, or any other naval or military force, or the defence of the realm . . .
(4) Treaties, or any relations, with Foreign States, or relations with other parts of His Majesty's dominions . . .
(5) Dignities or titles of honour . . .
(6) Treason, treason felony, alienage, naturalisation . . .
(7) Trade with any place out of Ireland . . .
(8) Any post services . . .
(9) Lighthouses, buoys, or beacons . . .
(10) Coinage . . .
(11) Trademarks . . .

3. In the exercise of their power to make laws under this Act the Irish Parliament shall not make a law so as either directly or indirectly to establish or endow any religion, or prohibit or restrict the free exercise thereof, or give a preference, privilege, or advantage, or impose any disability or disadvantage, on account of religious belief or religious or ecclesiastical status, or make any religious belief or religious ceremony a condition of the validity of any marriage, or affect prejudicially the right of any child to attend a school receiving public money without attending the religious instruction at that school, or alter the constitution of any religious body except where the alteration is approved on behalf of the religious body by the governing body thereof . . .

Source: Alan O'Day, *Irish Home Rule, 1867–1921*, Manchester: Manchester University Press, 1998, pp. 322–3.

THE ULSTER SOLEMN LEAGUE AND COVENANT AND THE WOMEN'S DECLARATION **Document 2**

The Ulster Covenant was signed by 237,268 men on Ulster Day, 28 September 1912. A separate Declaration was signed by 234,046 women.

Covenant:

Being convinced in our consciences that Home Rule would be disastrous to the material well-being of Ulster as well as the whole of Ireland, subversive of our civil and religious freedom, destructive of our citizenship, and perilous to the unity of the Empire, we, whose names are underwritten, men of Ulster loyal subjects of His Gracious Majesty King George V., humbly relying on the God whom our fathers in days of stress and trial confidently trusted, do hereby pledge ourselves in solemn Covenant, throughout this our time of threatened calamity, to stand by one another in defending, for ourselves and our children, our cherished position of equal citizenship in the United Kingdom, and in using all means which may be found necessary to defeat the present conspiracy to set up a Home Rule Parliament in Ireland. And in the event of such a Parliament being forced upon us, we further solemnly and mutually pledge ourselves to refuse to recognise its authority. In sure confidence that God will defend the right, we hereto subscribe our names.

And further, we individually declare that we have not already signed this Covenant.

Declaration:

We, whose names are underwritten, women of Ulster, and loyal subjects of our gracious King, being firmly persuaded that Home Rule would be disastrous to our Country, desire, to associate ourselves with the men of Ulster in their uncompromising opposition to the Home Rule Bill now before Parliament, whereby it is proposed to drive Ulster out of her cherished place in the constitution of the United Kingdom, and to place her under the domination and control of a Parliament in Ireland.

Praying that from this calamity God will save Ireland, we hereto subscribe our names.

Source: Archives of the Ulster Unionist Council, Public Record Office of Northern Ireland, http://www.proni.gov.uk/index/search_the_archives/ulster_covenant.htm

JOHN REDMOND'S WOODENBRIDGE SPEECH **Document 3**

A speech delivered by John Redmond, MP, leader of the Irish Parliamentary Party, to a group of 500 Irish Volunteers at Woodenbridge in County

Wicklow, on Sunday, 20 September 1914, encouraging Irish Volunteers to enlist in the army.

Wicklow Volunteers in spite of the peaceful happiness and beauty of the scene in which we stand, remember this country at this moment is in a state of war, and your duty is two-fold. Your duty is, at all costs to defend the shores of Ireland from foreign invasion. It is a duty, more than that of taking care that Irish valour proves itself on the field of war, as it has always proved itself in the past. The interests of Ireland as a whole are at stake in this war. This war is undertaken in defence of the highest principles of religion, morality and right, and it would be a disgrace for ever to our country, a reproach to her manhood, and a denial of the lessons of her history, if young Irishmen confined their efforts to remaining at home to defend the shores of Ireland from an unlikely invasion and shrinking from the duty of proving upon the field of battle that gallantry and courage which have distinguished your race all through its history. I say to you, therefore, your duty is two-fold. I am glad to see such magnificent material for soldiers around me, and I say to you, go on drilling and make yourselves efficient, and then account yourselves as men, not only in Ireland itself, but wherever the firing line extends in defence of right, of freedom and religion in this war.

Source: Irish Independent, 21 September 1914.

Document 4   FIANNA ÉIREANN AND THE RISING

Gary Holohan describes the attack on the Magazine Fort at the Phoenix Park by members of the Volunteers and Fianna Éireann disguised as footballers.

After a few minutes chat together, as if we were a football team with followers, we moved around the front of the [Magazine] Fort in a casual way, some of the lads kicking a ball from one to the other. When we got near the gate we rushed the sentry who was standing outside, and then another party rushed in and took the guard room completely by surprise. I was detailed off with Barney Mellows to take the sentry on the parapet. I rushed straight through the fort, which is a rather large place, and I had some difficulty in locating him. I eventually saw him looking at me over the roof. He came towards me with his bayonet pointed towards me. I fired a shot and he fell . . . We took the guard's rifles and went to the waiting hackney car . . . I followed behind the car on my bicycle. As the car turned towards the gate leading to the Chapelizod Road we noticed a youth of about 17 [*sic*] years of age running towards the gate.* He stopped and spoke to the policeman who was in the middle of the road directing traffic, and then ran away in the middle of the road toward Islandbridge. I left the hack and followed him, and when he got to the corner of Islandbridge Road he ran towards one of the big houses, evidently with the intention of giving the alarm. I jumped off my bicycle, and just as the door opened I shot him from the gate . . .

*This individual was erroneously identified as Gerald Playfair (14), son of the magazine fort's commandant. New research has shown that he was an elder brother, George Playfair (23) (Duffy, 2013: 35)

Source: Fearghal McGarry, *Rebels: Voices from the Easter Rising*, London: Penguin, 2011, p. 162.

THE 1916 PROCLAMATION   **Document 5**

The Proclamation of the Irish Republic, read by Patrick Pearse outside the General Post Office on Easter Monday, 1916.

POBLACHT NA H EIREANN
THE PROVISIONAL GOVERNMENT
of the
REPUBLIC OF IRELAND
TO THE PEOPLE OF IRELAND

IRISHMEN AND IRISHWOMEN. In the name of God and the dead generations from which she receives her old tradition of nationhood, Ireland, through us, summons her children to her flag and strikes for her freedom.

Having organised and trained her manhood through her secret revolutionary organisation, the Irish Republican Brotherhood, and through her open military organisations, the Irish Volunteers and the Irish Citizen Army, having patiently perfected her discipline, having resolutely waited for the right moment to reveal itself, she now seizes that moment, and, supported by her exiled children in America and by gallant allies in Europe, but relying in the first on her own strength, she strikes in full confidence of victory.

We declare the right of the people of Ireland to the ownership of Ireland, and to the unfettered control of Irish destinies, to be sovereign and indefeasible. The long usurpation of that right by a foreign people and government has not extinguished the right, nor can it ever be extinguished except by the destruction of the Irish people. In every generation the Irish people have asserted their right to national freedom and sovereignty, six times in the past three hundred years they have asserted it in arms. Standing on that fundamental right and again asserting it in arms in the face of the world, we hereby proclaim the Irish Republic as a Sovereign Independent State, and we pledge our lives and the lives of our comrades-in-arms to the cause of its freedom, of its welfare, and its exaltation among the nations.

The Irish Republic is entitled to, and herby claims, the allegiance of every Irishman and Irishwoman. The Republic guarantees religious and civil liberty, equal rights and equal opportunities to all its citizens, and declares its resolve to pursue the happiness and prosperity of the whole nation and of all its parts, cherishing all the children of the nation equally, and oblivious of the differences carefully fostered by an alien government, which have divided a minority from the majority in the past.

Until our arms have brought the opportune moment for the establishment of a permanent National Government, representative of the whole people of Ireland and elected by the suffrages of all her men and women, the Provisional Government, hereby constituted, will administer the civil and military affairs of the Republic in trust for the people.

We place the cause of the Irish Republic under the protection of the Most High God, Whose blessing we invoke upon our arms, and we pray that no one who serves that cause will dishonour it by cowardice, inhumanity, or rapine. In this supreme hour the Irish nation must, by its valour and discipline and by the readiness of its children to sacrifice themselves for the common good, prove itself worthy of the august destiny to which it is called

Signed on Behalf of the Provisional Government

THOMAS J. CLARKE, SEAN MacDIARMADA, THOMAS MacDONAGH, P. H. PEARSE, EAMONN CEANNT, JAMES CONNOLLY, JOSEPH PLUNKETT

Source: Liam de Paor, *On the Easter Proclamation and Other Declarations*, Dublin: Four Courts Press, 1997.

Document 6   THE DEMOCRATIC PROGRAMME

Document adopted by the First Dáil on 21 January 1919, setting out the Dáil's social policy.

We declare in the words of the Irish Republican Proclamation the right of the people of Ireland to the ownership of Ireland, and to the unfettered control of Irish destinies to be indefeasible, and in the language of our first President, Pádraig Mac Phiarais [Patrick Pearse], we declare that the nation's sovereignty extends not only to all men and women of the Nation, but to all its material possessions, the Nation's soil and all its resources, all the wealth and all the wealth-producing processes within the Nation, and with him we reaffirm that all right to private property must be subordinated to the public right and welfare.

We declare that we desire our country to be ruled in accordance with the principles of Liberty, Equality, and Justice for all, which alone can secure permanence of Government in the willing adhesion of the people.

We affirm the duty of every man and woman to give allegiance and service to the Commonwealth, and declare it is the duty of the Nation to assure that every citizen shall have opportunity to spend his or her strength and faculties in the service of the people. In return for willing service, we, in the name of the Republic, declare the right of every citizen to an adequate share of the produce of the Nation's labour.

It shall be the first duty of the Government of the Republic to make provision for the physical, mental and spiritual well-being of the children, to secure that no child shall suffer hunger or cold from lack of food, clothing, or shelter, but that all shall be provided with the means and facilities requisite for their proper education and training as Citizens of a Free and Gaelic Ireland.

The Irish Republic fully realises the necessity of abolishing the present odious, degrading and foreign Poor Law System, substituting therefore a sympathetic native scheme for the care of the Nation's aged and infirm, who shall not be regarded as a burden, but rather entitled to the Nation's gratitude and consideration. Likewise it shall be the duty of the Republic to take such measures as will safeguard the health of the people and ensure the physical as well as the moral well-being of the Nation.

It shall be our duty to promote the development of the Nation's resources, to increase the productivity of its soil, to exploit its mineral deposits, peat bogs, and fisheries, its waterways and harbours, in the interests and for the benefit of the Irish people.

It shall be the duty of the Republic to adopt all measures necessary for the recreation and invigoration of our Industries, and to ensure their being developed on the most beneficial and progressive co-operative and industrial lines. With the adoption of an extensive Irish Consular Service, trade with foreign Nations shall be revived on terms of mutual advantage and goodwill, and while undertaking the organisation of the Nation's trade, import and export, it shall be the duty of the Republic to prevent the shipment from Ireland of food and other necessaries until the wants of the Irish people are fully satisfied and the future provided for.

It shall also devolve upon the National Government to seek co-operation of the Governments of other countries in determining a standard of Social and Industrial Legislation with a view to a general and lasting improvement in the conditions under which the working classes live and labour.

Source: *Dáil Debates*, vol. F (21 January 1919), cols 22–3 historical-debates.oireachtas.ie.

Document 7   JOHN DILLON CRITICISES THE BRITISH RESPONSE TO THE RISING

On 11 May, the day before the last executions, John Dillon, the most senior figure in the IPP after Redmond, delivered a speech that highlighted how the executions and the killing of Francis Sheehy Skeffington were turning Irish public opinion against the government.

I asked the Prime Minister, first of all, whether he would give a pledge that the executions should stop. That he declined to give. Secondly, I asked him whether he could tell whether any executions had taken place in Ireland since Monday morning; the last we had official notification of before I left there. The reply of the Prime Minister was: 'No, Sir, so far as I know, not.' On Monday twelve executions had been made public. Since then, in spite of the statement of the Prime Minister, I have received word that a man named Kent had been executed in Fermoy, which is the first execution that has taken place outside Dublin. The fact is one which will create a very grave shock in Ireland, because it looks like a roving commission to carry these horrible executions all over the country.

. . . [on the killing of Francis Sheehy Skeffington] All Dublin was ringing with this affair for days. It came to our knowledge within two or three days after the shooting. And are we to be told that this is the excuse for what has occurred? A more lurid light on military law in Ireland could not possibly be imagined than that a man is to be shot in Portobello Barracks – it must have been known to at least 300 or 400 military men, the whole city of Dublin knew it, his poor wife was denied all knowledge of it until her husband was lying buried in the barrack yard for three or four days – and the military authorities in Dublin turn round and say they knew nothing whatever about it until the 6th of May.

. . . the horrible rumours which are current in Dublin, and which are doing untold and indescribable mischief, maddening the population of Dublin, who were your friends and loyal allies against this insurrection last week and who are rapidly becoming embittered by the stories afloat and these executions – I say the facts of this case [Sheehy Skeffington] disclose a most serious state of things.

. . . Yesterday a son of my own, a boy of seventeen and a half years of age, went to the military officer in Dublin to get a pass to enable him to go to Kingstown. He happens to be a lad who asked my own permission to allow him to join the British Army on his seventeenth birthday, and I gave him permission to join when he was eighteen. He will never join it now, and there are tens of thousands like him in Ireland.

. . . If you had passed a Military Service Bill for Ireland, it would have taken 150,000 men and three months' hard fighting to have dealt with it. It is not a Military Service Bill that you want in Ireland; it is to find a way to the hearts of the Irish people, and when you do that you will find that you have got a supply of the best troops in the whole world. How can we, in the face of these facts, accept the statement of the Prime Minister, that according to the best of his knowledge no men are being secretly shot in Ireland? The fact of the matter is that what is poisoning the mind of Ireland, and rapidly poisoning it, is the secrecy of these trials and the continuance of these executions.

. . . As I say, there were some very bad actions, but as regards the main body of the insurgents, their conduct was beyond reproach as fighting men. I admit they were wrong; I know they were wrong; but they fought a clean fight, and they fought with superb bravery and skill, and no act of savagery or act against the usual customs of war that I know of has been brought home to any leader or any organised body of insurgents. I have not heard of a single act. I may be wrong, but that is my impression.

. . . I do not come here to raise one word in defence of murder. If there be a case of cold-blooded murder, by all means try the man openly, before a court-martial if you like, but let the public know what the evidence is and prove that he is a murderer, and then do what you like with him. But it is not murderers who are being executed; it is insurgents who have fought a clean fight, a brave fight, however misguided, and it would be a damned good thing for you if your soldiers were able to put up as good a fight as did these men in Dublin – three thousand men against twenty thousand with machine-guns and artillery.

Source: *Hansard Parliamentary Debates, House of Commons*, 11 May 1916.

THE EXTENSION OF CONSCRIPTION TO IRELAND   **Document 8**

This Act made provision for the extension of conscription, introduced to Britain in 1916, to Ireland and raised the maximum age from 41 to 51. John Dillon led the IPP out of Parliament in protest at its enactment.

Military Service (No. 2) Act, 1918, 8 Geo. V, Ch. 5: An Act to make further provision with respect to Military Service during the present war.

Section 1. Every male British subject who has, at any time since the fourteenth day of August nineteen hundred and fifteen, been, or who for the time being is, in Great Britain, and who at the date of the passing of this Act has attained the age of eighteen years and has not attained the age of fifty-one years, or who at any subsequent date attains the age of eighteen years, shall, unless he is for the time being within the exceptions set out in the First Schedule to this Act*, be deemed . . . to have been duly enlisted in His Majesty's regular forces for general service . . .

Section 2. His Majesty may by Order in Council extend this Act to Ireland, and this Act if so extended shall, subject to such modifications and adaptations as made by the Order for the purpose of making it applicable to Ireland, have effect accordingly.

*Residents of the dominions; members of the regular or reserve forces; members of the Navy, Royal Marines or Air Force; disabled men; men in holy orders or ministers of religion.

Source: Statutes (1918), pp. 7–12.

Document 9   IRISH ROMAN CATHOLIC BISHOPS OPPOSE CONSCRIPTION

This unanimous statement was issued on behalf of the Irish Roman Catholic hierarchy on 9 April 1918, a week before the Military Service Bill to extend conscription to Ireland was passed.

Statements have recently been appearing in the Press to indicate that the Government intend to include this country in a measure of conscription. Whether there is any foundation for these rumours we know not at the moment. But since the outbreak of hostilities four years ago the War Office has shown such utter lack of real touch with Irish conditions that it is quite possible something may be now proposed which, if attempted, would only crown the disasters which want of knowledge and want of sympathy have already entailed. To enforce conscription here without the consent of the people would be perfectly unwarrantable, and would soon and inevitably end in defeating its own purposes.

Had the Government in any reasonable time given Ireland the benefit of the principles, which are declared to be at stake in the war, by the concession of a full measure of self-government, there would have been no occasion for contemplating forced levies from her now. What between mismanagement and mischief-making this country has already been deplorably upset, and it would be a fatal mistake, surpassing the worst blunders of the past four years, to furnish a telling plea now for desperate courses by an attempt to enforce conscription. With all the responsibility that attaches to our pastoral office we feel bound to warn the Government against entering upon a policy so disastrous to the public interest, and to all order, public and private.

Source: Irish Independent, 10 April 1918.

EXTRACTS FROM SINN FÉIN'S MANIFESTO FOR THE 1918   **Document 10**
GENERAL ELECTION

The manifesto issued by the Sinn Féin Party for the 1918 general election, outlining the party's intention to abstain from Westminster and establish a breakaway constituent assembly in Ireland.

GENERAL ELECTION. MANIFESTO TO THE IRISH PEOPLE
THE coming General Election is fraught with possibilities for the future of our nation. Ireland is faced with the question whether this generation wills it that she is to march out into the full sunlight of freedom, or is to remain in the shadow of a base imperialism that has brought and ever will bring in its train naught but evil for our race.

Sinn Féin gives Ireland the opportunity of vindicating her honour and pursuing with renewed confidence the path of national salvation by rallying to the flag of the Irish Republic.

Sinn Féin aims at securing the establishment of that Republic

1. By withdrawing the Irish Representation from the British Parliament and by denying the right and opposing the will of the British Government or any other foreign Government to legislate for Ireland.
2. By making use of any and every means available to render impotent the power of England to hold Ireland in subjection by military force or otherwise.
3. By the establishment of a constituent assembly comprising persons chosen by the Irish constituencies as the supreme national authority to speak and act in the name of the Irish people, and to develop Ireland's social, political and industrial life, for the welfare of the whole people of Ireland.
4. By appealing to the Peace Conference for the establishment of Ireland as an independent nation . . .

. . . ISSUED BY THE STANDING COMMITTEE OF SINN FÉIN

Source: National Library of Ireland, Ms. 25,588(54).

THE CONSTITUTION OF DÁIL ÉIREANN   **Document 11**

The constitution governing the legislative and executive functions of the First Dáil, read in Irish only at its inaugural meeting on 19 January 1921.

Article 1
All legislative powers shall be vested in Dáil Éireann, composed of Deputies, elected by the Irish people from the existing Irish Parliamentary constituencies.

Article 2

(a) All executive powers shall be vested in the members, for the time being, of the Ministry.

(b) The Ministry shall consist of a President of the Ministry, elected by Dáil Éireann, and four Executive Officers, viz:

A Secretary of Finance

A Secretary of Home Affairs

A Secretary of Foreign Affairs

A Secretary of National Defence

Each of whom the President shall nominate and have power to dismiss.

(c) Every member of the Ministry shall be a member of Dáil Éirean, and shall at all times be responsible to the Dáil.

(d) At the first meeting of Dáil Éireann after their nomination by the President, the names of the Executive Officers shall be separately submitted to Dáil Éireann for approval.

(e) The appointment of the President shall date from his election, and the appointment of each Executive Officer from the date of the approval by the Dáil of his nomination.

(f) The Ministry or any member thereof may at any time be removed by vote of the Dáil upon motion for that specific purpose, provided, that at least seven days notice in writing of that motion shall have been given.

Article 3

A Chairman elected annually by the Dáil, and in his absence a Deputy Chairman so elected, shall preside at all meetings of Dáil Éireann. Only members of the Dáil shall be eligible for these offices. In case of the absence of the Chairman and Deputy Chairman the Dáil shall fill the vacancies or elect a temporary Chairman.

Article 4

All monies required by the Ministry shall be obtained on vote of the Dáil. The Ministry shall be responsible to the Dáil for all monies so obtained, and shall present properly audited accounts for the expenditure of the same – twice yearly – in the months of May and November. The audit shall be conducted by an Auditor or Auditors appointed by the Dáil. No member of the Dáil shall be eligible for such appointment.

Article 5

This Constitution is provisional and is liable to alteration upon seven days written notice of motion for that specific purpose.

Source: B. Farrell, 'A note on the Dáil Constitution, 1919', in *Irish Jurist*, new series, vol. IV (1969), pp. 135–6.

THE DECLARATION OF INDEPENDENCE **Document 12**

One of the four foundation documents of the First Dáil, promulgated at its inaugural sitting on 21 January 1919, invoking Ireland's historic right to independence, recently asserted by the Easter Rising and the 1918 general election.

Whereas the Irish people is by right a free people:

And Whereas for seven hundred years the Irish people has never ceased to repudiate and has repeatedly protested in arms against foreign usurpation:

And Whereas English rule in this country is, and always has been, based upon force and fraud and maintained by military occupation against the declared will of the people:

And Whereas the Irish Republic was proclaimed in Dublin on Easter Monday, 1916, by the Irish Republican Army acting on behalf of the Irish people:

And Whereas the Irish people is resolved to secure and maintain its complete independence in order to promote the common weal, to re-establish justice, to provide for future defence, to insure peace at home and goodwill with all nations and to constitute a national polity based upon the people's will with equal right and equal opportunity for every citizen:

And Whereas at the threshold of a new era in history the Irish electorate has in the General Election of December, 1918, seized the first occasion to declare by an overwhelming majority its firm allegiance to the Irish Republic:

Now, therefore, we, the elected Representatives of the ancient Irish people in National Parliament assembled, do, in the name of the Irish nation, ratify the establishment of the Irish Republic and pledge ourselves and our people to make this declaration effective by every means at our command:

We ordain that the elected Representatives of the Irish people alone have power to make laws binding on the people of Ireland, and that the Irish Parliament is the only Parliament to which that people will give its allegiance:

We solemnly declare foreign government in Ireland to be an invasion of our national right which we will never tolerate, and we demand the evacuation of our country by the English Garrison:

We claim for our national independence the recognition and support of every free nation in the world, and we proclaim that independence to be a condition precedent to international peace hereafter:

In the name of the Irish people we humbly commit our destiny to Almighty God who gave our fathers the courage and determination to persevere through long centuries of a ruthless tyranny, and strong in the justice of the cause which they have handed down to us, we ask His divine blessing on this the last stage of the struggle we have pledged ourselves to carry through to Freedom.

Source: Documents on Irish Foreign Policy Project, http://www.difp.ie/docs/Volume1/1919/1.htm

Document 13   THE MESSAGE TO THE FREE NATIONS OF THE WORLD

Document promulgated by the First Dáil on 21 January 1919, calling for international support of Irish independence and recognition of it by the Paris Peace Conference.

To the Nations of the World!
Greeting.

The Nation of Ireland having proclaimed her national independence, calls through her elected representatives in Parliament assembled in the Irish Capital on January 21st, 1919, upon every free nation to support the Irish Republic by recognising Ireland's national status and her right to its vindication at the Peace Congress.

Nationally, the race, the language, the customs and traditions of Ireland are radically distinct from the English. Ireland is one of the most ancient nations in Europe, and she has preserved her national integrity, vigorous and intact, through seven centuries of foreign oppression: she has never relinquished her national rights, and throughout the long era of English usurpation she has in every generation defiantly proclaimed her inalienable right of nationhood down to her last glorious resort to arms in 1916.

Internationally, Ireland is the gateway of the Atlantic. Ireland is the last outpost of Europe towards the West: Ireland is the point upon which great trade routes between East and West converge: her independence is demanded by the Freedom of the Seas: her great harbours must be open to all nations, instead of being the monopoly of England. To-day these harbours are empty and idle solely because English policy is determined to retain Ireland as a barren bulwark for English aggrandisement, and the unique geographical position of this island, far from being a benefit and safeguard to Europe and America, is subjected to the purposes of England's policy of world domination.

Ireland to-day reasserts her historic nationhood the more confidently before the new world emerging from the War, because she believes in freedom and justice as the fundamental principles of international law, because she believes in a frank co-operation between the peoples for equal rights against the vested privileges of ancient tyrannies, because the permanent peace of Europe can never be secured by perpetuating military dominion for the profit of empire but only by establishing the control of government in every land upon the basis of the free will of a free people, and the existing state of war, between Ireland and England, can never be ended until Ireland is definitely evacuated by the armed forces of England.

For these among other reasons, Ireland – resolutely and irrevocably determined at the dawn of the promised era of self-determination and liberty that she will suffer foreign dominion no longer – calls upon every free nation to uphold her national claim to complete independence as an Irish Republic against the arrogant pretensions of England founded in fraud and sustained only by an overwhelming military occupation, and demands to be confronted publicly with England at the Congress of the Nations, in order that the civilised world having judged between English wrong and Irish right may guarantee to Ireland its permanent support for the maintenance of her national independence.

Source: Documents on Irish Foreign Policy Project, http://www.difp.ie/docs/Volume1/1919/2.htm

EXCERPTS FROM THE *IRISH BULLETIN*   **Document 14**

The Irish Bulletin was produced by the Dáil's Department of Publicity and edited by Desmond FitzGerald and later by Erskine Childers. It was the most important organ of republican publicity and propaganda during the revolution.

'Eighteen Innocent Men Murdered in Twenty-one Days'
By organised murder the English Military Government in Ireland is endeavouring to break the National Movement for independence. It is well to follow step by step this organisation of murder.

After twenty-seven Irish men and women had been done to death by English Agents during the 36 months of 1917–18–19 and the first three months of 1920, in March 1920 a murder gang was created within the English Police Force in Ireland. Its first victim was Alderman Thomas MacCurtain, Lord Mayor of Cork. Two others were murdered within the following week. Five were murdered in April; one in May and two up to June 19th. Progress was slow. The police feared public exposure before a Coroner's Court. On June 19th and on following days, an effort was made by their Chief Officials to reassure those timorous police. One of the Divisional Commissioners of the Royal Irish Constabulary informed the men stationed at various barracks in Munster that they might kill without fear. At Listowel, Co. Kerry, on June 19th he said:

'You may make mistakes occasionally and innocent persons may be shot, but that cannot be helped; and you are bound to get the right parties sometime. The more you shoot, the better I will like you, and I assure you, men, no policeman will get into trouble for shooting any man.'

. . . Similar statements are known to have been made to the police by other police officials in other parts of Ireland. These promises had a marked effect. The murders jumped from one in the month of May and three in the month of June to FIFTEEN in the month of July . . . SIXTY-TWO Irishmen and women – none of whom was killed in armed conflicts with English military or police – have been murdered in the nine months of 1920. The murderers, with one single exception, are still in active service of the English Military Government in Ireland.

Source: Irish Bulletin, 7 October 1920.

Document 15   ARTHUR GRIFFITH ON NATIONAL COURTS OF LAW

In 1906 Griffith published a pamphlet entitled 'The Sinn Féin Policy', outlining the policies that should be pursued by an independent Irish Parliament. These included the establishment of national arbitration courts, a policy that was subsequently implemented by the First Dáil.

And not less important to the nation than a National Civil Service are NATIONAL COURTS OF LAW . . . The prestige, the dignity, the strength such a national legal system would confer upon a movement for national independence is obvious; but in addition it would deprive the corrupt bar of Ireland of much of its incentive to corruption, save the pockets of our people, and materially help in bringing about that spirit of brotherhood – of national one-ness in Ireland which all who love their country desire to see . . . Eighty per cent of the cases which are now heard in the Civil Courts of Ireland, involving the expenditure by the people of an enormous sum of money which is utilised to keep up a corrupt judicial system, could be equally as *legally* decided in voluntary arbitration courts at no expense at all. The proposal then is this: That the Irish National Assembly shall appoint those of its members who by virtue of their positions are Justices of the Peace, but who decline to act as such under British law, to act as judges in the National Arbitration Courts, together with such men of character throughout the country, and such Irish barristers who have not devoted their time to hawking their souls for sale in the Four Courts, as it may be necessary to supplement them with as assessors or judges. No barristers or solicitors should be permitted to practice in the National Arbitration Courts, without the sanction of the Assembly, and without renouncing their practice in the foreign ones; and the Assembly should retain the same power over the Arbitration Judges that the British Parliament retains over the British and West-British Judiciary. Here, then, Ireland will have wrested the judicial system, now used to her detriment, and use it for her own protection. The course is legal and feasible – its advantages are great and obvious.

Source: Arthur Griffith, *The Sinn Féin Policy*, Dublin: National Council, 1906, pp. 22–3.

EXTRACTS FROM KEVIN O'SHIEL'S MEMOIR OF THE DÁIL LAND COURTS   **Document 16**

A memoir of the work of the Dáil land courts by one of its judges, Kevin O'Shiel, first published in the **Irish Times** *in 1966.*

From May until September 1920, I worked as a special judicial commissioner of Dáil Éireann for agrarian disputes and afterwards as a judicial commissioner of the Dáil Land Commission. I functioned in those posts for about a year and a half, during which I was constantly moving around the west, midlands and south of the country . . .

. . . The Dáil land courts were an amazing and unexpected success, completely justifying the optimism of their promoters. They survived the most violent attacks and carried on, and their order[s] were executed, even during the darkest period . . .

. . . The main reason for the surprising effect of those courts, dealing as they did with land, perhaps the most combustible subject in Ireland, was that the public had faith in their impartiality and were solidly behind them . . .

. . . Though we kept the land courts in operation all during that dreadful winter and spring, the intensive British attacks on us had their effects on our work. Early in 1921, Lloyd George addressed his Welsh constituents in exalted vein, claiming that, in Ireland, he had 'murder by the throat' and stating that 'six months ago the Irish republican organisation had all the symbols and realities of a government . . . Sinn Féin courts were held openly and attended by litigants, jurors and advocates, and their decisions were respected' . . . Today 'Sinn Féin controls, military and police, have gone. Sinn Féin courts have disappeared into cellars' . . . True, The Dáil courts were driven into cellars and sundry holes and corners; but they were certainly not obliterated. Nevertheless, there was undoubted substance in Lloyd George's boast, as our own statistics amply disclosed.

For example, in the period from May till the end of December, 1920, we dealt with 229 cases in 21 counties, involving an area of 49,600 acres and a purchase money of £140,330 whereas, in the succeeding six months, January to June, 1921, there was a steep drop in the returns, viz., 70 cases involving

13,400 acres, at a total purchase figure of but £88,700. Though, surprising as it was, in the circumstances, the work of the Dáil land courts hardly touched the fringe of the great agrarian problem, it can be claimed that it successfully checked a grave menace to property and life at a time of violent, revolutionary turmoil in the country.

Source: Fergus Campbell, 'The last land war? Kevin O'Shiel's memoir of the Irish revolution (1916–21)', in *Archivium Hibernicum*, 57 (2003), pp. 155–200.

Document 17   THE MUNITIONS STRIKE, 1920

Between May and December 1920 dockers and railway workers refused to unload or transport military equipment or personnel. The strike was supported by the ITGWU and represented one of the labour movement's most important contributions to the revolution.

'DOCKERS DOWN TOOLS. Decline To Deal With War Material.'
Dublin quayside workers have decided not to handle certain war material being imported into Ireland, and it is stated the Irish Transport and General Workers' Union have given instructions to this effect to all their members.

This is regarded as a grave development in the situation, and it is said that the policy of organised Labour will not be confined to the docks.

The decision, it is believed, was inspired by the action of the English dockers who are alleged to have refused at London, Hull, and other ports to ship munitions of war to aid the Polish campaign against Soviet Russia.

The policy was put into operation for the first time in Dublin last night.

A vessel from an English port, laden with motor cars and other articles for use by the Army in Ireland arrived at the North Wall.

She was berthed in the usual course by the Harbour authorities, but when it came to the question of discharge, and when the nature of her cargo became known . . . the workers belonging to the I.T. and G.W. Union refused to handle the cargo.

The result was that the vessel still remains at her berth undischarged.

A representative of the FREEMAN'S JOURNAL was informed on inquiry at the headquarters of the I.T. and G.W. Union, and amongst individuals, that under no circumstances would the cargo be handled locally, and should soldiers be employed in the discharge to-day, as in all probability they would, no facilities would be given.

Source: *Freeman's Journal*, 21 May 1920.

THE RESTORATION OF ORDER IN IRELAND ACT   **Document 18**

The Restoration of Order in Ireland Act was passed in August 1920 and re-applied many of the First World War Defence of the Realm Regulations to Ireland. The resort to these coercive measures marked a change in British policy to take harsher measures to quash the republican movement.

An Act to make provision for the Restoration and Maintenance of Order in Ireland, 10 & 11 Geo. V, Ch. 31 (9 August 1920)

1 (1) 'Where it appears to His Majesty in Council that, owing to the existence of a state of disorder in Ireland, the ordinary law is inadequate for the prevention and punishment of crime or the maintenance of order, His Majesty in Council may issue regulations under the Defence of the Realm Consolidation Act, 1914 . . . for securing the restoration and maintenance of order in Ireland . . .

(3) Regulations so made may also –

. . .

(b) confer on a court-martial the powers and jurisdiction exercisable by justices or any other civil court for binding persons to keep the peace or be of good behaviour . . . and for compelling persons to give evidence and to produce documents before the court;

. . .

(e) authorise the conveyance to and detention in any of His Majesty's prisons in any part of the United Kingdom of any persons upon whom a sentence of imprisonment has been passed in Ireland, whether before or after the passing of this Act;

(f) provide for any of the duties of a coroner or coroner's jury being performed by a court of inquiry constituted under the Army Act instead of by the coroner and jury;

. . .

(h) authorise the trial without a jury of any action, counter claim, civil bill, issue, cause, or matter in the High Court or a county court in Ireland which, apart from this provision, would be triable with jury; . . .

Source: Statutes (1920), pp. 222–5.

EXTRACTS FROM THE DIARIES OF MARK STURGIS   **Document 19**

Mark Sturgis was one of a group of British civil servants sent to Ireland in 1920 to make the Dublin Castle administration more effective in dealing with the Republican campaign. While there he kept a diary covering the period from July 1920 to January 1922. The original five volumes are held in the National Archives in Kew.

1920

[*Sunday night 21 November*]

It has been a day of black murder.

. . . What happened was that at least a battalion of the IRA, perhaps more, systematically raided the houses occupied by Military officers – mostly either those who had been employed by Courts Martial or Secret Service men – in parties of twelve and upwards at 9 a.m. this morning. They have murdered ten officers, two civilians . . . and two of Tudor's Auxiliaries. Many of these were caught in bed and probably all unarmed and defenceless, and some were killed in the presence of their wives.

. . . We have heard some account but no substantiated detail of shooting this afternoon at the Hurley Match at Croke Park. It was arranged some time ago . . . to round up the crowd and search them for bad men and arms on the assumption that a large number of such, both from Dublin and Tipperary, might well be expected there . . . the police found a SF picket at the gate who fired on them – they returned the fire and ten were killed, eleven seriously wounded and about 50 slightly . . . 30 revolvers were said to have been picked up on the ground by the police afterwards.

[*Monday 22 November*] A strange and possibly unpleasant affair in the guard room at our Gates is the incident of to-day. Three men, Clancy, McKee, Vice Commandant, Dublin Brigade, IRA and a man Clune, classed as bad were prisoners there. This morning they were in charge of three or four Auxiliaries and were to have gone to Mountjoy [prison] to-night. It is reported that they suddenly made a desperate attack on the guards whose rifles were beside them as they sat reading – one got hold of a rifle and fired two shots another seized a spade and in the fight all were shot dead by the guard.

Source: Michael Hopkinson (ed.), *The Last Days of Dublin Castle: The Diaries of Mark Sturgis*, Dublin: Irish Academic Press, 1999, pp. 76–9.

Document 20   EXTRACTS FROM *AN TÓGLACH* ON GUERRILLA WARFARE

The Irish Volunteer/IRA journal An tÓglach (The Volunteer) *was edited by Piaras Béaslaí during the War of Independence and acted as both a propaganda organ and a training manual, providing instructions on strategies for effective guerrilla warfare, training in the handling of explosives and printing details of successful engagements to encourage others to follow these examples.*

Editorial on 'Guerrilla Warfare'

It has been already pointed out that the position of the Irish Volunteers has now come to resemble a native army waging guerrilla warfare against a foreign army of occupation. It is the duty of Volunteers to take this fact seriously to heart, and to recognise in all their plans, in their methods of training and study, and in their general outlook, the existence of this state of guerrilla warfare and all that it implies. It is our business to develop those guerrilla tactics which we have found most serviceable in dealing with actual conditions in Ireland at present, and to bring them to the highest pitch of perfection of which they are capable. It is our business to wage war against the forces of the invaders whenever and however we find it can be done most effectively . . .

It is an axiom of warfare that one must reserve one's strength in order to strike when and where one is able to do so most effectively. A force greatly inferior to the enemy in numbers, armament, and equipment may strike very heavy blows against their enemy and ultimately render his position in the country untenable by the adoption of guerrilla tactics . . . Of all the forms of 'small wars,' that most dreaded by Imperialist armies of conquest is a prolonged guerrilla warfare in which they are unable to obtain a moment's security nor gain any opportunity of effectively crushing their ubiquitous foe. Particularly do they dread the adoption of well-organised guerrilla tactics by a civilised foe of keen intelligence and courage. Surprises, ambushes, raids on their fortified positions, sniping at their stragglers, capture of their arms and equipment, interruption of their communications, interference with their intelligence, are to be apprehended by them daily; and their forces are driven more and more into the position of invested garrisons in the midst of a hostile country, afraid to venture from their strongholds except in force, living in a state of perpetual apprehension. That such a state of affairs exists to a great extent in Ireland at present is obvious to all; and it is the business of the Irish Volunteers to see that it continues, grows more intense and more menacing to the invader.

'The Roscarberry Triumph'

This is in many respects the most instructive operation recently carried out by our troops. The complete destruction of a large and strong fort has had a marked effect on the enemy in the adjoining area . . .

Tactically the operation serves as model for a Night Attack on a Strong Post. 'The barracks was a detached building, three storied, of a frontage of about 45 feet and a width of about 50 feet. It was a stone building fortified in the usual way – steel roof, shutters, sandbags, and barbed wire. It had a flat roof also sandbagged on which were mounted 2 Lewis guns and a punt gun able to fire fifty pellets a long distance. There were three houses in front of the building about 20 yards away. The nearest house to a flank was the Post Office about 30 yards to the West. The barracks faced South and a wall about 5 feet high extended from the Post Office to within three yards of the barrack door.' The garrison consisted of 22 RIC.

The attack was carried out by an Active Service Unit of 28 men. The operation was covered in the outlying zone by three companies – each guarding its own sector towards East, North, and West. The fighting lasted about two hours and three quarters and about another half hour was occupied in posting the troops in their Action Stations and laying the charge. All details of the plan of attack were carefully thought out beforehand, and there was no unnecessary delay.

The design was to make a stormable breach by blowing in the door with 50lb of gun cotton and sending forward a Storming Party. Suitably positioned riflemen covered the assault . . . The charge was laid and the fuses . . . lit. The Storming Party lay flat on the ground 30 yards away. After the explosion the Party waited five seconds to escape falling splinters etc. On arriving at the breach it was found to be partly blocked by wreckage making a rush impossible. With admirable promptness and resource the method of attack was changed. It was now decided to destroy the barracks by bombing attacks directed against the breach and shutters . . . Covering rifle fire was opened from each party in reply to fire from the garrison. After a time the garrison was bombed out of the front of the building, and adopted a treacherous ruse – feigning to surrender and then opening fire again.

Eventually with help of the petrol and paraffin the building was fired, the attacking party closing in to 30 yards and eventually 10 yards. In future it would be more convenient to have a supply of pint bottles with petrol or paraffin as they could easily be thrown into the building.

The action was finished by 5am when the roof fell in leaving the barracks a mere shell. The enemy losses must have been nineteen . . . Our troops suffered no casualties – a fact in itself proving the carefulness of the planning and the efficiency of the carrying out.

Points to Note:

Use of local companies to cover Operation.
Careful previous thinking out of details.
Equipment and instructions for Storming Party.
Economy of cartridges by Direct Covering Party.
Stockinged feet to ensure silence.
Precautions to escape splinters.
Readiness to adopt an alternative plan.
Co-operation of covering riflemen.
Need for petrol and paraffin bottles.

Source: An tÓglach (The Volunteer), 15 January 1920 and 22 April 1921.

VIOLENCE AGAINST WOMEN DURING THE WAR OF INDEPENDENCE

Document 21

The following extracts from the report of the British Labour Party's commission that visited Ireland in 1920 highlight the nature of violence carried out against women during the War of Independence by both crown forces and the IRA. There is a clear hint that some of that violence was sexual in nature.

Some members of the Commission visited the home of a widow whose house has been raided twice. On the first occasion, about a dozen Auxiliaries rushed into the house and asked for her son. Some of them terrified a delicate daughter whom they covered with revolvers and asked where two of her brothers were. As the Auxiliaries were unable to obtain any information they went away. On the following night at 11.30 p.m., Auxiliaries again came to the house. They broke in the panel of the door and shouted for the son for whom they had inquired on the previous day. The widow replied that the boys had been home to tea but she had not seen them since. One of the party went upstairs and sat on the bed. He pointed a revolver at the daughter who was ill in bed and demanded to know the whereabouts of her brothers, but she could not tell him. Downstairs the men roughly handled the old widow, saying that if she did not tell them where her boys were they would burn down the house. They placed a tin of petrol on the floor. The woman told the Auxiliaries that her son _____ was in prison, but she did not know where . . . The widow told those of our members who visited her that she prayed for mercy. The men left the house swearing that there was 'no bloody God'.

This rough and brutal treatment of women is by no means the worst that is to be said against men in the service of the British Crown. It is, however, extremely difficult to obtain direct evidence of incidents affecting females, for the women of Ireland are reticent on such subjects. The following case is one which came under our notice. A young woman who was sleeping alone in premises which were raided by the Crown forces was compelled to get out of bed and her nightdress was ripped open from top to bottom.

Victimisation of Policemen's Wives and Barrack Servants
April 16, 1920
An armed party visited the house of Misses _____ and took the two girls out in their night attire. They were marched some distance and a court martial held on them 'for walking with the Peelers'. They were sentenced to be shot, but it was mitigated and their hair cut off instead.

The motive for this outrage was that these two girls were on friendly terms with the young members of the RIC at _____ .

June 25, 1920

A party of about twenty armed and disguised men entered the house of Mrs _____ (a policeman's wife), seized herself and four children who were under six years of age, and put them out on the road. The furniture was then put out. Being raining at the time, Mrs _____ sought refuge at the local post office, but the raiders informed her she would not be allowed to remain in the parish another night. She had then to cycle to _____ wet through, in a deplorable condition, where her husband was stationed.

August 7, 1920

Four men entered the house of an injured person. Two of them seized her by the hands and feet while another put his hands over her mouth. They then put three pig rings into her buttocks with pincers. She had been supplying the police with milk.

Source: *Report of the Labour Commission to Ireland*, London: Caledonian Press, 1922, pp. 28–9 and 80–81.

Document 22   UNIONIST ACCEPTANCE OF THE GOVERNMENT OF IRELAND ACT

A speech by Captain Charles Curtis Craig, brother of Sir James Craig, in the House of Commons on 29 March 1920, explaining why Ulster Unionists were prepared to accept self-government for the six counties.

We would much prefer to remain part and parcel of the United Kingdom. We have prospered, we have made our province prosperous under the Union, and under the laws passed by this House and administered by officers appointed by this House. We do not in any way desire to recede from a position which has been in every way satisfactory to us, but we have many enemies in this country, and we feel that an Ulster without a Parliament of its own would not be in nearly as strong a position as one in which a Parliament had been set up where the Executive had been appointed and where above all the paraphernalia of Government was already in existence. We believe that so long as we were without a Parliament of our own constant attacks would be made upon us, and constant attempts would be made . . . to draw us into a Dublin Parliament, and that is the last thing in the world that we desire to see happen. We profoundly distrust the Labour party and we profoundly distrust the right hon. Gentleman the Member for Paisley (Mr Asquith). We believe that if either of those parties, or the two in combination, were once more in power our chances of remaining a part of the United Kingdom would be very small indeed. We see our safety, therefore, in having a Parliament of our own, for we believe that once a Parliament is set up and working well, as I have no doubt it would in Ulster, we should fear no one, and we feel that we then would be in a position of absolute security . . .

Source: Hansard, 29 March 1920, cols 989–90.

THE GOVERNMENT OF IRELAND ACT (1920)   **Document 23**

The Government of Ireland Act partitioned Ireland, creating two home rule states of Northern Ireland and Southern Ireland. It was effectively the constitution of Northern Ireland from 1921 until 1972.

An Act to Provide for the Better Government of Ireland, 10 & 11 Geo. V. Ch. 67 (23 December 1920)

Establishment of Parliaments for Southern Ireland and Northern Ireland and a Council of Ireland
1 (1) On and after the appointed day there shall be established for Southern Ireland a Parliament to be called the Parliament of Southern Ireland con- sisting of His Majesty, the Senate of Southern Ireland, and the House of Commons of Southern Ireland, and there shall be established for Northern Ireland a Parliament to be called the Parliament of Northern Ireland con- sisting of His Majesty, the Senate of Northern Ireland, and the House of Commons of Northern Ireland . . .
2 (1) With a view to the eventual establishment of a Parliament for the whole of Ireland, and to bringing about harmonious action between the parliaments and governments of Southern Ireland and Northern Ireland, and to the pro- motion of mutual intercourse and uniformity in relation to matters affecting the whole of Ireland . . . there shall be constituted . . . a Council to be called the Council of Ireland. . . .

Power to Establish a Parliament for the Whole of Ireland
3 (1) The Parliaments of Southern Ireland and Northern Ireland may, by identical Acts agreed to by an absolute majority of members of the House of Commons of each Parliament . . . establish, in lieu of the Council of Ireland, a Parliament for the whole of Ireland, consisting of His Majesty and two Houses . . .

Legislative Powers of Irish Parliaments
4 (1) . . . the Parliament of Southern Ireland and the Parliament of Northern Ireland shall respectively have power to make laws for the peace, order, and

good government of Southern Ireland and Northern Ireland with the following limitations, namely, that they shall not have power to make laws except in respect of matters exclusively relating to the portion of Ireland within their jurisdiction . . . and that they shall not have power to make laws in respect of the following matters in particular, namely:

(1) The Crown, or the succession to the Crown, or a regency, or the property of the Crown . . . or the Lord Lieutenant . . .
(2) The making of peace or war, or matters arising from a state of war . . .
(3) The navy, the army, the air force, the territorial force, or any other naval, military, or air force, or the defence of the realm, or any other naval, military, or air force matter . . .
(4) Treaties, or any relations with foreign states . . .
(5) Dignities, or titles of honour . . .
(6) Treason, treason felony, alienage, naturalization, or aliens . . .
(7) Trade with any place out of the part of Ireland within their jurisdiction . . .
(8) Submarine cables
(9) Wireless telegraphy
(10) Aerial navigation
(11) Lighthouses, buoys, or beacons . . .
(12) Coinage; legal tender; negotiable instruments (including bank notes) . . .
(13) Trade marks, designs, merchandise marks, copyright, or patent rights . . .

Prohibition of laws interfering with religious equality . . .
5 (1) In the exercise of their power to make laws under this Act neither the Parliament of Southern Ireland nor the Parliament of Northern Ireland shall make a law so as either directly or indirectly to establish or endow any religion, or prohibit or restrict the free exercise thereof, or give a preference, privilege, or advantage, or impose any disability or disadvantage, on account of religious belief or religious or ecclesiastical status, or make any religious belief or religious ceremony a condition of the validity of any marriage, or affect prejudicially the right of any child to attend a school receiving public money without attending the religious instruction at that school, or alter the constitution of any religious body . . . or divert from any religious denomination the fabric of cathedral churches . . . or take any property without compensation. . . .

Powers of the Council of Ireland
10 . . . (3) The Council may consider any questions which may appear in any way to bear on the welfare of both Southern Ireland and Northern Ireland, and may, by resolution, make suggestions in relation thereto as they may think proper, but suggestions so made shall have no legislative effect . . .

Constitution of the Houses of Commons

14 . . . (2) The House of Commons of Northern Ireland shall consist of fifty-two members . . .

(3) The members shall be elected . . . according to the principle of proportional representation, each elector having one transferable vote . . .

. . .

Powers of taxation

22 (1) The imposing, charging, levying, and collection of customs duties and of excise duties on articles manufactures and produced . . . and collection of income tax . . . and excess profits duty, corporation profits tax, and any other tax on profits shall be reserved matters, and the proceeds of those duties and taxes shall be paid into the Consolidated Fund of the United Kingdom.

Source: http://www.legislation.gov.uk/ukpga/1920/67/pdfs/ukpga_19200067_en.pdf

THE ANGLO-IRISH TREATY   **Document 24**

The Anglo-Irish Treaty was signed at 10 Downing Street on 6 December 1921 by the Irish and British Treaty delegations. The 26 counties of Southern Ireland became the Irish Free State, a self-governing dominion of the British Commonwealth. The King remained as head of state and members of the Free State Parliament had to swear an oath fealty to him. Britain also retained a naval presence in three Irish ports and the Free State undertook to pay a portion of Britain's imperial debt.

Articles of Agreement for a Treaty between Great Britain and
Ireland signed in London on the 6th of December 1921

1. Ireland shall have the same constitutional status in the Community of Nations known as the British Empire as the Dominion of Canada, the Commonwealth of Australia, the Dominion of New Zealand and the Union of South Africa, with a Parliament having powers to make laws for the peace, order and good government of Ireland and an Executive responsible to that Parliament, and shall be styled and known as the Irish Free State.

. . .

3. The representative of the Crown in Ireland shall be appointed in like manner as the Governor-General of Canada and in accordance with the practice observed in the making of such appointments.

4. The oath to be taken by Members of the Parliament of the Irish Free State shall be in the following form:

I .... do solemnly swear true faith and allegiance to the Constitution of the Irish Free State as by law established and that I will be faithful to H.M. King George V, his heirs and successors by law, in virtue of the common citizenship of Ireland with Great Britain and her adherence to and membership of the group of nations forming the British Commonwealth of Nations.

5. The Irish Free State shall assume liability for the service of the Public Debt of the United Kingdom as existing at the date hereof and towards the payment of war pensions as existing at that date in such proportion as may be fair and equitable, having regard to any just claims on the part of Ireland by way of set-off or counter-claim, the amount of such sums being determined in default of agreement by the arbitration of one or more independent persons being citizens of the British Empire.

. . .

7. The Government of the Irish Free State shall afford to His Majesty's Imperial Forces:
(a) In time of peace such harbour and other facilities as are indicated in the Annex hereto, or such other facilities as may from time to time be agreed between the British Government and the Government of the Irish Free State; and
(b) In time of war or of strained relations with a Foreign Power such harbour and other facilities as the British Government may require for the purposes of such defence as aforesaid.

. . .

10. The Government of the Irish Free State agrees to pay fair compensation on terms not less favourable than those accorded by the Act of 1920 to judges, officials, members of Police Forces and other Public Servants who are discharged by it or who retire in consequence of the change of Government effected in pursuance hereof.

. . .

12. If . . . an address is presented to His Majesty by both Houses of the Parliament of Northern Ireland to that effect, the powers of the Parliament and Government of the Irish Free State shall no longer extend to Northern Ireland, and the provisions of the Government of Ireland Act, 1920 (including those relating to the Council of Ireland) shall, so far as they relate to Northern Ireland continue to be of full force and effect, and this instrument shall have effect subject to the necessary modifications.

Provided that if such an address is so presented a Commission consisting of three Persons, one to be appointed by the Government of the Irish Free State, one to be appointed by the Government of Northern Ireland and one who shall be Chairman to be appointed by the British Government shall determine in accordance with the wishes of the inhabitants, so far as may be compatible with economic and geographic conditions, the boundaries between Northern Ireland and the rest of Ireland, and for the purposes of the Government of Ireland Act, 1920, and of this instrument, the boundary of Northern Ireland shall be such as may be determined by such Commission.

14. . . . if no such address as is mentioned in Article 12 hereof is Presented, the Parliament and Government of Northern Ireland shall continue to exercise as respects Northern Ireland the powers conferred on them by the Government of Ireland Act, 1920, but the Parliament and Government of the Irish Free State shall in Northern Ireland have in relation to matters in respect of which the Parliament of Northern Ireland has not power to make laws under that Act (including matters which under the said Act are within the jurisdiction of the Council of Ireland) the same powers as in the rest of Ireland, subject to such other provisions as may he agreed in manner hereinafter appearing.

On behalf of the British Delegation	On behalf of the Irish Delegation
Signed	*Signed*
D. Lloyd George	Art Ó Gríobhtha (Arthur Griffith)
Austen Chamberlain	Micheál Ó Coileáin (Michael Collins)
Birkenhead	Riobard Bartún (Robert Barton)
Winston S. Churchill	Eudhmonn S. Ó Dugainn (Eamonn
L. Worthington-Evans	Duggan)
Hamar Greenwood	Seoirse Gabhann Ó Dubhaigh
Gordon Hewart	(George Gavan Duffy)

ANNEX

1. The following are the specific facilities required:

Dockyard Port at Berehaven

(a) Admiralty property and rights to be retained as at the rate hereof. Harbour defences to remain in charge of British care and maintenance parties.

Queenstown

(b) Harbour defences to remain in charge of British care and maintenance parties. Certain mooring buoys to be retained for use of His Majesty's ships.

Belfast Lough

(c) Harbour defences to remain in charge of British care and maintenance parties.

Lough Swilly

(d) Harbour defences to remain in charge of British care and maintenance parties.

Aviation

(e) Facilities in the neighbourhood of the above Ports for coastal defence by air.

Source: National Archives of Ireland website treaty exhibition, http://treaty.nationalarchives.ie/document-gallery/anglo-irish-treaty-6-december-1921

Document 25   EXTRACTS FROM THE DÁIL TREATY DEBATE

The Anglo-Irish Treaty was debated in the Dáil between 14 December 1921 and 7 January 1922. Mary MacSwiney spoke for two hours and 40 minutes outlining the opposition to the treaty because it failed to confer a republic. It was a heated debate with many personal exchanges such as those between Brugha and Collins and Griffith and Childers.

Mary MacSwiney

I speak for the living Republic, the Republic that cannot die. That document will never kill it, never. The Irish Republic was proclaimed and established by the men of Easter Week, 1916. The Irish Republican Government was established in January, 1919, and it has functioned since under such conditions that no country ever worked under before. That Republican Government is not now going to be fooled and destroyed by the Wizard of Wales. We beat him before and we shall beat him again, and I pray with all my heart and soul that a majority of the Members of this assembly will throw out that Treaty and that the minority will stand shoulder to shoulder with us in the fight to regain the position we held on the 4th of this month. I pray that once more; I pray that we will stand together, and the country will stand behind us. I have no doubt of that. I know the women of Ireland, and I know what they will say to the men that want to surrender, and therefore I beg of you to take the decision to throw out that Treaty. Register your votes against it, and do not commit the one unforgivable crime that has ever been committed by the representatives of the people of Ireland (applause).

Source: *Dáil Debates*, vol. T, 21 December 1921, cols 126–27.

Cathal Brugha

A Deputy from Tipperary and Waterford, one of my own colleagues, has sent me in a question which I will read. 'In view of the fact that many members and several people are biased in favour of this proposed Treaty because the Minister of Finance is in favour of ratification, and in view of the fact that many of these people, and many of these members, are of opinion that Mr. Michael Collins is a leader of the army and has fought many fights for the Republic, I think it is of great importance that an authoritative statement be made (*a*) defining the real position Mr. Michael Collins held in the army, (*b*) telling what fights he has taken an active part in, provided this can be done without injustice to himself or danger to the country; or can it be authoritatively stated that he ever fired a shot at any enemy of Ireland?'

. . . It is necessary for me to define Michael Collins' position in the army. Now, I have my department divided up into sections. I have the ordinary Ministerial part of it; the civil part of it; the liaison part of it; and then the Head Quarters Staff. The Head Quarters Staff is divided up again; at the head is the Chief of Staff; and at the head of each section of the Head Quarters Staff is another man working under the Chief of Staff. One of those heads of the subsections is Mr. Michael Collins; and to use a word which he has on more than one occasion used, and which he is fond of using, he is merely a subordinate in the Department of Defence.

While the war was in progress I could not praise too highly the work done by the Head Quarters Staff. The Chief of Staff and each of the leaders of the subsections – the members of the Head Quarters Staff – were the best men we could get for the positions; each of them carried out efficiently, so far as I know, the work that was entrusted to him they worked conscientiously and patriotic-ally for Ireland without seeking any notoriety, with one exception; whether he is responsible or not for the notoriety I am not going to say (cries of 'Shame' and 'Get on with the Treaty'). There is little more for me to say. One member was specially selected by the Press and the people to put him into a position which he never held; he was made a romantic figure, a mystical character such as this person certainly is not; the gentleman I refer to is Mr. Michael Collins——

Source: *Dáil Debates*, vol. T, 7 January 1922, cols 325–26.

Arthur Griffith and Erskine Childers
PRESIDENT A. GRIFFITH: Before this proceeds any further, I want to say that President de Valera made a statement – a generous statement – and I replied. Now (striking the table) I will not reply to any Englishman in this Dáil (applause).

. . .

MR. ERSKINE CHILDERS: My nationality is a matter for myself and for the constituents that sent me here.

PRESIDENT A. GRIFFITH: Your constituents did not know what your nationality was.

MR. ERSKINE CHILDERS: They have known me from my boyhood days – since I was about half a dozen years of age.

PRESIDENT A. GRIFFITH: I will not reply to any damned Englishman in this Assembly.

. . .

MR. ERSKINE CHILDERS: I hardly think you will say this is out of order (cries of 'Chair! Chair!'). It is hardly out of order to say something to an interjection like that made by the President. I am not going to defend my nationality, but I would be delighted to show the President privately that I am not, in the true sense of the word, an Englishman, as he knows. He banged the table. If he had banged the table before Lloyd George in the way he banged it here, things might have been different (cries of 'Order!' and applause).

PRESIDENT A. GRIFFITH: I banged the table before your countryman, Mr. Lloyd George.

MADAME MARKIEVICZ: And Griffith is a Welsh name.

Source: Dáil Debates, vol. T, 10 January 1922, col. 416.

Document 26   DOCUMENT NO. 2

Extracts from de Valera's alternative to the treaty that proposed an external relationship between the Irish Free State and the Commonwealth that would recognise the King as head of the Commonwealth but not the Free State.

In order to bring to an end the long and ruinous conflict between Great Britain and Ireland by a sure and lasting peace honourable to both nations, it is agreed

1. That the legislative, executive, and judicial authority of Ireland shall be derived solely from the people of Ireland.
2. That, for purposes of common concern, Ireland shall be associated with the States of the British Commonwealth, viz: the Kingdom of Great Britain, the Dominion of Canada, the Commonwealth of Australia, the Dominion of New Zealand, and the Union of South Africa.
3. That when acting as an associate the rights, status, and privileges of Ireland shall be in no respect less than those enjoyed by any of the component states of the British Commonwealth . . .

. . .

6. That, for purposes of the Association, Ireland shall recognise His Britannic Majesty as head of the Association.

7. That, so far as her resources permit, Ireland shall provide for her own defence by sea, land and air, and shall repel by force any attempt by a foreign power to violate the integrity of her soil and territorial waters, or to use them for any purpose hostile to Great Britain and the other associated States.

Source: *Dáil Debates*, vol. T, 10 January 1922, http://historical-debates.oireachtas.ie/ D/DT/D.P.A.170001.html

THE ARMY EMERGENCY POWERS RESOLUTION   **Document 27**

This resolution was passed by the Dáil on 28 September 1922, conferring extensive judicial and punitive powers on military courts, including the controversial right to impose the death penalty that resulted in 77 executions during the Civil War.

(1) WHEREAS the Government has entrusted to the Army the duty of securing the public safety and restoring order throughout the country and has placed on the army the responsibility for the establishment of the authority of the Government in all parts of the country in which that authority is challenged by force.

(2) AND WHEREAS the Army Council has represented to the Government that in order to discharge effectively the duty and responsibility so placed on them it is essential that the Army Council should have power to set up Military Courts or Committees with full powers of enquiring into charges and inflicting punishments on persons found guilty of acts calculated to interfere with or delay the effective establishment of the authority of the Government, and that the Army Council should have power to authorise the detention in places whether within or without the jurisdiction of the Government of persons in Military custody and power to control the dealing in and possession of fire arms.

(3) AND WHEREAS the Government recognising the force of such representations had sanctioned the doing under the authority of the Army Council of all or any of the following matters and things.

a. The setting up of Military Courts or Committees for the enquiring into charges against persons in respect of any of the offences hereinafter mentioned . . .

(1) Taking part in or aiding or abetting any attack upon or using force against the National Forces.

(2) Looting arson destruction seizure unlawful possession or removal of or damage to any public or private property.

(3) Having possession without proper authority of any bomb or any dynamite gelignite or other explosive substance or any revolver rifle gun or other fire arm or lethal weapon or any ammunition for such fire arm.

(4) The breach of any general order or regulation made by the Army Council.

and the infliction by such Military Courts or Committees of the punishment of death or of penal servitude for any period or of imprisonment for any period or of a fine of any amount either with or without imprisonment on any person found guilty by such Court or Committee of any of the offences aforesaid . . .

Source: Iris Oifigiúil (The Dublin Gazette), Tuesday, 3 October 1922.

References

aan de Wiel, J. (2003) *The Catholic Church in Ireland, 1914–1918: War and Politics*, Dublin: Irish Academic Press.

Abbott, R. (2000) *Police Casualties in Ireland, 1919–1922*, Dublin/Cork: Mercier.

Andrews, C. S. (1979) *Dublin Made Me*, Dublin/Cork: Mercier.

Augusteijn, J. (1990) 'The importance of being Irish. Ideas and the Volunteers in Mayo and Tipperary', in D. Fitzpatrick (ed.), *Revolution? Ireland 1917–1923*, Dublin: Trinity History Workshop, pp. 25–42.

Augusteijn, J. (1996) *From Public Defiance to Guerrilla Warfare: The Experience of Ordinary Volunteers in the Irish War of Independence, 1916–1921*, Dublin: Irish Academic Press.

Augusteijn, J. (2010) *Patrick Pearse: The Making of a Revolutionary*, Basingstoke: Palgrave.

Barry, T. (1981) *Guerrilla Days in Ireland*, Dublin: Anvil.

Barton, B. (2002) *From Behind a Closed Door: Secret Court Martial Records of the 1916 Easter Rising*, Belfast: Blackstaff.

Bew, P. (1996) *John Redmond*, Dundalk: Dundalgan.

Borgonovo, J. (ed.) (2006) *Florence and Josephine O'Donoghue's War of Independence: A Destiny that Shapes Our Ends*, Dublin: Irish Academic Press.

Bowen, K. (1983) *Protestants in a Catholic State: Ireland's Privileged Minority*, Montreal/Kingston: McGill-Queen's University Press.

Bowman, T. (2003) *Irish Regiments in the Great War*, Manchester: Manchester University Press.

Bowman, T. (2007) *Carson's Army: The Ulster Volunteer Force, 1910–22*, Manchester: Manchester University Press.

Boyce, D. G. (2002) ' "That party politics should divide our tents": Nationalism, unionism and the First World War', in A. Gregory and S. Pašeta (eds), *Ireland and the Great War: 'A War to Unite Us All?'*, Manchester: Manchester University Press, pp. 190–216.

Breen, D. (1981) *My Fight for Irish Freedom*, Dublin: Anvil.

Brennan, M. (1980) *The War in Clare, 1911–21*, Dublin: Four Courts Press.

Buckland, P. (1973) *Irish Unionism 2: Ulster Unionism and the Origins of Northern Ireland, 1886 to 1922*, Dublin: Gill and Macmillan.

Buckely, D. (2008) *The Battle of Tourmakeady*, Dublin: Nonsuch.

Campbell, C. (1994) *Emergency Law in Ireland, 1918–1925*, Oxford: Clarendon Press.

Campbell, F. (2003) 'The last land War? Kevin O'Shiel's memoir of the Irish Revolution', *Archivum Hibernicum*, 57, pp. 155–200.

Carey, T. and de Búrca, M. (2003) 'Bloody Sunday 1920: New evidence', *History Ireland*, 11: 2, pp. 10–16.

Carroll, F. M. (1978) *American Opinion and the Irish Question, 1910–23*, Dublin: Gill and Macmillan.

Carroll, F. M. (1985) 'The American Commission on Irish Independence and the Paris Peace Conference of 1919', *Irish Studies in International Affairs*, 2: 1, pp. 103–18.

Carroll, F. M. (2002) *Money for Ireland: Finance, Diplomacy, Politics and the First Dáil Éireann Loans, 1919–1936*, London: Praeger.

Casey, J. (1970) 'Republican courts in Ireland, 1919–1922', *Irish Jurist*, 5, pp. 319–42.

Childers, E. (1921) *The Constructive Work of Dáil Éireann – No. 1*, Dublin: Talbot.

Clarke, K. (2008) *Revolutionary Woman*, Dublin: O'Brien.

Coakley, J. (1994) 'The election that made the First Dáil', in B. Farrell (ed.), *The Creation of the Dáil*, Dublin: Blackwater, pp. 31–46.

Coleman, M. (2003) *County Longford and the Irish Revolution, 1910–1923*, Dublin: Irish Academic Press.

Comerford, James J. (1978) *My Kilkenny IRA Days*, Kilkenny: Dinan.

Coogan, T. P. (1990) *Michael Collins*, London: Hutchinson.

Costello, F. (1990) 'The Republican Courts and the decline of British rule in Ireland, 1919–1921', *Éire-Ireland*, 25: 2, pp. 36–55.

Costello, F. (2003) *The Irish Revolution and Its Aftermath, 1916–1923: Years of Revolt*, Dublin: Irish Academic Press.

Daly, M. E. (1997) *The Buffer State: The Historical Roots of the Department of the Environment*, Dublin: Institute of Public Administration.

Davitt, C. (1968) 'The Civil Jurisdiction of the Courts of Justice of the Irish Republic' *Irish Jurist*, 3, pp. 112–30.

Deasy, L. (1973) *Towards Ireland Free*, Dublin/Cork: Mercier.

de Paor, L. (1997) *On the Easter Proclamation and Other Declarations*, Dublin: Four Courts Press.

Dolan, A. (2003) *Commemorating the Irish Civil War*, Cambridge: Cambridge University Press.

Dolan, A. (2006) 'Killing and Bloody Sunday, November 1920', *Historical Journal*, 49: 3, pp. 789–810.

Dooley, T. (2000) *The Plight of Monaghan Protestants*, Dublin: Irish Academic Press.

Dooley, T. (2004) *The Land for the People: The Land Question in Independent Ireland*, Dublin: UCD Press.

Duffy, J. (2013) 'Children of the revolution', *History Ireland*, 21: 3, pp. 34–5.

Dungan, M. (1997) *They Shall Not Grow Old: Irish Soldiers and the Great War*, Dublin: Four Courts Press.

Dunphy, R. (1995) *The Making of Fianna Fáil Power in Ireland, 1923–48*, Oxford: Clarendon Press.

English, R. (1998) *Ernie O'Malley: IRA Intellectual*, Oxford: Oxford University Press.

Fanning, R. (1978) *The Irish Department of Finance, 1922–58*, Dublin: Institute of Public Administration.

Fanning, R. (2013) *Fatal Path: British Government and Irish Revolution*, London: Faber and Faber.

Farrell, B. (1971) *The Founding of Dáil Éireann: Parliament and Nation Building*, Dublin: Gill and Macmillan.

Farrell, B. (1988) 'From First Dáil through Irish Free State', in B. Farrell (ed.), *De Valera's Constitution and Ours*, Dublin: Gill and Macmillan, pp. 18–32.

Farry, M. (2012) *The Irish Revolution, 1912–23: Sligo*, Dublin: Four Courts Press.

Ferriter, Diarmaid (2007) *Judging DeV*, Dublin: Royal Irish Academy.

Fitzpatrick, D. (1977) *Politics and Irish Life, 1913–21: Provincial Experience of War and Revolution*, Dublin: Gill and Macmillan.

Fitzpatrick, D. (1978) 'The geography of Irish nationalism', *Past and Present*, 78, pp. 113–44.

Fitzpatrick, D. (1980) 'Strikes in Ireland, 1914–21', *Saothar: Journal of the Irish Labour History Society*, 6, pp. 26–39.

Fitzpatrick, D. (1996) 'Militarism in Ireland, 1900–1922', in T. Bartlett and K. Jeffery (eds), *A Military History of Ireland*, Cambridge: Cambridge University Press, pp. 379–406.

Fitzpatrick, D. (2003) *Harry Boland's Irish Revolution*, Cork: Cork University Press.

Fitzpatrick, D. (ed.) (1990) *Revolution? Ireland, 1917–1923*, Dublin: Trinity History Workshop Publications.

Foy, M. (2006) *Michael Collins's Intelligence War: The Struggle between the British and the IRA, 1919–1921*, Stroud: Sutton.

Foy, M. and Barton, B. (1999) *The Easter Rising*, Stroud: Sutton.

Gallagher, M. (1977) 'Socialism and the nationalist tradition in Ireland, 1798–1918', *Éire-Ireland*, 12: 2, pp. 63–102.

Gallagher, M. (1979) 'The pact general election of 1922', *Irish Historical Studies*, 21: 84, 404–21.

Garvin, T. (1981) *The Evolution of Irish Nationalist Politics*, Dublin: Gill and Macmillan.

Hanley, B. (2008) 'Fear and loathing at Coolacrease', *History Ireland* (Jan.– Feb. 2008), pp. 5–6.

Hannigan, D. (2008) *De Valera in America: The Rebel President's 1919 Campaign*, Dublin: O'Brien.

Hart, P. (1998) *The IRA and Its Enemies: Violence and Community in Cork, 1916–1923*, Oxford: Oxford University Press.

Hart, P. (2003) *The IRA at War, 1916–1923*, Oxford: Oxford University Press.

Hart, P. (2005) *Mick: The Real Michael Collins*, London: Macmillan.

Hayes-McCoy, G. A. (1969) 'A military history of the 1916 Rising', in K. B. Nowlan (ed.), *The Making of 1916: Studies in the History of the Rising*, Dublin: Stationery Office, pp. 255–338.

Hennessey, T. (1997) *A History of Northern Ireland, 1920–1996*, Dublin: Gill and Macmillan.

Hepburn, A. C. (2008) *Catholic Belfast and Nationalist Ireland in the Era of Joe Devlin, 1871–1934*, Oxford: Oxford University Press.

Higgins, R. (2012) *Transforming 1916: Meaning, Memory and the Fiftieth Anniversary of the Easter Rising*, Cork: Cork University Press.

Hopkinson, M. (1988) *Green Against Green: The Irish Civil War*, Dublin: Gill and Macmillan.

Hopkinson, M. (1993) 'President Woodrow Wilson and the Irish Question', *Studia Hibernica*, 32, pp. 89–111.

Hopkinson, M. (2002) *The Irish War of Independence*, Dublin: Gill and Macmillan.

Hopkinson, M. (ed.) (1999) *The Last Days of Dublin Castle: The Diaries of Mark Sturgis*, Dublin: Irish Academic Press.

Horne, J. (2008) 'Our war, our history: Ireland at war', in J. Horne (ed.), *Our War: Ireland and the Great War*, Dublin: Royal Irish Academy, pp. 1–34.

Inoue, K. (1998) 'Dáil propaganda and the Irish self-determination League of Great Britain during the Anglo-Irish War' *Irish Studies Review*, 6: 1, pp. 47–53.

Inoue, K. (2002) 'Propaganda of Dáil Éireann', in J. Augusteijn (ed.), *The Irish Revolution, 1913–1923*, Basingstoke: Palgrave, pp. 87–102.

Jackson, A. (1993) *Sir Edward Carson*, Dundalk: Dundalgan.

Jackson, A. (1999) *Ireland, 1798–1998*, Oxford: Blackwell.

Jackson, A. (2003) *Home Rule: An Irish History, 1800–2000*, London: Weidenfeld & Nicolson.

Jeffery, K. (1994) 'British Security Policy in Ireland, 1919–21', in P. Collins (ed.), *Unionism and Nationalism: Conflict in Ireland, 1885–1921*, Belfast: Queen's University, pp. 163–75.

Jeffery, K. (2000) *Ireland and the Great War*, Cambridge: Cambridge University Press.

Jeffery, K. (2006a) *The GPO and the Easter Rising*, Dublin: Irish Academic Press.

Jeffery, K. (2006b) *Field Marshal Sir Henry Wilson: A Political Soldier*, Oxford: Oxford University Press.

Kautt, W. H. (2010) *Ambushes and Armour: The Irish Rebellion, 1919–1921*, Dublin: Irish Academic Press.

Kelly, M. J. (2006) *The Fenian Ideal and Irish Nationalism*, Woodbridge: Boydell and Brewer.

Kenneally, I. (2008) *The Paper Wall: Newspapers and Propaganda in Ireland, 1919–21*, Cork: Collins Press.

Keogh, D. (1986) *The Vatican, the Bishops and Irish Politics, 1919–39*, Cambridge: Cambridge University Press.

Kissane, Bill. (2005) *The Politics of the Irish Civil War*, Oxford: Oxford University Press.

Knirck, Jason (2006) *Imagining Ireland's Independence: The Debates Over the Anglo-Irish Treaty of 1921*, Plymouth: Rowman and Littlefield.

Kotsonouris, M. (1994) *Retreat from Revolution: The Dáil Courts, 1920–24*, Dublin: Four Courts Press.

Kotsonouris, M. (2004) *The Winding Up of the Dáil Courts, 1922–1925: An Obvious Duty*, Dublin: Four Courts Press.

Laffan, M. (1983) *The Partition of Ireland, 1911–1925*, Dundalk: Dundalgan Press.

Laffan, M. (1985) ' "Labour must wait": Ireland's conservative revolution', in P. Corish (ed.), *Radicals, Rebels and Establishments*, Belfast: Appletree Press, pp. 203–22.

Laffan, M. (1999) *The Resurrection of Ireland: The Sinn Féin Party, 1916–1923*, Cambridge: Cambridge University Press.

Leeson, D. M. (2003) 'Death in the afternoon: The Croke Park Massacre, 21 November 1920', *Canadian Journal of History*, 38, pp. 43–67.

Leeson, D. M. (2011) *The Black and Tans: British Police and Auxiliaries in the Irish War of Independence*, Oxford: Oxford University Press.

Leonard, J. (1990) 'Getting them at last: The IRA and ex-servicemen', in D. Fitzpatrick (ed.), *Revolution? Ireland 1917–1923*, Dublin: Trinity History Workshop, pp. 118–29.

Leonard, J. (2012) ' "English dogs" or "poor devils"? The dead of Bloody Sunday morning', in D. Fitzpatrick (ed.), *Terror in Ireland, 1916–1923*, Dublin: Lilliput, pp. 102–40.

Loughlin, J. (1986) *Gladstone, Home Rule and the Ulster Question, 1882–93*, Dublin: Gill and Macmillan.

Lynch, P. (1966) 'The social revolution that never was', in D. Williams (ed.), *The Irish Struggle, 1916–1926*, London: Routledge and Kegan Paul, pp. 41–54.

Lynch, R. (2006) *The Northern IRA and the Early Years of Partition, 1920–1922*, Dublin: Irish Academic Press.

Lynch, R. (2010) 'Explaining the Altnaveigh Massacre', *Éire-Ireland*, 45: 3–4, pp. 184–210.

Lyons, F. S. L. (1968a) 'Fenianism, 1867–1916', in T. W. Moody (ed.), *The Fenian Movement*, Dublin/Cork: Mercier, pp. 37–48.

Lyons, F. S. L. (1968b) *John Dillon: A Biography*, London: Routledge and Kegan Paul.

McCarthy, C. (2007) *Cumann na mBan and the Irish Revolution*, Cork: Collins Press.

McCoole, S. (2003) *No Ordinary Women: Irish Female Activists in the Revolutionary Years, 1900–1923*, Dublin: O'Brien Press.

McGarry, F. (2005) *Eoin O'Duffy: Self-Made Hero*, Oxford: Oxford University Press.

McGarry, F. (2010) *The Rising. Ireland: Easter 1916*, Oxford: Oxford University Press.

McGarry, F. (2011) *Rebels: Voices from the Easter Rising*, London: Penguin.

McGarry, F. (2012) 'Violence and the Easter Rising', in D. Fitzpatrick (ed.), *Terror in Ireland, 1916–1923*, Dublin: Lilliput, pp. 39–57.

McGee, O. (2005) *The IRB: The Irish Republican Brotherhood from Land League to Sinn Féin*, Dublin: Four Courts Press.

Macready, C. F. N. (1924) *Annals of an Active Life*, Vol. II, London: Hutchinson.

Matthew, H. C. G. (1986) *Gladstone, 1809–1874*, Oxford: Clarendon Press.

Matthews, A. (2010) *Renegades: Irish Republican Women, 1900–1922*, Dublin/Cork: Mercier.

Miller, D. W. (1973) *Church, State and Nation in Ireland, 1898–1921*, Dublin: Gill and Macmillan.

Mitchell, A. (1974) *Labour in Irish Politics, 1890–1930: The Irish Labour Movement in an Age of Revolution*, Dublin: Gill and Macmillan.

Mitchell, A. (1995) *Revolutionary Government in Ireland: Dáil Éireann 1919–22*, Dublin: Gill and Macmillan.

Mitchell, A. (2002) 'Alternative government: "Exit Britannia" – the formation of the Irish national state, 1918–1921', in J. Augusteijn (ed.), *The Irish Revolution, 1913–1923*, Basingstoke: Palgrave, pp. 70–86.

Mooney Eichacker, J. (2003) *Irish Republican Women in America: Lecture Tours, 1916–1925*, Dublin: Irish Academic Press.

Murphy, B. P. (1991) *Patrick Pearse and the Lost Republican Ideal*, Dublin: James Duffy.

Murray, P. (2000) *Oracles of God: The Roman Catholic Church and Irish Politics, 1922–37*, Dublin: UCD Press.

O'Callaghan, J. (2010) *Revolutionary Limerick: The Republican Campaign for Independence, Limerick, 1913–1921*, Dublin: Irish Academic Press.

O'Connor, B. (1929) *With Michael Collins in the Fight for Irish Independence*, London: P. Davies.

O'Day, A. (1998) *Irish Home Rule, 1867–1921*, Manchester: Manchester University Press.

O'Donoghue, F. (1954) *No Other Law: The Story of Liam Lynch and the Irish Republican Army*, Dublin: Irish Press.

O'Halpin, E. (1987) *The Decline of the Union: British Government in Ireland, 1892–1920*, Dublin: Gill and Macmillan.

O'Halpin, E. (1999) *Defending Ireland: The Irish State and Its Enemies Since 1922*, Oxford: Oxford University Press.

O'Halpin, E. (2012) 'Counting terror: Bloody Sunday and the dead of the Irish Revolution', in D. Fitzpatrick (ed.), *Terror in Ireland, 1916–1923*, Dublin: Lilliput, pp. 141–57.

O'Leary, C. (1979) *Irish Elections, 1918–1977: Parties, Voters and Proportional Representation*, Dublin: Gill and Macmillan.

O'Mahony, R. (2012) 'The sack of Balbriggan and tit-for-tat terror', in D. Fitzpatrick (ed.), *Terror in Ireland, 1916–1923*, Dublin: Lilliput, pp. 58–74.

O'Neill, T. (2006) *The Battle of Clonmult: The IRA's Worst Defeat*, Dublin: Nonsuch.

Ó Suilleabháin, M. (1965) *Where Mountainy Men Have Sown*, Tralee: Anvil Books.

Pakenham, F. (Lord Longford) (1972), *Peace by Ordeal: The Negotiation of the Anglo-Irish Treaty, 1921*, London: Sidgwick and Jackson.

Pašeta, S. (2008) *Thomas Kettle*, Dublin: UCD Press.

Regan, J. M. (1999) *The Irish Counter-Revolution, 1921–1936*, Dublin: Gill and Macmillan.

Ryan, L. (2000) '"Drunken Tans": Representations of sex and violence in the Anglo-Irish War', *Feminist Review*, 66, pp. 73–94.

Ryan, L. (2001) 'Splendidly silent: Representing Irish republican women, 1919–23', in A. Gallagher *et al.* (eds), *Re-presenting the Past: Women and History*, Harlow: Longman, pp. 23–43.

Smith, J. (2000) *The Tories and Ireland, 1910–1914: Conservative Party Politics and the Home Rule Crisis*, Dublin: Irish Academic Press.

Stanley, A. (2005) *I Met Murder on the Way: The Story of the Pearsons of Coolacrease*, Carlow: Alan Stanley.

Taillon, R. (1996) *When History Was Made: The Women of 1916*, Belfast: Beyond the Pale.

Thornley, D. (1964) *Isaac Butt and Home Rule*, London: MacGibbon and Kee.

Townshend, C. (1975) *The British Campaign in Ireland, 1919–1921: The Development of Political and Military Policies*, Oxford: Oxford University Press.

Townshend, C. (1979a) 'The Irish railway strike of 1920: Industrial action and civil resistance in the struggle for independence', *Irish Historical Studies*, 21: 83, pp. 265–82.

Townshend, C. (1979b) 'The Irish Republican Army and the development of guerrilla warfare, 1916–1921', *English Historical Review*, xciv, pp. 318–45.

Townshend, C. (1984) *Political Violence in Ireland: Government and Resistance since 1848*, Oxford: Oxford University Press.

Townshend, C. (2005) *Easter 1916: The Irish Rebellion*, London: Penguin.

Travers, P. (1983) 'The priest in politics: The case of conscription', in O. MacDonagh *et al.* (eds), *Irish Culture and Nationalism, 1750–1950*, Dublin: Gill and Macmillan, pp. 161–81.

Valiulis, M. G. (1992) *Portrait of a Revolutionary: General Richard Mulcahy and the Founding of the Irish Free State*, Dublin: Irish Academic Press.

Walsh, M. (2008) *The News from Ireland: Foreign Correspondents and the Irish Revolution*, London: I. B. Tauris.

Ward, A. J. (1974) 'Lloyd George and the 1918 Irish conscription risis', *Historical Journal*, 17:1, pp. 107–29.

Ward, M. (1995) *Unmanageable Revolutionaries: Women in Irish Nationalism*, London: Pluto Press.

Whelan, B. (2006) *United States Foreign Policy and Ireland, 1913–29*, Dublin: Four Courts Press.

Wills, C. (2009) *Dublin, 1916: The Siege of the GPO*, London: Profile.

Index

Act of Union 3
Agar-Robartes, T.G. 8
Aiken, Frank 80, 110–11, 115
ambushes 67–9, 71–3, 81–4, 89
American Association for the Recognition of the
    Irish Republic (AARIR) 52
American Commission on Conditions in Ireland
    49, 91
American Declaration of Independence 24, 46
amnesties 3
An tÓglach (the Volunteer) 54, 68, 81, 140–2
Ancient Order of Hibernians 34, 41
Anderson, John 97, 100–1
Andrews, Todd 54, 76
Anglo-Irish Treaty 1921 100–14
    Dáil cabinet 103–5, 108
    Dáil debate 104–6, 150–2
    draft treaty 103–4
    external association, proposal for 105–6, 152–3
    geographical boundaries 103–4, 118
    Irish Free State, creation of 102–4, 108
    Irish War of Independence 100–12
    Northern Ireland 102–4, 109–11, 118
    oath of fealty to monarchy 103–4, 109
    revision 109
    signature 104–5, 109
    Sinn Féin 105–6, 108–9, 115–16
    split 104–12, 114–16
    text 147–50
    truce ending War of Independence 100–12
    vote 106
Anglo-Irish War *see* Irish War of Independence
arbitration courts 16, 54, 57, 136–7
arms and ammunition 9, 17–22, 51–3, 67–9, 73, 79,
    81–3, 90, 100, 112 *see also* bombings
    and explosives

arrests and round-ups 18, 23, 26–8, 34–5, 39–40,
    64, 73, 100
Ashe, Thomas 22, 35
Asquith, Herbert 6, 8–9, 144
assassinations 56, 69, 89, 92–3, 111, 116
Auxiliaries 70–1, 73, 80, 83, 85–8, 92–3, 97

'B' Specials 80 (*see also* Ulster Special Constabulary),
    110–11
Balbriggan, sack of 85–7
Bandon Valley massacre 93
Barry, Tom 71–3, 81, 83, 112
Barton, Robert 102, 104, 108, 149
Béaslaí, Piaras 47, 54, 86, 140–2
Belfast boycott 80, 110
Bell, Alan 56, 89
Black and Tans 70, 72, 80, 83, 85–8, 92–3, 97
Bloody Sunday 71–2, 84, 88–9, 93, 100
Boland, Harry 39–40, 48, 77, 82, 101, 116
bombings and explosives 15, 21, 67, 81–3, 110,
    112, 114–15
Bonar Law, Andrew 7, 104
Boundary Commission 103–4, 118
Breen, Dan 67, 75–6, 109
Brennan, Michael 73, 82, 106
Broy, Ned 86, 88–9
Brugha, Cathal 45, 47, 55, 79–80, 85, 103–5, 112,
    116, 150–2
Butt, Isaac 3–4
by-elections 16, 31–5, 39, 46

cabinet government model 45–6
Campbell-Bannerman, Henry 6
Carson, Edward 7, 8, 11, 37
Casement, Roger 17–19, 27, 39
casualties 22–4, 26, 67–8, 81–6, 96–7, 110

Catholics and Catholic Church
  Anglo-Irish Treaty 1921, support for 113
  clergy 4, 10, 32, 36, 38–41, 50, 57–8, 77, 84,
    105, 113
  conscription 38–9, 84, 129
  Dáil Éireann, recogniition of 50, 84
  First World War 10, 33, 38, 129
  IRA 74, 76, 84
  Ne Temere papal decree of 1908 7, 94
  Northern Ireland 110, 117–18
  socialism 44
  university education 6
Ceann Comhairle 45–6
Ceannt, Eamonn 16–17, 20, 126
Celtic Literary Society 16
censorship 54–5, 94
Chamberlain, Austen 86, 102, 149
Childers, Erskine 36, 54, 58, 74, 102, 105, 108,
  114, 135–6, 150–2
children, participation of in Easter Rising 22, 23
Christian Brothers 76
Churchill, Winston 86, 102, 149
Civil Authorities (Special Powers) Act 1922 117–18
Civil War, 1922–3 106, 109, 111–16, 153–4
Clan na Gael, United States 25, 51–2
Clancy, George 93
Clancy, Peadar 71, 86, 89, 140
Clarke, Kathleen 23, 92, 105, 108
Clarke, Thomas 15, 17, 19, 126
class and social background 26, 60, 74–8, 79, 92
clerical workers and intelligence work 88–90
Clonmult, Battle of 72
Clune, Conor 71, 100
Clune, Patrick 84, 100–1
Cohalan, Daniel F. 52, 84
Collins, Michael 33, 35–6, 39–40, 47–8, 55–6, 71,
  76–8, 80, 84–6, 90, 100, 103–11, 113–16,
  149, 150–2
Commonwealth 50, 104–5, 109
Connolly, James 17, 20, 23, 25, 28, 64, 126
Connolly, Seán 21, 64
conscription 17, 18, 33, 37–40, 43, 75, 98, 129
Conservatives 5–6, 98–9, 100, 104
conservatism 44, 46–7, 59–60
consolidation of two Irelands, 1923–5 116–18
Constitution 25, 45–7, 109, 111–12, 131–2
constitutional nationalism 9, 15, 28, 43
constitutional status of Southern Ireland 102–3
constructive unionism 6, 36
Cooneyites 94
Cork City, burning of 86
coroners 70, 88

Cosgrave, W.T. 16, 33, 55, 104, 113
county option 98
courts martial 23–4, 27, 70
Craig, Charles Curtis 144–5
Craig, James 7, 102, 110, 117, 144
Creel, George 48
Criminal Investigation Department (CID) 115
Croke Park shootings 86
Crossbarry, Battle of 72
crown courts 57–9, 70
cultural revival 15–16, 77
Cumann na mBan 22–3, 38–9, 58, 75, 90–2, 106,
  113
Cumann na nGaedheal 115–17
Curragh Mutiny 8
Curzon, George (Lord Curzon) 50

Dáil Courts 57–60, 61, 63, 69–70, 97, 137–8
Dáil Éireann
  Anglo-Irish Treaty 1921 103–6, 108
  Catholic clergy's refusal to recognise 84
  Democratic Programme 25, 46–7, 63, 126–7
  departments 45, 47–8
  domestic policy 55–63, 137–8
  First Dáil 16, 25, 45–63, 67–8, 126–7
  finance and budget 55–7
  foreign policy 48–55
  Labour Party 44
  local government 61–2
  oaths 61–2, 85
  recognition 49–50, 100
  Second Dáil 92, 99, 107–8, 113
  Sinn Féin 16, 45, 47, 100, 106, 108–9
  Third Dáil 113–14
  women 47
Daly, Edward 27
Daly, P.T. 15, 20
Davitt, Cahir 58, 60
de Valera, Eamon 20, 22, 24, 27–8, 33–4, 38–41,
  45, 47, 49, 51, 52–3, 72, 100, 105–8, 116,
  152–3
Declaration of Independence 46, 48, 133–4
Defence of the Realm Act 1914 35, 54, 70
Democratic Programme 25, 46–7, 63, 126–7
Devine, T.J. 32, 41
Devlin, Joe 34, 41–2
Dillon, John 28, 36–8, 40–1, 128–30
disarmament 100
disestablishment of Church of Ireland 4, 7
district courts 57–8
Dolan, Charles 16
domestic policy of Dáil Éireann 55–63, 137–8

dominion status 48, 50, 101–2
dual-monarchy, proposal for 16, 34
Dublin Castle 17–18, 21, 56, 71, 88–9, 96–7, 100, 106, 139–40
Dublin Corporation 16, 18, 55, 62
Dublin lock-out 1913 17, 26, 63
Dublin Metropolitan Police (DMP) 68, 99
Duggan, Eamonn 86, 102, 104, 149
Dungannon Clubs 16

Easter, 1916. Yeats, W.B. 28
Easter Rising, 1916 15–29, 81
   arms and ammunition, acquisition of 17–19, 21–2
   arrests and punishments 23, 26–8, 34–5, 64
   casualties 22–4, 26
   commemorations 25–6
   death penalty 23, 27–8, 64
   Easter Week 19–24
   funding 25, 52
   General Post Office 20–1, 23–4
   Germany 17–19, 22, 25
   IVF 16–23, 64, 77
   locations, choice of 20–1
   martial law 21, 27, 35–6
   military council 17–19, 24–5
   mobilisation 20–2
   planning 16–21, 24
   Proclamation 1916 24–6, 27, 47, 125–6
   public support 26–8, 33, 128–9
   reactions 26–9, 31, 33
   women 22–3, 25, 26, 27
education 4, 7, 47, 74, 76–7, 99
elections
   by-elections 16, 31–5, 39, 46
   general elections 5, 31, 40–4, 46, 108–9, 116–17, 131
   local government 61–3
   partition 99–100
emergency powers resolution 113–14, 153–4
emigration 57, 75, 94
Emmet, Robert 24–5
English, Ada 105, 108
English, Richard 76
evictions 5, 57
executions 23, 27–8, 33, 64, 70–1, 76, 83–4, 89, 92–4, 110, 114, 117–18
explosives and bombings 15, 21, 67, 81–3, 110, 112, 114–15
external association, proposal for 105–6, 152–3

fair rent, free sale and fixity of tenure (three 'f's) 5
family connections 26, 75, 78, 91–2

Fenians *see* Irish Republican Brotherhood (IRB)
Fianna Éireann 23, 124–5
Fianna Fáil 43–4, 53, 115–17
financing
   Civil War, 1922–3 113
   Dáil Éireann 45, 55–7
   Easter Rising, 1916 25, 52
   Irish Convention 1917–18 36
   local government 62–3
   United States 51–3, 56
   women 91–2
Fine Gael 43, 115–16
First World War 9–11, 19, 32
   agricultural sector, benefits to 57, 63, 94
   Catholic Church 10, 33, 38, 129
   conscription 17, 18, 33, 37–40, 43, 75, 98, 129
   Easter Rising, 1916 16–17
   enlistment in British Army 10–11, 26
   Paris Peace Conference 46
   Protestants, decline in population of 94
   reprisals 87
   republican resurgence 35–40
   separation women 26
   third Home Rule Bill 6, 9, 122
Fisher, Warren 97
FitzGerald, Desmond 53, 54, 135–6
Fitzpatrick, David 74, 79
flying columns or active service units 71–2, 91
force-feeding 35
foreign policy of Dáil Éireann 48–55
Forlan, Peter 86
Four Courts 20, 60, 107, 111–12
French Declaration of the Rights of Man 24
French, John (the Viscount French) 69, 89, 96
Friends of Irish Freedom (FOIF) 52
Frongoch prison camp 35

Gaelic Athletic Association (GAA) 16, 77
Gaelic cultural revival 15–16, 77
Gaelic League 16, 18, 25, 68, 76–7
Gallagher Resolution 48–9
Garvin, Tom 80
Gavan Duffy, George 102, 104, 149
gender *see* women
general elections 5, 31, 40–4, 46, 108–9, 116–17, 131
General Post Office, Dublin 20–1, 23–4
general strikes 38, 64
Geoghegan-Quinn, Máire 47
geographical boundaries 103–4, 118
geography of War of Irish Independence 78–81
Germany 17–19, 22, 25, 39–40, 64, 88, 116

Gladstone, William 4–7
Governor General 109
Government of Ireland Act 1920 44, 96–100, 118
Greenwood, Hamar 97, 101–2, 149
Griffin, Michael 84
Griffith, Arthur 16, 34, 38–9, 47, 49, 57, 77, 100, 102–5, 113, 116, 136–7, 149
guerrilla warfare 67–9, 71–5, 78–9, 81–94, 101, 104, 112–13

habeas corpus 60
Hagan, John 50
Harland and Wolff 80
Hart, Peter 71, 74–5, 79, 93–4
Henderson, Arthur 87
Heslin, Michael 90
Hogan, Seán 68, 76
Holohan, Gary 23, 124–5
Home Government Association (HGA) 3–4
home rule 3–9, 15, 28–9
    first bill 5
    second bill 6
    third bill 6, 7, 36, 98, 122
Home Rule League 4–5
House of Lords 6–8
hunger-strikes 35, 68, 71

ideology, role of 77–8
Independent Irish Party 3
Independence War see Irish War of Independence
informers 17, 94
intelligence 18, 39, 54–6, 68–9, 71–2, 84, 88–92, 101, 115 see also spies
internment 26–7, 35, 39–40, 70, 89, 117–18
IRA (Irish Republican Army) (see also Irish Volunteer Force)
    agricultural background 74–5
    Anglo-Irish Treaty 106–14
    Catholic Church 74, 76, 84, 113
    children 23
    Civil War, 1922–3 106, 111–16
    convention 106–7, 110–11
    Dáil Éireann 59, 85
    flying columns or active service units 71–2, 91
    GHQ 72, 78–82, 88, 90, 106, 110
    guerrilla warfare 81–5, 87–9, 96, 104
    intelligence 88–92
    Irish Bulletin 54
    Irish War of Independence 67–74, 78–80, 90–1, 96–7, 100
    local government 62–3

RIC 58, 67–70, 97, 106
    rural base 74–6
    sectarianism 93
    social composition and motivation 74–8
    split 106–8, 110–12, 116
    women 91–2
Irish Bulletin 53–5, 93, 135–6
Irish Citizen Army (ICA) 17, 20–3, 25–8, 64
Irish Civil War, 1922–3 106, 109, 111–16, 153–4
Irish Convention 1917–18 36–7
Irish Free State, creation of 102–4, 108
Irish National League (INL) 5, 31
Irish Parliamentary Party (IPP) 4–8, 11, 16, 29, 31–43, 49, 61, 98
Irish Republican Army (IRA) see IRA (Irish Republican Army)
Irish Republican Brotherhood (IRB) 3, 15–17, 19, 35, 40, 80, 85, 104, 109
Irish Republican Police (IRP) 58
Irish Self-Determination League (ISDL) 55
Irish Transport and General Workers Union (ITGWU) 17, 64, 138
Irish Volunteer Force (IVF) 9, 16–23, 35–6, 39–40, 77 (see also IRA)
Irish War of Independence 67–94
    Anglo-Irish Treaty 1921 100–12
    Auxiliaries 70–1, 73, 97
    Bloody Sunday 71–2, 84, 88–9, 93, 100
    British policy 70–3, 96–7
    casualties 67–8, 70–3
    Dublin Castle administration 96–7, 139–40
    expenditure 56
    First Dáil Éireann 67–8, 131–2
    gender 90–3, 113
    geography of war 78–81
    guerrilla warfare and violence 67–9, 71–5, 78–9, 81–93, 96, 101
    intelligence 88–92
    IRA 67–78, 90–1, 96–7, 100
    law and order, breakdown in 69–70, 96
    local government 62
    partition 97–100, 102–4
    peace negotiations 100–4
    political campaign for independence, 1919–21 56, 58
    Restoration of Order in Ireland Act (ROIA) 1920 70, 139
    RIC, attacks on 67–72, 79, 97
    sectarianism 80–1, 93–4
    truce 73, 80, 87, 89, 94, 100–12
Irish White Cross 91

Johnson, Thomas 46, 50, 64

labour and trade union movements 17, 26, 34, 38, 57–8, 63–5
Labour Commission to Ireland 92–3, 143–4
Labour Party (British) 87, 92, 143–4
Labour Party (Irish) 38, 43–4, 46, 50, 61, 64, 99–100, 108, 109, 116
land and land reform 4–5, 7, 15, 57–60, 63, 94, 137–8
Land League 5, 32, 56, 57–8
Land War 4–5
language 25, 76–7
Larkin, Jim 17, 44, 64
law and order, breakdown in 58, 69–70, 96
Lemass, Noel 115
Lemass, Seán 23, 115
Liberal Party 4–6, 11, 98
Lloyd George, David 6, 28–9, 37–9, 49–50, 60, 97–8, 100–4, 137, 149
local government reform 6, 60–2
Logue, Michael 84
Long Committee 98–9
Long, Walter 59, 96, 98–9
Longford 33–5, 58, 60, 62
Lord Lieutenant, attempted assassination of 69, 89
Lynch, Liam 68–9, 85, 106–7, 115
Lynn, Kathleen 22
Lyons, Brigid 22, 90, 92

MacCurtain, Tomás 81, 92, 135–6
MacDermott (MacDiarmada), Seán 15–17, 126
MacDonagh, Thomas 20, 23, 126
MacEoin, Sean 72, 75, 83, 106
MacMahons, massacre of 110–11
MacNeill, Brian 115
MacNeill, Eoin 10, 16, 18–20, 24–5, 34–5, 47, 77, 115, 118
MacNeillite Volunteers 16–17
MacPherson, Ian 96–7
Macready, Nevil 68, 97, 101
MacSwiney, Mary 91, 92, 105, 108, 150–2
MacSwiney, Terence 71, 86, 91
Magner, Thomas 84
Maguire, Conor 59–60
Maguire, John 114
Maguire, Tom 74, 79, 114
Mallin, Michael 22, 27
Mannix, Daniel 84
Markievicz, Constance 22, 23, 26–7, 40, 43, 47, 92, 105, 108
martial law 21, 27, 35–6

martyrdom 28
McCartan, Patrick 50, 52
McCullough, Denis 15–16, 22
McGuill, James 111
McGuinness, Joseph 32–3, 92
McKee, Dick 71, 86, 89, 140
Mellows, Liam 22, 108, 112, 114
Mernin, Lily 86
'Message to the Free Nations of the World' 46, 48, 134–5
military campaign for independence *see* Irish War of Independence 67–94
monarchy 16, 34, 102–5, 109
Monroe Doctrine 52
Moore, Maurice 50, 101
Mountjoy Prison, Dublin 35, 114, 140
Moylett, Patrick 100
Mulcahy, Richard 22, 35–6, 39–40, 79–80, 85, 88, 106, 114
Munitions Strike, 1920 64, 138
mutinies 8, 116

Nathan, Matthew 21
National Aid Association 56
National Council 16
national courts, establishment of 136–7
nationalism 9, 15, 18, 28–9, 34, 36, 43, 74, 78
Ne Temere papal decree of 1908 7, 94
Northern Ireland 102–4, 109–11, 118 *see also* Ulster
Norway, Arthur Hamilton 21

oaths 61–2, 103–4, 109, 117
O'Callaghan, Kate 92, 108
O'Callaghan, Michael 93
O'Casey, Seán 28
O'Connell, Daniel 3
O'Connell, J.J. ('Ginger') 81, 106, 111
O'Connor, Art 59–60
O'Connor, Rory 106–7, 111
O'Donoghue, Florence 73–4, 75, 77, 79
O'Donovan, James 83
O'Farrell, Elizabeth 22
Offaly Brigade 94
O'Flanagan, Michael 32, 40, 84
Ó hÉigeartuigh, Diarmuid 55
O'Higgins, Kevin 47, 113, 115–17
O'Kelly, Seán 16, 46, 48
O'Malley, Ernie 76, 84, 107
O'Mara, James 51–2
O'Shiel, Kevin 59–60, 137–8
ostracisation 67–8
Ó Sulleabháin, Micheál 75

Paris Peace Conference 46, 49–50, 68
parish courts 57–8
Parker, Dehra 48
Parliament Act 1911 6, 7–8
Parnell, Charles Stewart 4–5, 41–2
partition 44, 28–9, 33–7, 97–104, 116–18, 144–5
peace negotiations 100–4
Pearse, Margaret 92, 105, 108
Pearse, Patrick 16–17, 19–20, 22, 24–5, 27, 77,
    125–6
Pearse, Willie 27
Pearson, Abraham 92–4
Pearson, Richard 92–4
people's budget 6
Plough and the Stars, the. O'Casey, Seán 28
Plunkett, George 60
Plunkett, George Noble (Count Plunkett) 32–3,
    47, 49, 60
Plunkett, Horace 36
Plunkett, Joseph 17–18, 28, 32–3, 126
political campaign for independence, 1919–21
    45–65
  Dáil courts 57–60, 61, 63, 69–70, 97, 137–8
  domestic policy 55–63, 137–8
  First Dáil Éireann 45–64, 88, 133–5
  foreign policy 48–55
  land reform 57–9, 63
  social conflict in revolutionary Ireland 63–5
poor law, abolition of 16, 47, 63
ports, British naval presence in Irish 103, 109
Privy Council 109
Proclamation 1916 24–6, 27, 47, 125–6
propaganda and publicity 53–5, 87, 91, 93
proportional representation 42, 61, 99, 108–9, 147
Protestants 3–4, 6, 8, 10, 26, 28–9, 74, 80–2,
    92–4, 99
Provisional Government and Army 111–15
psychological effect of violence 24, 87–8, 89, 92–3, 94
public debt 103
public ownership 25
Public Record Office, destruction of 112
public opinion and support 26–8, 33, 37, 83–7,
    128–9

Redmond, John 9–10, 11, 28–9, 31–4, 36–7, 41,
    49, 123–4
Redmond, William Archer 34–5, 41
Redmond, Willie 32–3
religion *see also* Catholics and Catholic Church
  disestablishment of Church of Ireland 4, 7
  Easter Rising, 1916 25, 26

partition 99
  sectarianism 80–1, 92, 93–4, 111
repression 27–9, 31, 33, 60, 65, 68, 117
reprisals 69, 71, 79, 83, 85–8, 92, 114–15
republicanism
  by-elections of 1917 and 1918 31–5, 39, 46
  Catholic church 84
  conscription crisis 33, 37–40, 43
  First World War 35–40
  ideology 77–8
  Irish Convention 1917–1918 36–7
  nationalism 78
  partition 33–4, 36–7
  radical 39–40
  resurgence 31–44
  Sinn Féin 31–44, 46
Restoration of Order in Ireland Act 1920 54, 70, 139
revisionism 71
revolutionary nationalism 15
road and bridges, damage caused to 62, 73
Robinson, Seamus 67, 109
Roman Catholics *see* Catholics and Catholic Church
Roscarberry 141–2
Royal Irish Constabulary (RIC) 22, 67–72, 79, 82–3,
    87, 97, 110
Royal Ulster Constabulary (RUC), founding of 117
Ryan, Michael J. 49

sectarianism 80–1, 92, 93–4, 111
secretaries of state 96–7
self-determination 46, 48–52
sexual assault 93, 143–4
Sheehy-Skeffington, Francis 24, 128–9
Sheehy-Skeffington, Hanna 40, 58
Sheehy-Skeffington, Owen 92
Sherwood Foresters, ambush of 24
Shortt, Edward 96
Sinn Féin
  Anglo-Irish Treaty 105–6, 108–9, 115–16
  ard fheis (annual national conventions) 34, 35
  by-elections 31–5, 39, 46
  Civil War, 1922–3 106, 115–16
  conscription 33, 38–9
  Dáil Éireann 16, 45, 47, 100, 106, 108–9
  Easter Rising, 1916 18, 27, 31
  executions 83–4, 94
  formation 16
  general elections 40–4, 46, 108–9, 116, 131
  German plot 39–40
  Government of Ireland Act 1920 99–101
  guerrilla warfare 83–4, 94

Sinn Féin (*continued*)
   internment 26, 39–40
   Irish Convention 1917–18, boycott of 36–7
   Irish War of Independence 68, 97
   IVF 35, 39, 40
   land reform 57
   local government 61–2
   national courts, establishment of 136–7
   partition 33–4, 116–17
   republican resurgence 31–44
   social conflict 65
   split 105–6, 108–9
   Westminster Parliament, abstention from 16, 33, 40–1, 43, 45, 131
Skinnider, Margaret 23
Smuts, Jan 50, 101
social conflict 63–5
social conservatism 26, 47
socialism 25, 44, 46–7
Soloheadbeg ambush 67
Somme, Battle of the 10–11
spies 83–4, 88–9, 92, 94 *see also* intelligence
Squad, the 56, 71, 89
Stack, Austin 60, 103–4
Statute of Westminster 1929 106
Sturgis, Mark 97, 101, 139–40

Teachtaí Dála (TDs) 47, 56, 105, 109, 113–14
Teeling circle of the IRB 77
trade unionists 17, 26, 34, 38, 57–8, 63–5
treachery 18, 27, 98
Treacy, Seán 67, 75
Tudor, Hugh 70, 97

Ulster *see also* Northern Ireland
   casualties 85
   Catholics 80–1
   Crisis, 1912–14 7–9, 17, 19
   Dáil courts 59
   First World War 98
   General Election of 1918 40–2
   IRA 80–1
   partition 44, 28–9, 33–7, 97–104, 116–18, 144–5
   Protestants 80–1
   Provisional Government 8, 25
   Royal Ulster Constabulary (RUC), founding of 117
   Ulster Special Constabulary (USC) 80
   Ulster Unionist Party (UPP) 99–100
   unionists 25, 40–2, 98–101
   violence of 1922 85, 110–11

Ulster Volunteer Force (UVF) 9, 10–11, 16–18, 80
Ulster Solemn League and Covenant, text of 123
unionism 6–8, 25, 36, 40–2, 96–101, 144–5
United Irish League 41, 49
United Irish revolt 1798 15, 18
United States 25, 48–53, 56, 91–2
universal suffrage 25

violence
   assassinations 69, 89, 111
   Easter Rising, 1916 24
   conscription 38, 39
   guerrilla warfare 67–9, 71–5, 78–9, 81–94, 101, 104, 112–13
   Irish War of Independence 67–9, 71–5, 78–9, 81–93, 96, 101
   partition 117
   psychological effect 24, 92–3, 94
   Ulster 8–9, 85
   women, against 92–3, 143–4

War of Independence *see* Irish War of Independence
Westminster Parliament, abstention from 16, 33, 40–1, 43, 45, 131
Wilson, Woodrow 46, 48, 51
Woodenbridge speech by John Redmond 9–10, 123–4
women
   Cumann na mBan 22–3, 38–9, 58, 75, 90–2, 106, 113
   Dáil Éireann 47
   despatch carriers, women as 22–3, 113
   Easter Rising, 1916 22–3, 25, 26, 27
   elections 34, 40
   family connections 91–2
   General Election of 1918 40
   hair, cutting 92
   intelligence 90–2
   Irish War of Independence 90–3, 113
   political campaigning 91–2
   psychological impact of deaths of relatives 87–8, 89, 92–3, 94
   separation women 26
   sexual assault 93, 143–4
   social backgrounds 92
   violence against women 92–3, 143–4
   Women's Declaration, text of 123
Workman, Clark and Co 80

Yeats, W.B. 28